**CSR for HR**

A Necessary Partnership for Advancing Responsible Business Practices

**Elaine Cohen** is passionate about CSR, HR, sustainability reporting and social justice. She is the co-founder and managing consultant of Beyond Business Ltd, a leading CSR consulting and sustainability reporting firm, serving a long list of international companies and non-profit clients. Prior to work in this field, Elaine gained over 20 years of business experience with Procter & Gamble (eight years in supply chain executive roles in Europe), with Unilever (eight years as VP for Human Resources with Unilever Israel) and a range of other roles with smaller companies. Elaine served as Manager of the Israeli Society for Human Resources Management during the period 2005–2007. Elaine makes a contribution to the community as a Board Member of a women's empowerment non-profit and by offering sustainability services to non-profits. Elaine lectures widely on CSR and the connection between CSR and human resources, is a committed blogger on sustainability reporting via her blog (www.csr-reporting.blogspot.com), provides Expert Reviews of sustainability reports for CorporateRegister.com (www.corporateregister.com) and *Ethical Corporation Magazine*, writes editorials and book reviews for CSRwire.com (www.csrwire.com), records CSR commentary and insights for 3BL TV (www.3BLmedia.com) and writes for many printed journals and websites. She is a frequent Tweeter on CSR issues at @elainecohen. Elaine holds a (double) Honours BA Degree in Modern Languages from Bradford University, is Manchester (UK) born and has lived in Israel since 1990. She is married with two children. Oh, and she is addicted to ice cream!

# CSR FOR HR

## A NECESSARY PARTNERSHIP FOR ADVANCING RESPONSIBLE BUSINESS PRACTICES

### Elaine Cohen

Greenleaf
PUBLISHING

This book is dedicated to my children, Eden and Amit Cohen, so that they may grow up in a more sustainable world. Also, they will love seeing their name in print!

© 2010 Greenleaf Publishing Limited

Published by Greenleaf Publishing Limited
Aizlewood's Mill
Nursery Street
Sheffield S3 8GG
UK
**www.greenleaf-publishing.com**

Printed in Great Britain on acid-free paper by
CPI Antony Rowe, Chippenham and Eastbourne

Cover by LaliAbril.com

British Library Cataloguing in Publication Data:
A catalogue record for this book is available from the British Library.

ISBN-13: 9781906093464

# Contents

# Thanks!

Many thanks to: Unilever, for providing me with an opportunity to learn and practise the human resources profession for eight years and with my first opportunity to learn about and work in the field of corporate social responsibility (CSR); my husband, Judah Cohen, for infinite love and tireless support; my mother, Trudy Carlick, because she deserves my deep gratitude for all she has ever done for me; John Stuart at Greenleaf Publishing, for the opportunity to become a published author, and Dean Bargh for diligent and professional work on the manuscript; Liad Ortar, my business partner, for environmental insights and general support; Carmel Kaminer, who worked on the analysis of women in business mentioned in Chapter 7; Cathy Joseph, for reading my draft manuscript and alerting me to errors and inconsistencies, and providing invaluable insights and suggestions on content; those who have contributed to different chapters: Amy Hall of Eileen Fisher, Nirit Cohen and Revital Bitan of Intel, Chris Jarvis and Angela Parker of Realized Worth, Ellen Weinreb of Sustainable Jobs, Ilana Atlas and Alison Ewings of Westpac, Melissa Swanson of Gap Inc., Ellen Resnick and Carol Casazza Herman of Resnick Consulting, Julie Urlaub of Taiga Company and Deborah Fleischer of Green Impact. I would also like to express gratitude to Professor Wayne Visser for advice on publishers; the CSR community on Twitter for a constant stream of valuable updates and information, in particular some champion tweeps @FabianPattberg, @DavidCoethica, @ChristineArena, @RealizedWorth, @3BLMedia, @Cathyj131, @Jan_Morgan, @susanmcp1, @Taigacompany and many, many more; my consulting firm clients in Israel and abroad for the privilege of working with them; all the companies mentioned in this book which provided me with insight and inspiration and sources of information; and, finally, to the entire community of CSR and human resources professionals who, each in their own way, contribute to making business a positive driver of change for world benefit.

# Introduction

This book is both a wake-up call for the human resources (HR) profession and a toolkit written to help members of that profession to act. Its objective is to stimulate the interest of HR professionals in a way that is informative and engaging, and hopefully to prompt more HR managers to action with regard to the social and environmental aspects of their function and the way they perform their roles in organisations.

Corporate social responsibility (CSR), a (largely) voluntary business approach that goes beyond the letter of the law and accepts accountability and transparency with regard to a business organisation's impacts on people, society and the environment, has now become one of the main preoccupations of corporate leaders. Based on the fundamentals of good governance, ethics and compliance with the law, CSR offers additional opportunities for businesses to mitigate business risk, enhance business reputation and take advantage of new business developments. In adopting a CSR strategy, businesses can contribute not only to the sustainability of the planet, but also to their own sustainability as businesses. This approach is changing the way businesses develop strategy, take decisions, execute processes, engage with employers, consumers, external pressure groups and communities and respond not only to shareholders, but also to all stakeholders in different ways and through new channels of communication. Indeed, excellence in stakeholder engagement has become a key driver for sustainable business.

CSR has a role to play in response to huge global issues such as climate change and poverty and is transforming organisations, their professional capabilities and the skills needed to lead or even develop an adequate response. The low-carbon economy, for example, is just one area in which a host of new job functions requiring new expertise have mushroomed in businesses around the world. Job titles such as vice president for corporate sustainability, CSR director, corporate responsibility officer and many others are now a feature of most leading companies. Just ten years ago, these roles did not exist. There is now growing evidence that this is not a fad and that CSR is mainstream and not just something that companies do to look good. It is a fundamental cornerstone of long-term success, highly visible to a wider range of stakeholders than ever before, expected and rewarded by stakeholders if done well and punished by stakeholders if fake or tin-hearted.

The fundamental bedrock of a company's ability to perform in line with the principles of sustainability, responsibility, accountability and transparency is its internal organisational leadership, values, culture, capabilities and communications. The talk today is about embedding CSR in all parts of the organisation. The prerequisite of having an employee community engaged in CSR strategy and practice is not negotiable. Leaders must ensure that their primary stakeholder group, the one that most influences the company's business results and that is most influenced by the company's business practices — its employees — understands, engages with and proactively advances the business CSR agenda.

For too long, CSR (or corporate social and environmental responsibility) has been seen as something companies engage with issue by issue: reducing the company's carbon footprint; contributing to the community; or developing a cause-marketing programme. Many companies have now realised that these 'projects' cannot exist in isolation as stand-alone activities. There is an interconnectedness about such business activities that requires a discipline of total systems thinking and integration into the baseline culture of the way a business does business. This can only be achieved when a company educates, engages and empowers its entire workforce. The HR function is a critical partner in making this happen. Arguably, the HR function is the *key* partner in making this happen. This book proposes that the HR function has a responsibility to be proactive in leading the way in establishing a CSR-enabled culture within any business.

And yet this is not happening. HR managers are preoccupied with their traditional roles of organisational development, recruitment, training and compensation, and are failing to see the opportunities that CSR brings for them as professionals, for their organisations and for global sustainability. HR professionals are just emerging from the transactional nature of their roles into the business-partnership transformation mind-set, and have not yet understood that the business focus has moved on to a level that requires CSR thinking and practice. For HR professionals to become true and valued business partners, a fundamental understanding of CSR and its interface with their function is essential. They need to move from a certain preoccupation with their own importance and achieve a higher level of stakeholder engagement. Paradoxically, the function in the organisation that should be leading cultural change for sustainability is the last to realise the role it must play. HR professionals must wake up to CSR and start learning how to do things differently. It is my expectation that, once they do, they will materially affect business results in a more positive way, and reap personal and professional benefits, catapulting the HR function, perhaps for the first time, into one that all businesses understand is necessary for them to thrive through the long term and fulfil their overarching responsibilities.

Change is not easy, and changing paradigms even less so. In talking to HR professionals, it is important to know how they think, what challenges they face and what obstacles they need to overcome, both in terms of their own mind-set and in terms of how they see their functional contribution in the organisation. My role as a country VP for Human Resources with Unilever over a period of eight years, as well as over 15 years of executive operational management experience in other (global) businesses, has enabled me to talk to HR professionals as a person who understands the business context, identifies with HR people and their needs, and has faced the challenges of operating as a member of an executive management team in a dynamic business. I know what it takes to get things done in HR. I feel the criticisms levelled at the HR function and the continuing professional search for a meaningful place in corporate dialogues and decision-making processes. I understand the dichotomy between profit centre and cost centre, and the need to prove that the HR contribution is cost-positive. I have felt the frustrations of wanting to advance HR processes without adequate tools to measure their financial contribution to business success. I have heard negative reactions of colleagues to the 'psychologistics' of organisational processes. I have debated with HR colleagues over the ways in which to 'sell' HR to management. The HR function itself is still uncomfortable with the way its role is regarded in organisations and conflicted about its ability to impact. I therefore understand the strong leap of faith I am asking of HR managers in presenting this book to them. HR has barely navigated the challenges of establishing the transformational HR role in organisations and here I am saying, 'Wake up, CSR is here!' For those that are open to it, my concept of *corporate social human resources* (CSHR) management may just provide the key to addressing many of the other fundamental insecurities of HR people and the inadequacies of the way HR impacts in organisations.

This book is presented through the eyes and mind of an HR manager. Most of us know the power of storytelling in getting messages through. This book leverages that power by telling the story of the metamorphosis of an 'HR manager' into a 'CSHR manager', whose HR practices are driven by a responsiveness to the needs of all HR stakeholders, which include society and environment. The chief protagonist in this story is Sharon, a fictional HR manager to whom I became quite endeared as I wrote the book. Sharon has the good fortune to meet an experienced (fictional) 'CSHR' manager called Arena Dardelle, who begins to coach Sharon on the principles of CSR and how HR is impacted by them. During the months that follow, Sharon systematically and methodically works her way through each aspect of her role as an HR manager, identifying the inter-relationships between CSR and HR, and finds, or develops, (with my help) tools for implementing the CSHR way. In relating Sharon's challenges and opportunities, the book examines internal conflicts and questions about the relevance of CSR to HR and the possibility for HR to act in a new, purposeful way in the organisation. The dialogue reflects the many discussions I have had as an HR and CSR practitioner and the problems I have experienced with a wide range of HR managers in my role as a consultant to companies. Ultimately, and perhaps this is one of the most important insights to be gained from this book, Sharon realises she doesn't need to sit around and wait for her CEO or executive team to develop a comprehensive CSR strategy for the HR function. She realises that there is much that she, as the professional guardian of organisational culture and capability, can and *must* do to establish the organisational readiness for a CSR approach and contribute to the advancement of business objectives in the meantime. Sharon's methodological process forms a practical guide for all HR professionals, offering many cases and tools that can be used.

As Sharon embarks on her journey of discovery, she meets many 'teachers' along the way. While some of these are my own inventions, several are real-life professionals who generously agreed to contribute to this book from their own experience. The footnotes tell the full story. One such real professional is Ilana Atlas, Group Executive, People and Performance, Westpac Banking Group, Australia (now retired), who offered terrific insights into the synergy between HR and CSR in practice. Another is Nirit Cohen, HR Manager at Intel, who wrote an illuminating piece on the integration of CSR and HR at Intel.

Some HR managers may identify readily with Sharon, some a little less. In some cases, she might even seem a little ingenuous. I had to make Sharon a complete novice in the field of CSR at the outset in order to enable full discussion of the different concepts throughout the book. I hope I haven't insulted anyone! However, I do feel that Sharon, once on board, becomes a model for the HR profession, so in that sense, I hope that HR managers will gain inspiration and a similar desire to respond to the wake-up call, as Sharon did.

The intended audience for this book is anyone practising, teaching, learning or aspiring to be involved in the HR function. The concepts and tools apply to all HR people, in organisations of all types and all sizes. Others will also find the book useful: for example, leaders of companies who are responsible for directing the HR contribution in the business, and managers who must partner with HR managers in order to deliver results. This book will serve as an aid to them to assist in determining what they should expect from their HR function. I also think that this book will appeal to CSR managers, practitioners and consultants and to all those involved in the sustainability transformation of business today. And this book might also appeal to anyone who simply likes a good business story with a happy ending!

One final point: there is much more that I could have included in this book. There are many more examples that I could have quoted, many more people that I could have interviewed or invented and much more material that pops up daily on my PC screen from my thousands of sources via the World Wide Web. As with any publication, the author must make trade-offs and set limits.

My main limit was the time I had available to devote to research and writing and the deadline set by my generous publishers, Greenleaf Publishing, which I only slightly overshot! I apologise in advance for the fact that this is not a totally exhaustive guide. However, I believe it is the most detailed guide for the HR manager available today on this subject and as comprehensive as any HR manager needs in an initial exposure to CSR.

I would love to hear reactions from all readers, HR professionals or otherwise, and invite you to contribute to the new CSR for HR blog, www.csrforhr.com.

I hope you enjoy this book. Thank you for reading! Now it's time to meet Sharon and her CSHR manager teacher, Arena . . .

*Elaine Cohen, August 2010*

# Curriculum Vitae
## HR Professional: Arena Dardelle[1]

**Key personal qualities:** Values-driven, strategic, mediator, analytical, mentor, optimist.

## Professional experience:

**2002–present: VP Human Resources, Europe, International Food Company Ltd (IFC Ltd)**

IFC is a leading packaged foods manufacturer, headquartered in London, with operations in 25 countries, employing 43,000 people, with a turnover of £5 billion. In my role, I am responsible for HR strategy and leadership, and the HR business contribution. In addition to my HR role, I also partner the Corporate Responsibility function closely, to align HR and CSR processes. Key achievements in recent years have been:

- Annual employee survey since 2005, with **year on year noticeable improvement in employee engagement and satisfaction results**.

- **Reduced employee absenteeism (by 34%) and top talent turnover (by 48%) over 5 years.**

- **New diversity strategy and diversity recruitment solutions** delivering cost savings of over £250k per year. Winner of the annual Europe Diversity Awards for 2005 and 2007.

- **Revised values and performance linked compensation and benefit plans** for all employees, at no additional cost to the business. Employees demonstrated satisfaction with the new plans in the corporate Employees survey.

- **New global top talent development process** resulting in 90% internal promotions during last 5 years.

## Prior roles:

**1998–2002: Cosmetics Plus: Global Organisation Development Manager.** Cosmetics Plus is a $6billion company, headquartered in the UK, owning several leading global cosmetic and perfume brands. In this role, I led the global rollout of several HR initiatives including a new Performance Evaluation Process, and HR Skills development. I led the assimilation of the corporate mission and values, and community involvement.

**1993–1997: Riley PetFoods, UK: HR Manager.** Riley PetFoods is a large national branded pet foods manufacturer. I was responsible for supporting all HR needs for national operations.

---

1 This curriculum vitae is entirely fictional, as is the character of Arena Dardelle. The CV is shown for illustration purposes and is not based on any known HR professional career path. All the companies mentioned are fictional and have no connection to existing companies.

**1988–1992: Human resources management** and supporting roles in medium-sized companies (details provided on request).


## Education:

1987: INSEAD, France: Masters of Business Administration

1982–1986: Cambridge University, UK: MA Politics, Psychology and Sociology Tripos


## Community activities:

Volunteer project work at Oxfam

Greenpeace volunteer — administrative campaign work

Monthly visits to read to the blind


## Languages:

French/English (bilingual), proficiency in German and Italian

# Curriculum Vitae
## Sharon Black[2]

## Professional experience:

### 2004–present: Director of Human Resources, Andromex Ltd

Andromex is a privately owned software developer, employing 2,500 people in the UK, with outsourced activities in India and offices in several East European countries. My role covers HR strategy, policy and performance for the global operations.

**Responsible for:** Human Resources strategy and all HR processes. Member of Executive Committee. HR Team of 20.

**Key achievements:**

- Development of recruitment strategy delivering improved attraction and retention.

- Establishment of core HR processes for performance evaluation and employee development.

- Development of training systems throughout the business.

## Prior roles

### 1999–2003: Hawthornes Ltd: Human Resources Manager

Hawthornes is a privately owned business in the technology sector employing 700 people in the UK.

**Responsible for:** Human Resources strategy and development.

**Key achievement:** Development of talent management strategy to ensure talent mobility and promotion from within the company. Internal placements and promotions increased from 27% in 1999 to 58% in 2003.

### 1996–1998: El-Tec Ltd: Employee Development Manager: El-Tec is a national software company operating in the UK, provider to major global electronics companies, privately owned, employing close to 1,000 people.

**Responsible for:** Identifying training and development needs, designing solutions and ensuring effective implementation.

**Key achievement:** Development and implementation of a Senior Leadership programme for all high potential Managers

---

2  This curriculum vitae is entirely fictional, as is the character of Sharon Black. The CV is shown for illustration purposes and is not based on any known HR professional career path. All the companies mentioned are fictional and bear no connection to existing companies.

**<u>1993–1995: Armstrong's UK: Factory HR Manager</u>**

**Responsible for:** Implementation of all HR policies and programmes in main furniture plant and assembly plant employing 550 people.

**Key achievement:** Significant improvement in plant employee turnover rates.

## Education

**1992–1993: Bradford University School of Management:** MBA

**1988–1991: Manchester University:** BA Social Sciences and Sciences & Psychology

**Member of:** Chartered Institute of Personnel Development

# Part I
# HR: a critical partner for CSR

# 1

# HR meets CSR

She is a human resources manager of a medium-sized company, operating globally on a limited scale. Her company is called Andromex Ltd and is a privately owned software developer, headquartered in Bristol, UK, employing 2,500 people, with several operations outsourced to India and other countries. She is skilled, with 13 years of HR management experience. She has studied organisational behaviour, training and organisation design, read every one of Dave Ulrich's books[1] and attended a coaching course to equip her to career-coach managers at Andromex Ltd. She hasn't missed the leading national annual HR conference in the past four years and has even presented a couple of papers. She is well respected as a business partner in the Andromex management team. She runs a tight HR organisation, providing training, welfare, career development programmes, internal communications, recruitment and support for business processes. Her team of 20 people are highly regarded and acclaimed for doing a good job. She and her team won the HR Excellence prize last year for an exceptional new recruitment model she developed and implemented. She loves the HR profession and sees herself progressing into larger roles in the future. She knows that HR is strategic, and a necessary enabler for business development and growth. She truly feels that she does a job that is critical to helping the business succeed, and very worthwhile. At last, her CEO has agreed to her attending the ASTD conference[2] in the USA — a major expense for a business run on a tight budget, and she is looking forward to the trip.

Little did she know, it would change her life as an HR manager.

---

1 Professor Dave Ulrich is an HR 'guru' and has written several ground-breaking books on HR management.
2 The American Society for Training and Development (www. astd.org) holds highly regarded annual conferences on training and associated HR subjects.

By the way, her name is Sharon.

As she boards the connecting flight from London to the conference, refreshed after a brief shopping spree in Heathrow airport and armed with a newly acquired copy of *Guts!* by Jackie and Kevin Freiberg,[3] a book that has come highly recommended to her, she searches for her aisle seat in business class, grateful for the fact that the company revised its policy on economy flights for long-hauls. She found herself seated next to a woman, a few years older than her, poring over a book whose title she couldn't quite make out, something 'unusual'. The woman looked up and smiled, and reverted to her book. An hour or so later, as lunch is served, the woman started a conversation:

**The woman:** Where are you travelling to?

**Sharon:** I'm going to a conference in San Diego. It's a conference about training, the ASTD conference. I work in human resources.

**The woman:** Is that right? Incredible! You won't believe it, but I am travelling to the same conference. I go every year. I am also in human resources. I work for International Food Company Ltd (IFC). I am the European HR VP. My name is Arena.

**Sharon:** Really? What a coincidence! Pleased to meet you. I'm Sharon.

Sharon and Arena started talking. Sharon noticed that the book Arena was reading was *Business as Unusual* by Anita Roddick, the pioneering business woman and social activist who created and led The Body Shop,[4] one of the first ethical businesses to become globally successful and defy traditional ways of doing business. Arena noticed her looking at Anita Roddick's picture on the cover.

**Arena:** I admire Anita Roddick. She died in 2007, at the age of 64. A tragedy. One of those deaths, for me at least, where you remember exactly where you were when you heard. She was such an inspiration for us all. This is the second time I am reading this book. The values Anita Roddick led at The Body Shop and the way she integrated them throughout the business were quite revolutionary at that time, though now, no respectable business can afford not to take notice of social and environmental issues. It has become quite a movement, corporate social responsibility. It has changed the way I think and work so much over the past few years, as an HR professional. Anita Roddick said 'we

### The values of The Body Shop

- Activate self-esteem
- Protect our planet
- Against animal testing
- Support community trade
- Defend human rights

www.thebodyshop.com

---

3  Kevin Freiberg and Jackie Freiberg, *Guts! Companies That Blow the Doors Off Business-as-usual* (New York: Broadway Business, 2006).

4  Anita Roddick, *Business as Unusual: My Entrepreneurial Journey — Profits with Principles* (UK: Anita Roddick Books, new edn, 2005).

were searching for employees but people turned up instead'[5] — and you know, that is really what social responsibility is all about. Ensuring that we not only respect people and our environment, but also take time to understand their concerns and aspirations, and enable them to maintain a respectable standard of living. Take their issues into account as we plan and develop. I was thinking of calling myself a CSHR manager — corporate social human resources manager, as I seem to be doing as much CSR as I am HR these days. There was a quote from a couple of people at Canadian Business for Social Responsibility[6] who said that **CSR minus HR is PR**.[7] Do you understand that? If a company tries to behave as a corporate socially responsible company but doesn't take the time to ensure all the HR processes are aligned, and that people are respected, then CSR becomes nothing more than a public relations exercise. But I'm preaching. That's what happens when you enjoy your work, I suppose. Anyway, Sharon, what do you do about corporate social responsibility in your business?

**Sharon:** er . . .

Sharon had to admit that she didn't do anything very much about corporate social responsibility in her business. In fact, she had to admit that she didn't really know what it all meant. It was a little embarrassing really. She knew CSR had something to do with contributing to the community, such as sending employees out to do maintenance on old people's houses, or organising volunteer days. She had thought of doing something like that in her company, because it seemed like an interesting approach for an employee Fun Day, but there were always so many other things to do. As long as the CEO wasn't demanding a community programme, Sharon didn't feel it was part of the core HR role to initiate these things. 'I am busy enough as it is,' she thought.

**Sharon:** I have to admit that I don't really know what corporate social responsibility involves. I am not sure why it's important. Contributing to the community and improving the environment is fine, but I don't see it as something that the HR function should recommend. I am proud of what we have achieved as an HR team. We have developed a strong position in the company because we work closely aligned to business strategy, and we have started to track metrics, such as training effectiveness, so that the management team knows how we are adding value. We have become accepted as business partners. I don't think it's right that we should start recommending allocation of time and budgets to contribute to the community. The CSR concept sounds like someone else's area of responsibility, like public relations or marketing. It sounds to me like

5  Roddick, *Business as Unusual*: 55.

6  www.cbsr.ca.

7  A quote from Adine Mees and Jamie Bunham of Canadian Business for Social Responsibility appearing in World Business Council for Sustainable Development *Driving Success: Human Resources and Sustainable Development* (Geneva: WBCSD, 2005, www.wbcsd.org/web/publications/hr.pdf).

a lot of effort and I am not sure what it contributes to the business. I agree that it would be nice to make a donation to the community here and there, but frankly, my boss will not release money for this. We just don't have the funds. We are a privately owned company and budgets are tightly controlled. It took me four years just to get him to let me go to this conference in the USA.

**Arena:** Sharon, you sound just like me a few years back, before I joined International Food. That's exactly how I thought about things. But today, well, I couldn't work for a company that didn't have a social and environmental responsibility strategy. I couldn't do an HR job without being part of a CSR team. CSR has helped me understand the real meaning of sustainable business. It has helped me realise that my job as a human resources manager is even more meaningful. Today, CSR is a key element of managing risk, developing new business opportunities and protecting and enhancing the company reputation. For us HR managers, it's a core element of our company culture, and has major strategic value. But it also means that we have to learn new skills and do things a little differently than we did in the past. So for HR, CSR represents new challenges. It's exciting! Look. We have a few hours ahead of us. Let me tell you a little about CSR and why HR managers can't afford to ignore it, OK?

**Sharon:** I did want to catch the new Richard Gere film on Channel 2.

**Arena** (laughing)**:** Believe me, Richard Gere might give you a quick thrill, but CSR will change your personal and professional life forever. In any case, I saw that movie already and, believe me, Richard Gere is not what he used to be.

**Sharon:** OK, Arena. I am always happy to listen. Thanks.

Despite Sharon's seeming reluctance, Arena started to educate Sharon on corporate social responsibility. First, she shared the following definitions:

**Corporate social responsibility (CSR).** A way of doing business that is based on ethical principles and structured management controls, and that takes into account social and environmental considerations alongside economic considerations when making business decisions, and attempts to create positive impacts on all stakeholders. CSR is a voluntary approach, going beyond compliance with laws and regulations.

**Sustainability.** Sustainable development of business means 'satisfying the needs of the present without compromising the ability of future generations to meet their own needs'. This is the most commonly quoted definition of sustainability, coined by the Brundtland Commission[8] in 1983.

8  The Brundtland Commission, formally the World Commission on Environment and Development (WCED), known by the name of its chair, Gro Harlem Brundtland, was convened by the United Nations in 1983. The commission was created to address growing concern 'about the accelerating deterioration of the human

**Arena:** These two terms are often used interchangeably, but they are rather different. CSR is about how a business does things and impacts on people, society and environment. It involves an evaluation of the way the business impacts on all stakeholders and adoption of business practices to improve these impacts. It requires engaging stakeholders in dialogue about their concerns and aspirations, and what they expect from the business. CSR also involves identifying ways in which the business can succeed in the long term by addressing these expectations, so as to deliver positive outcomes for all as far as possible, including positive outcomes for the business, of course. It's about businesses taking responsibility and being accountable for their impacts on people, communities and the environment. Obeying the law is not enough. CSR goes beyond the requirements of the law. Sustainability, on the other hand, tends to refer to the ability of the business to sustain itself through time, while contributing to the improvement of society and the planet as a whole.

**Sharon:** I don't understand the difference.

**Arena:** OK. Take Gap Inc. Gap is a large business with a strong reputation for CSR. I see you are wearing a GAP sweatshirt. Gap Inc.[9] has a complex supply chain that is outsourced, mainly to Asian suppliers. There are hundreds of thousands of employees in the Gap Inc. supply chain in over 2,500 contract factories. We know that human rights in these businesses are often abused and difficult to control. Gap Inc. instigated a major supplier auditing and training programme and required suppliers to adhere to strict ethical standards. This is CSR. The focus is on directly managing the way the company does business in order to ensure it does no harm and even makes a positive overall contribution. On the other hand, Gap Inc. has been active in building government, third sector[10] and industry coalitions to address the global issues of human rights and child labour in outsourced factories. They have been involved in setting standards for eliminating exploitation of workers in Asian countries, addressing problems of child labour, enabling freedom of association, setting appropriate hygiene standards and so on. These are industry issues that are wider than one business alone can influence and that have an impact on the global economy and

> **Gap Inc. values**
>
> Integrity, respect, open-mindedness, quality and balance
>
> www.gapinc.com

environment and natural resources and the consequences of that deterioration for economic and social development'. In establishing the commission, the UN General Assembly recognised that environmental problems were global in nature and determined that it was in the common interest of all nations to establish policies for sustainable development. Source: en.wikipedia.org/wiki/Brundtland (accessed 10 June 2010).

9   Gap Inc. is a global apparel supplier, with revenues of $16 billion, employing over 150,000 people. Key brands are GAP, Old Navy and Banana Republic.

10  A term used to refer collectively to organised civil society and non-governmental groups and organisations (NGOs).

well-being. Gap Inc. has gone beyond the direct boundaries of its own business to invest in creating major change to strengthen communities and social fabric in the world as a whole, and not just those directly impacted by their own specific business activities. This is sustainability. CSR is an essential core element of overall sustainability strategy.

**Sharon:** I get it. CSR is about the way the company does business. Sustainability is more about collaboration to address world issues which may affect society over the long term. Businesses can do CSR on their own, but they will tend to do sustainability in partnership.

**Arena:** That's more or less right, although even certain aspects of CSR involve partnership. The main thing is that CSR is more about what the business controls. Its own products, interactions, processes, practices and the results of its own business decisions. Sustainability is more about the responsibility of business to contribute to addressing broader societal issues, such as global warming, poverty, access to water, access to healthcare, human rights, development needs, climate change and so on. These things are far-reaching and require cross-sector collaboration and industry coalitions and partnerships for long-term systemic change. CSR is key to sustainability because, first, all businesses must accept responsibility for the way they themselves operate and the impacts they generate directly.

**Sharon:** Before they save the planet.

**Arena:** Right.

**Sharon:** So CSR is like a Boy Scout, building character, behaving well and making a positive contribution, while sustainability is Superman, going out of his way to save the planet.

**Arena:** Funny. Good analogy. That's not so far from the truth. However, businesses do not exist to save the planet. That's not their goal. But because the scale of many businesses is so great, and the power business wields to transform the way we live and work is so dominant, it makes sense for businesses to use this power in a positive way for the good of society. In doing so, they contribute to the long-term well-being of the business.

**Sharon:** But what's all that got to do with HR? I don't see my company saving the planet any time soon. I am not responsible for outsourcing as in the Gap Inc. example you mentioned. I can understand if major global corporations who employ hundreds of thousands of people and make billions of dollars in profits and operate in every community in the world feel they have a role to play in reducing world poverty, but what has all that go to do with HR?

**Arena:** I will explain. Let's go back to the outsourcing example. Gap Inc. employs a large team of people in CSR — over 90 people worldwide. Several are factory auditors — vendor compliance officers. Who recruits them?

Who ensures they have appropriate training? Gap Inc. employs 30,000 people directly. Who ensures they are employed in a fair and responsible manner, and set an example for outsourced operations? Who determines their safety at work? Who determines the process for their performance evaluation? Gap Inc.'s vendor compliance officers need to understand the local operations. The team come from different backgrounds with over 25 different nationalities. How do you champion a culture of diversity and acceptance of others within the business? Ethical behaviour of our own employees is based on strong values — what processes do you lead to ensure assimilation of common values and ethics? All these questions relate to core elements of CSR, and the fact that HR has an important role to play in ensuring employees are engaged. Finally, CSR is about transparency. Gap Inc., for example, publishes a social responsibility report. This is an annual or biennial report that summarises all the things a company is doing under the heading of CSR or sustainability. I mentioned that the use of the terms CSR and sustainability are often interchangeable, didn't I? Some companies don't make such a distinction between the two, so from now I will just talk about CSR, OK? International Food, where I work, produces a CSR report every two years. As HR managers, we are responsible for providing input to that report. The report is an important tool for building trust and ensuring that all stakeholders are aware of what we do, so that they can make informed decisions about whether to buy our product, whether to invest in our company or whether to apply for a job. I use our report at International Food as a core tool in recruitment, for example. More and more students these days are looking to work for companies that they perceive as ethical. I also ensure the report is communicated internally, so that our employees know about IFC's efforts to be a responsible and sustainable business. This helps them engage, support and stay motivated by more than just their pay packet.

**Sharon:** Look, as I said, this may be relevant for a big global business with a major element of outsourcing. I work for a local company. We employ 2,500 people and run a few small operations overseas. We are not traded on the stock markets and we don't have consumer brands or operate retail stores selling direct to the consumer. We can't save the world. I agree that CSR sounds important, but it doesn't seem so relevant for me in my HR role at the company I work for. I don't see any pressure on us to develop this approach. My executive leadership team is not demanding this.

**Arena:** Yes, clearly CSR is more complex in global businesses. But even in a small business, or one that doesn't sell consumer brands as we do, employee engagement is critical, strong local communities are important, protecting the local environment is fundamental and creating trust with all stakeholders enables management of risk and identification of opportunities. HR plays a crucial role in ensuring the right corporate climate and practices which enable the business to succeed in a responsible way. This is important for every business, small or large, consumer-facing or B2B.[11]

I ought to add that CSR is a voluntary approach. Businesses choose to adopt a CSR way, because they see benefit or because it seems morally right to them, beyond what the law prescribes. For example, the law may prescribe a minimum wage, but many companies pay unskilled workers more than the prescribed minimum wage, in order to ensure they can have a reasonable standard of living. Sometimes the benefit of CSR is a sort of defence strategy — businesses have been, and continue to be, attacked for irresponsible practices and CSR then becomes their defence. This happened with most of the apparel and fashion businesses in the 1990s, which were attacked for unethical labour conditions. Nike, Adidas, Puma and, yes, even Gap Inc., were all targeted by activist groups and angry consumers when it was discovered that they employed child labour and violated human rights in their outsourced manufacturing supply chains in countries like Bangladesh and India and China. Their best defence was CSR. Later, their defence turned to advocacy and now, these companies have very strict standards and employ people internally and externally to monitor suppliers' adherence to these standards, and they collaborate across the industry to raise the standards for everyone.

Then there are CSR strategists — those companies who see the real long-term business benefit — General Electric's Ecomagination[12] range was a clear strategic opportunity. This was a range of products built according to the highest environmental principles using environmentally friendly technologies. GE Chairman and CEO Jeff Immelt said

> Ecomagination is one of the most successful cross-company business initiatives in our recent history. It is a clear amplifier of our strong reputation for innovation and execution, harnessing the strength of every GE business to maximise returns for GE investors while minimising our own energy use and greenhouse gas emissions.

GE saw an increase in its brand value by more than US$6.0 billion since 2005[13] after the introduction of Ecomagination.

Finally, there are the values-driven businesses such as The Body Shop,

---

11  B2B (business to business) — business that sells its services or products to other businesses and not to consumers. This would include a company such as the fictional Andromex where Sharon works, which sells software programs to other businesses for their internal business processes.
12  ge.ecomagination.com.
13  Paula Oliveira and Andrea Sullivan, 'Sustainability and Its Impact on Brand Value', in *Best Global Brands 2008* (Interbrand: 15), www.interbrand.com/images/BGB_reports/BGB_2008_EURO_Format.pdf, accessed 1 June 2010.

## Ben & Jerry's values

We have a progressive, nonpartisan social mission that seeks to meet human needs and eliminate injustices in our local, national and international communities by integrating these concerns into our day-to-day business activities. Our focus is on children and families, the environment and sustainable agriculture on family farms.

www.benjerry.com

## Eileen Fisher values

- Individual growth and well-being
- Collaboration and teamwork
- Joyful atmosphere
- Social consciousness

www.eileenfisher.com

## Patagonia mission statement

Build the best product, cause no unnecessary harm, use business to inspire and implement solutions to the environmental crisis.

www.patagonia.com

Ben & Jerry's,[14] Patagonia,[15] Eileen Fisher,[16] and comme il faut[17] in Israel. I visited Israel last summer and got to know this small fashion business called comme il faut and I was very impressed! They were even included in the 2010 list of '100 World's Most Ethical Companies' published by Ethisphere,[18] which is quite some recognition for a smaller privately owned business outside of the USA or northern Europe. These companies, and several others, started out as ethical businesses because of the vision and passion of the founding managers who wanted to see their personal values reflected in the way they did business. Whatever the reason, CSR is voluntary and goes beyond compliance. This means that these companies adopt policies and practices that go further than the letter of the law. The law doesn't always create an adequate social and environmentally sound framework as I have said. Take diversity and inclusion, for instance. Except for the USA where there is affirmative action legislation, most governments do not legislate for diversity. But for many reasons, diversity is good CSR practice that goes further than the law requires.

**Sharon:** Who are stakeholders, exactly?

**Arena:** Another definition:

**Stakeholders.** All those who have an effect on a business, and all those who are affected by a business. Stakeholders may be individuals or groups. Typical stakeholders of most businesses include shareholders, employees, customers, suppliers and external groups such as NGOs or social/environmental activists. Differentiate stakeholders from shareholders — shareholders own stocks in the company but stakeholders may not.

Employees are core stakeholders. They need to be engaged intensively in order to ensure they uphold responsible business practices. They

14  www.benjerry.com.
15  www.patagonia.com.
16  www.eileenfisher.com.
17  www.comme-il-faut.com.
18  ethisphere.com/wme2010, accessed 10 June 2010.

need to be taught how to engage with other stakeholders such as customers and suppliers. All this is part of the social fabric of responsible corporate culture, which you as an HR manager lead.

**Sharon:** Risk and opportunity? What do you mean by that?

**Arena:** If you do not provide a working environment that treats your employees equitably, beyond the letter of the law, they may leave. That's a business risk. If you provide a recruiting platform which emphasises the company's positive impacts on society and environment, you will attract top talent, as more and more statistics today show that people are looking for more than just earning a living; they are looking for meaningful ways to make a difference while at work. This is a business opportunity.

**comme il faut mission statement**

We believe in the power of women to influence.

We choose to take a stand, based on our business and personal responsibility. Our company is a home for learning, action and leadership, in which every woman can feel special, significant and influential.

www.comme-il-faut.com

**Sharon:** So CSR is also about values, employing people responsibly and offering development opportunities. Sounds like HR to me.

**Arena:** Well, it goes beyond traditional HR, and it encompasses the entire business. And it's more than nice values. It's strategy, coupled with values. Take a look at this diagram. It's a CSR roadmap from a great sustainability consulting firm that we work with.

## CSR Roadmap

Let's run through the key terms.

**Materiality.** What matters most. These are issues that are critical for the success of the business and issues, which are of prime importance to stakeholders, who influence and are influenced by the business. Business cannot be expected to address every single issue that arises. An analysis of material issues evaluates and prioritises the key areas for sustainability, with a view to ensuring these are addressed responsibly and transparently.

Let's look at an example of materiality:

A material issue for Gap Inc. that was identified through discussion with stakeholders was energy conservation. It is very clear that consumers require businesses to be more active in protecting the environment. It is clear that Gap can considerably reduce costs and become more competitive by reducing the energy required in production and transportation throughout the supply chain. This might sound like common-sense good business, and it is. Most businesses don't identify this as a core priority if they don't have motivation to consider their environmental impacts.

Some of the measures Gap is taking to conserve energy include:[19] participating in a US Environmental Agency programme to reduce greenhouse gas emissions, year-on-year reduction of energy used in Gap stores (over 3,000 stores around the world), reducing energy usage in distribution centres and changing transportation arrangements for employees including providing shuttles to work, carpooling and cycling to work. I had a discussion with Kindley Walsh-Lawlor, Senior Director of Strategy and Communications and Environmental Affairs at Gap Inc. She said:

> Whether we're saving costs by reducing energy consumption or creating covetable products through innovative, sustainable design, we believe that reducing our impact on the environment can also result in positive business benefits. Our environmental strategy is focused on three key areas where we believe our efforts can have the greatest positive impact: Energy conservation, Cotton/sustainable design and Output/waste reduction, or ECO for short. Gap Inc. has been recognized by the San Francisco Bay Area Council for best practices as a Regional Transportation Initiative Employer for the wide range of employee transportation options we support. Gap Inc. utilizes company shuttles between headquarters locations, encourages carpooling by offering commuter benefits and provides facilities for employees who commute by bicycle. In addition, the company recently partnered with Zipcar to provide free membership and discounted rates to employees anywhere Zipcar is located, including San Francisco, New York, Toronto and London. These benefits are communicated to employees regularly in our headquarters buildings and through our company intranet, GapWeb, as well as annually as part of our benefits open enrollment period.[20]

19  www.gapinc.com/socialresponsibility, accessed 10 June 2010.
20  Quotation provided by Melissa Swanson of Gap Inc. Public Affairs, 20 October 2008.

Now. How does a company make changes to employee arrangements for getting to work without engaging employees by creating a policy, procedures, and a comprehensive communication programme? And who does that? The HR team. And who reports the results? The HR team. And who sets a personal example? The HR team. Believe me, I have saved enough to take a holiday in Hawaii since I started shuttling to work.

The process of CSR starts with the business identifying its core stakeholders, engaging them in dialogue, assessing the material issues, developing a strategy to improve its impacts on stakeholders, integrated of course with business strategy, doing it, measuring it, and then reporting. Reporting is the necessary element of transparency that creates trust and informed consumerism. The more businesses that do this, the more business will be sustainable and the more all stakeholder groups and the world in general will benefit. This whole process relies on committed leadership, and rests on a strong culture of ethics and good governance. And of course it never ends, because the external context is always dynamic and stakeholder priorities change. So the cycle is repeated, and, each time, the HR manager is presented with new challenges. CSR is a long-term thing, not just something you do as a short-term project.

**Sharon:** And governance is?

> **Governance.** Corporate governance is about the way in which boards oversee the running of a company by its managers, and how board members are in turn accountable to shareholders and the company. This has implications for company behaviour towards employees, shareholders, customers and banks. Good corporate governance plays a vital role in underpinning the integrity and efficiency of financial markets. Poor corporate governance weakens a company's potential and at worst can pave the way for financial difficulties and even fraud. If companies are well governed, they will usually outperform other companies and will be able to attract investors whose support can help to finance further growth.[21]

**Arena:** I don't have too much to do with governance, but I know that the Board for International Food and Agricultural Development regularly reviews IFC's social responsibility performance and there is a Governance Committee which reports to the Board of Directors. Anyway, that's how it goes. Any thoughts?

**Sharon:** Yes, of course. I understand that CSR is a new approach to doing business. One that takes into account more than the traditional targets of growth, profit and shareholder return. It needs a strong culture to support it, and awareness of different behaviours. Given that HR is the business

21  OECD (Organisation for Economic Cooperation and Development) Directorate for Financial and Enterprise Affairs, 'Improving Business Behaviour: Why We Need Corporate Governance', Speech following the adoption of the 2004 Review of the OECD Principles of Corporate Governance, www.oecd.org/document/37/0,3343,en_2649_34813_31838821_1_1_1_1,00.html, accessed 1 June 2010.

function charged with leading culture and processes, and championing the interests of employees, HR has to be a core partner. CSR benefits the business by mitigating risk and creating opportunity. And for HR managers to take all that on board, they need to understand more and learn new things. All in all, everyone wins. Sounds too good to be true. What's the catch?

**Arena:** Wow, you picked all that up quickly, Sharon. The catch is that, well, the immediate benefits are not always quantifiable. CSR is a bit like an insurance policy. If you don't need it, you don't invest your time, energy and money. This is how most CEOs think. If they are not being pressured and pounded by analysts, customers, Greenpeace or lawsuits, it's easy for them to think they are immune and avoid the extra energy involved in developing CSR because they cannot justify the expense and cannot quantify the benefits precisely. In any event, the benefits are longer term and not in the current fiscal period, more often than not. So CEOs either don't understand or choose not to act. But those who do reap clear benefits. There is a lot of data available today, which supports the fact, that CSR, or sustainability, is good for business. Interface,[22] the carpet people, adopted an environmental strategy long before most of the market, and in general they attribute their significant success to a CSR strategy. Ray Anderson, Chairman of Interface, said: 'From the top line through the bottom line we have benefited from this approach.'[23] A.T. Kearney, the consulting firm, performed an analysis of how companies performed during the 2008 financial crisis and found that in 16 out of 18 industries studied, companies committed to sustainability outperformed industry averages by 15% over the six months from May through November 2008.[24]

The other catch is that it's easy to get caught up in the PR web and start to use CSR as a PR tool rather than as a fundamental strategy. This creates the opposite effect — cynicism and mistrust. Finally, CSR needs to be managed or it doesn't happen. But other than that, CSR just makes sense. It puzzles me that so many businesses just don't get it, actually. And HR managers are way behind. In some businesses, HR managers have taken the initiative and driven CSR forward in many ways. But it is not really HR's role to lead CSR. This is a CEO or executive team responsibility. But HR is an undisputable and crucial partner.

**Sharon:** I want to hear more. More detail. How does it work from day to day? What does a corporate responsible business do in the workplace, for example, that is different from regular HR practices?

**Arena:** Great, I am so glad you want to know more. But first, would you

---

22  www.interfaceinc.com.
23  Quoted in Christina Arena, *Cause for Success* (Novato, CA: New World Library, 2004): 16.
24  www.atkearney.com/index.php/News-media/companies-with-a-commitment-to-sustainability-tend-to-outperform-their-peers-during-the-financial-crisis.html, accessed 1 June 2010.

mind if we took a break? I want to take a short nap. We've got ten more hours of flying time. Let's pick up again in an hour or so, and we will cover responsible workplace things like CSR in the recruitment process, diversity and inclusion, labour rights, rewards and benefits, lay-offs, training and development, internal communications, health and safety, work–life balance, and supporting an ethical culture. All of these topics have new meanings when you consider the social and environmental aspects of the responsible workplace.

**Sharon:** OK. Sweet dreams. Let's continue after your beauty sleep.

Sharon was hooked. Fascinated. So many terms she had heard before and not really stopped to consider were now clear. Perhaps for the first time, she understood that, as an HR manager, CSR could be part of her role and not just another task. She had a lot to think about, but first, she thought to herself, 'Let's see if I can catch the end of that Richard Gere movie!'

# 2

# The CSHR manager and the responsible workplace

**Sharon:** Sleep well?

**Arena:** Yes thanks, I needed that hour. How are you doing? Did you sleep?

**Sharon:** I would rather not say.

**Arena:** Huh?

**Sharon:** I watched the end of Richard Gere.

**Arena:** Ah, I might have guessed. I hope you enjoyed it.

**Sharon:** Now that I am learning about how to become a CSHR manager, I reckon that I have to remain abreast of all sorts of influences and trends.

**Arena:** Not so fast, Sharon, my dear. We have just touched the tip of the iceberg. There's a whole lot more you need to know before you become a CSHR manager.

**Sharon:** So what are we waiting for?

**Arena:** Responsible workplace. What does that mean to you?

**Sharon:** Good, I like tests. A responsible workplace:

- Pays employees on time
- Looks out for the safety of all employees
- Doesn't discriminate

- Honours commitments made to employees
- Provides job security
- Provides benefits other than salary
- Operates in a fair and equitable manner

That's all I can think of right now, for starters. I am sure there must be more.

**Arena:** Great. That's certainly a good start. That is more or less what I would have said some years ago, before I was a CSHR manager. Now that I consider HR management as completely intertwined with corporate social responsibility practices, I tend to look at things a little differently. Remember we talked about stakeholders? Well, who are the most significant stakeholders of any business? By significant, I mean influential.

**Sharon:** The ones owning the shares – the shareholders?

**Arena:** Ah yes. Maybe they would like to think they are the most significant, and it's true that those who invest the money assist the business to keep developing and growing. The business has an obligation to shareholders to ensure they get a good return on their investment. But the people who have the most influence on the business, and are the most affected by the business, in general, on a daily basis, are the employees. Of course, every stakeholder is important, but some are more important, right?

Employees are the group of stakeholders who keep the business running. Without engaged, committed, motivated, capable and competent employees, working together towards a common goal, none of the other stakeholders would benefit because the business would not succeed at an optimum level. In order for a business to be socially responsible, each one of the employees engaged in its activities must be committed to the social responsibility of that business. So one of the first areas a business needs to consider when it is planning its roadmap for social responsibility is what sort of a workplace it creates for its employees. How can you expect your employees to understand and support corporate socially responsible practices if they themselves are not treated in a responsible way? As the old saying goes: social responsibility begins at home. Or something like that.

I have some survey results here in my notebook. In a survey conducted by Sirota in 2007,[1] the results show that '86% of employees who are satisfied with their organization's CSR commitment have high levels of engagement. When employees are negative about their employer's CSR approach, only 37% are highly engaged.' Douglas Klein, the President of Sirota Survey Intelligence, said: 'To employees, CSR and business success

---

1 www.newunionism.net/library/working%20life/Sirota%20-%20Corporate%20 Social%20Responsibility%20Survey%20-%202007.pdf, accessed 6 August 2010.

go together. Companies that enhance their reputations through CSR perform better, and generate greater employee loyalty from workers.' The survey conducted by Sirota involving 1.6 million employees from more than 70 organisations found that

> Employees who have a favourable view of an organisation's corporate social responsibility commitment are also positive about other factors important to its success, including:
>
> • Senior management's integrity,
>
> • Senior management's inspirational sense of direction,
>
> • Organization's competitiveness in the marketplace,
>
> • Company's interest in employees' well-being,
>
> • Employees' engagement or pride in their organization.[2]

An organisation I particularly admire in terms of employee engagement and social responsibility is the Australian bank ANZ.[3] In their corporate social responsibility report for 2007, they report an employee engagement level of 64%. They say that research by Hewitt Associates shows companies that have an engagement score of 60% or higher have an average five-year total shareholder return of greater than 20%.[4] ANZ has rolled out a programme called Breakout, which is designed to create greater trust between bank employees and all stakeholders and realigning around values. They invested significant efforts in putting high numbers of employees through the programme and gained engagement with core values such as customer satisfaction and community involvement.

**Sharon:** I see. Employee engagement is the result of creating a responsible workplace. In a responsible workplace, employees advance the business as well as advancing the corporate social responsibility of the business.

**Arena:** Absolutely.

**Sharon:** I hadn't thought of it that way before.

**Arena:** Between dialogue and engagement, there are a number of standards for a responsible workplace that must be met. Take a look at this next diagram from our CSR consultants.

---

2  Elad Levinson, 'Authentic CSR Creates Higher Employee Engagement', Interaction Associates, www.interactionassociates.com/ideas/authentic-csr-creates-higher-employee-engagement, accessed 1 June 2010.

3  www.anz.com.au.

4  ANZ, 'What's the Difference? Corporate Social Responsibility Report 2007',www.anz.com.au/aus/Corporate-Responsibility-2007/default.asp, accessed 1 June 2010.

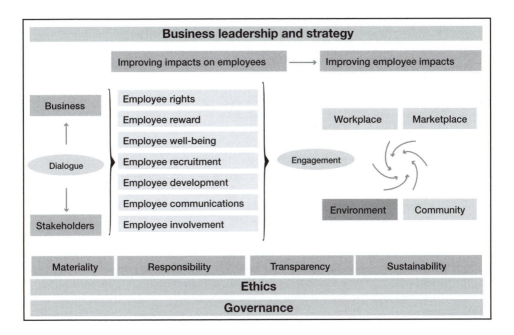

**Arena:** What do you make of this?

**Sharon:** The first thing that strikes me is that we go from improving impacts **on** employees to improving impacts **of** employees. That suggests to me that when employees are feeling that the business is treating them well, they will treat others well. In a CSR context, this means not only contributing more towards the achievement of business objectives, as they relate to the marketplace, customers and suppliers, for example, but in other areas too: in the workplace, by playing an active role in the culture we want to create; in the community, by getting involved and sharing their skills and energies in volunteer activity; and in protecting the environment both inside and outside the workplace.

**Arena:** You are absolutely correct! Most people don't understand this scope. You have hit the nail on the head. CSR begins with creating a responsible workplace, where the business takes responsibility for its impacts on employees and their families. This process starts with maintaining dialogue with employees about what they want from the business, and translates into actions that improve impacts on employees and thereby engages them, so that they can represent the responsible business to all their stakeholders and interfaces.

**Sharon:** Yes, that makes sense to me, though I am not sure about the dialogue bit. Surely you don't expect us to let the employees dictate how the business is run. It's not a democracy, after all. We have done our best to prevent unionisation of our business. They wanted to form a union but the CEO said that if they did, he would make sure everyone went back to earning minimum wage and strictly legal minimum benefits. They soon backed down. I was pleased in a way. I really don't want to be spending all my time negotiating with unions. At our company, the management team is responsible for deciding business strategy, and I am the one in charge of HR policies. Dialogue with employees seems to be a little risky, doesn't it?

**Arena:** Yes, of course it's risky! We might just hear something we'd prefer to avoid. But then, isn't that what taking responsibility is all about? How can we be responsible if we don't face reality? How can we fulfil our obligations to employees if we don't ask them about their expectations? How can we create an open and trusting environment if we are not open enough to hear what employees expect of us? I don't mean chatter in the corridor or around the water-cooler. I mean a structured process for gaining information from employees. This is scary, I admit.

I agree with you that business is not necessarily a democracy. The CEO and the management team make the decisions. Dialogue assists them to make **informed** decisions. To decide based on reality, not assumptions. Dialogue does not imply that the management must implement every suggestion or request. But it does imply a deep desire to understand and acknowledge the aspirations and concerns of employees. This is the first step.

**Sharon:** How do you go about creating this sort of dialogue?

**Arena:** There are many ways of creating dialogue. Remember, it's not just dialogue about business issues. It's also dialogue about the corporate responsibility of the business. There are many opportunities for dialogue, formal and informal — in fact this is an entire subject in itself. Let's park it for a while, and come back to it. I want to make sure you understand the entire scope of how HR interacts with CSR and the issues it needs to address. Then we can talk about them one by one.

**Sharon:** OK. That sounds great. Would you mind just hanging on while I check if there is another movie. I hardly get the time to go to the cinema these days, except when the kids want to see something that usually makes me fall asleep. Brad Pitt is on Channel 10 in 20 minutes. Do you think we will have covered the HR scope by then?

**Arena:** I see you are a real movie freak. You ought to work for this big pharmaceutical company I know. As part of their employee well-being programme, they have a film club. Once every month or so, they hire out a whole cinema and premiere a new film. Employees are entitled to purchase four tickets at extremely subsidised rates. It's a great way to provide a benefit to employees, and creates another opportunity for people in the business to get to know each other on an informal level.

**Sharon:** That sounds great. But surely CSR is not just about dialogue and films?

**Arena:** Correct! Responsible workplace covers a range of topics, as you saw in the diagram.

I will start with **employee rights**. Does the business actively uphold employee rights? Does the business proactively ensure that employees are informed of their rights? Do the employees in your business know their rights? A responsible business takes active steps to ensure employees are informed about and understand what they should be able to expect from their employer both in terms of the law and in terms of additional employee policies and practices which apply in the workplace. Some of these rights are protected by the Universal Declaration of Human Rights, some by the Global Compact of the United Nations, some by International Labour Organisation standards, some by local law and some by the company's code of ethics.

This may sound obvious, right? It's more than just obeying the law. It's taking a proactive approach to informing employees so that they can make responsible choices about things that concern them. Even if the employee does not make a specific effort to know what his or her rights are, the business has a duty to make sure this information is available to him or her.

**Sharon:** I agree, that as an HR manager, I haven't given this much thought. I don't know if the employees in my business truly know what they are entitled to. From the sort of questions I get asked, I tend to think they believe they are entitled to a whole lot more that they actually are. In fact, having them know what their rights are would save me a lot of time, and I am sure it would earn the company points for transparency. Perhaps it would even save us money in claims and arbitration. Last month, I spent hours and hours in meetings because an employee claimed he did not receive compensation for moving to work in another company location. He was definitely not entitled to compensation as the new location is only 10 km away from the old one, but he had heard that the law says he is, and he wrote a long letter demanding compensation. We had no obligation to pay, but had we taken a more proactive approach in communicating his rights upfront, we might have been able to avoid the loss of time and energy.

**Arena:** Another area of responsible workplace practices is **employee reward**. Do you pay minimum wage or more than minimum wage? I read recently that millions of people in the UK are known as the working poor.[5] Isn't that a tragedy? Nearly two out of five low-earners struggle to meet bills and honour credit commitments. You work your guts off and still don't have enough money to feed your family and pay your mortgage. I can't think of anything more depressing. What is the responsibility of business to ensure employees earn a living wage, and how can this be dealt with in order to ensure the sustainability of the business? Who defines what a living wage is?

5   Jeff Prestridge, 'The Working Poor in Fight for Survival', *Mail Online*, 6 March 2010, www.dailymail.co.uk/money/article-1256048/The-working-poor-fight-survival. html, accessed 1 June 2010.

The Swiss pharmaceutical company Novartis did a brilliant job of defining a living wage and implementing a global programme to ensure that all people employed in their business are paid accordingly. This is something I took from their website:

> Traditionally, companies respect minimum wages set by law and use competitive salaries to attract talent. The living wage concept is a diversion from this model, creating a new 'minimum' based on the cost of living. A living wage reflects the local cost of a basket of goods considered to provide an adequate standard of living and is generally higher than the legal minimum wage. Novartis is one of the first international companies to have defined and implemented a living wage globally, and worked with Business for Social Responsibility (BSR) to create a methodology to determine a living wage standard.[6]

BSR[7] is a non-profit organisation supporting CSR in America. Novartis, working in partnership with a range of social organisations to define what that standard should be, created a new methodology and applied it all over their business in more than 40 countries. The initial analysis of Novartis's 90,000 employees showed that 93 employees were underpaid against this new standard, which Novartis corrected accordingly. What do you say to that, Sharon? Isn't that taking a very proactive approach to employee rights?

**Sharon:** Sure! That's impressive!

**Arena:** Guess who led the implementation of this programme? Which function in the business? This is another quote from their case study:[8] 'The Novartis guideline on fair working conditions had focused on a uniform principle to be applied to all employees worldwide — so Human Resources (HR) was the obvious global line function to take responsibility for implementation of the living wage commitment.' See how HR and CSR are connected? A business that is not CSR-oriented would just not think about things in this way. What a great piece of HR work.

On a wider level, CSR thinking also considers the company's remuneration and reward policy and how it is applied in the business. Who are the top wage earners and what levels of salary do they earn in relation to the rest of the employees in the business? A major issue in the debate around the global financial crisis that came to a peak in the last quarter of 2008 was the inflated salaries of senior business people — chairmen of boards of directors, CEOs, senior management — and the

6 Novartis, 'Novartis shares living wage experience at UN Global Compact Leaders Summit', 2007, www.corporatecitizenship.novartis.com/news/2007-07-06_living-wage.shtml, accessed 10 June 2010.

7 www.bsr.org.

8 Novartis, 'Implementing a Living Wage Globally: The Novartis Approach', (Basle, Switzerland: Novartis, 2006, www.corporatecitizenship.novartis.com/downloads/cc-in-action/Living_Wage.pdf, accessed 10 June 2010).

terms and conditions they were awarded including many different types
of personal benefits. They were flying off to meetings in their private jets
while the factory workers were not able to afford the basic essentials.
There are big debates about how ethical that is. Is there a difference
between remuneration levels for men and women? What is in the
remuneration package besides salary? What about options programmes
and profit-sharing? What about transparency in the area of remuneration?
How are pay reviews decided and administered? Does the person who
shouts the loudest get the highest pay rise? To what extent is pay linked
to performance? All of these issues are core to the responsible and
sustainable approach. Who drives policy and practice in all of these areas?
Not the CFO, of course. If it were left to the CFO, the only people who would
get pay increases would be finance people!

**Sharon:** Funny. But I know what you mean. We have a remuneration policy
and it seems fair to me. All the HR people earn three times as much as
everybody else!

**Arena:** What?

**Sharon:** That was a JOKE! Or wishful thinking.

**Arena:** Ah OK, I was just about to ask you for a job.

**Sharon:** You're hired.

**Arena:** Seems like I already have a full-time job teaching you about CSR.

**Sharon:** You are really giving me a new perspective on my role as an HR
manager. Thanks!

**Arena:** OK, save the thanks for the time being. Let's keep moving. Another
area of responsible workplace practices relates to **employee well-being**.
This covers a whole range of things, including safety at work. How do you
ensure your employees' safety is protected while they are at work? Not
just workers in factories, where there are obvious safety hazards and
risks. Office employees too. When was the last time you talked to your office
staff on safety practices at work? What about road safety? How much time
do you spend training employees in safe working practices? What about
the physical working environment? Ergonomics. Do you have a policy on
ergonomics?

**Sharon** (laughing)**:** Ergonomics? Come on. We HR people don't like using
big words. We did make a check once about the way people sit in front of
their computer screens. The Safety Manager recommended it. We replaced
a few chairs but that was it.

**Arena:** Good, but there's more. Did you know that half of employee health
problems that lead to time off work are caused by poor ergonomics?
Companies lose millions of dollars through lost work time resulting from
employee accidents and injuries. The responsible thing to do is create a
working environment in which the company can benefit from maximum

healthy time at work and the employees can work in an environment which contributes to their good health instead of destroying it. I could talk for hours on this. I probably will if you don't stop me.

**Sharon:** I won't stop you, unless they bring that Brad Pitt movie forward.

**Arena:** Funny. More on well-being. How do you create a drug-free, smoke-free, alcohol-free, violence-free working environment? How do you positively encourage employees to look after their own health? This is in the business interest of course — healthier employees are usually happier, more productive, and take less time off sick. They cost you less and they deliver more. This is how CSHR-led programmes can have a direct impact on the bottom-line profitability of the business. Studies conducted at some of the world's leading corporations, such as General Motors, Johnson & Johnson, Procter & Gamble and Chevron, have demonstrated that well-being programmes can be cost-beneficial — they can save more money than they cost, thus producing a positive return on investment. A recent study that compared the programmes of ten Fortune 500 companies found that the median return on investment (ROI) was $3 in benefits per dollar spent.[9]

It's not just enough to ensure the employee is safe and healthy at work. Employees must be safe from security problems too. This is particularly important in jobs where there is exposure to the general public. Some businesses train employees in service roles to deal with violence from the general public. Well-being also includes welfare and social benefits — how does your company deal with employees in a more holistic sense? What about the ways in which employees are encouraged to balance their work with the rest of their life activities? We often refer to work–life balance. Who determines balance? In my company we talk about work–life management: the extent to which the company assists employees in handing work responsibilities in harmony with the responsibilities they have in all the other areas of their lives. This is a whole area in its own right. There are many companies today who promote work–life management programmes and find that they gain immeasurable benefits in many ways. This is a truly advanced approach to responsible workplace practice.

I was reading the Aviva[10] social responsibility report for 2008.[11] Seems like a really positive company. This is what they say about employee well-being:

> We are equally supportive of people's individual well-being, and promote 'lifestyle awareness' topics such as fitness, posture, relaxation, stress management and healthy eating. In many of our business units, company-sponsored Employee Assistance Programmes provide staff and their families with support, ranging from guid-

---

9  www.well-being-at-work.co.uk/corporate-well-being.php, accessed 10 June 2010.
10  Aviva is the world's fifth largest insurance company: www.aviva.com.
11  www.aviva.com/reports/csr08/page109, accessed 24 August 2010.

ance on parenting, education and finance through to professional counselling services for emotional and addiction issues. In several locations, including Australia, employees receive company-funded vaccinations against influenza, and we offer seminars at our global headquarters in London to help employees who want to stop smoking. Employees with back pain at Aviva Czech Republic can relax on a hydro jet bed during lunch breaks and out of work hours, while Hibernian held 'Sleep Factor' and 'Beat the Energy Slump' workshops.

Wish I knew how to beat that energy slump. I fixed a meeting with the Aviva Training Manager, who will be at the ASTD conference, to try to find out how HR can justify this, and how they assess the effects.

What about spirituality in the workplace? How does the company provide for spiritual growth of its people? Does that seem strange? Since when did spirituality have a place in the office?

**Sharon:** You mean, except for when people shout 'Oh my God' when something goes wrong?

**Arena** (laughing): Yeah, I mean a little more than that. You will be surprised to know that it does have a place in the office. At Bank Leumi's[12] head office in Tel Aviv, there is a synagogue. There are many companies around the world with places of worship and many activities for employees of a spiritual nature. Spiritual, religious, whatever you want to call it, leaders of responsible workplaces are starting to realise that their employees contribute better if they respond to a more holistic set of needs rather than focusing on the pay packet alone.

These are just some of the aspects of employee well-being which go beyond the things that laws usually dictate, but serve to ensure that the core stakeholder group of employees are treated in a manner which will enable them to be healthy, productive and motivated.

**Sharon:** Yes, I see. I mean, this is not entirely new to me. As an HR manager in my previous job, I ran a diet class. I had Weightwatchers come in and run an in-house programme. And the group also went walking together. People really appreciated it. So much so that they asked for the meals served in the company dining room to be calorie-labelled. Two of the group actually said they had improved cholesterol levels as a result. These are things that we do anyway in HR. Why suddenly call it social responsibility or CSR?

**Arena:** Yes, you are right. Much of what we call social responsibility is often just part of the way things get done. Many companies, for example, don't like to measure or talk about their employee volunteering programmes because it's just something they do. They don't want to brand it, or leverage it; they just believe it's the right thing. The point about social responsibility is that it's part of the business strategy and it

12 www.leumi.co.il.

requires a stakeholder mind-set. It requires the business to consider all of its impacts and review the risk and opportunity in each. Many businesses act in a socially responsible way in part of their activities. The holistic approach relates to considering the entire spectrum and prioritising and aligning. A business which runs a diet class but at the same time practises discrimination in the hiring process is not adopting a comprehensive level of corporate responsibility regarding its impacts on employees.

Here's an example from another business function: marketing. A company a friend of mine used to work for, Unilever, is a great marketing company. In recent years, Unilever has been attacked for hypocrisy in its marketing processes.[13] One the one hand, there is the Dove Real Women campaign, which promotes real beauty and denounces the beauty industry as promoting unrealistic female stereotypes and influencing young people in a negative way. This was a wonderful campaign supported by the Dove Self-Esteem Fund,[14] a programme to help build self-esteem in women. Great stuff. On the other hand, the same company ran a series of ads for Axe deodorant for men, that's Lynx in the UK, and the ads portrayed women as dropping everything to chase after men wearing this mystical deodorant as if they were wild animals. Very demeaning for women. How can a company run two ads with opposing social messages? And what were the social considerations in the Axe ad? What message was that ad giving to the women working at Unilever? Or was the financial bottom line the only consideration when that campaign was approved?

So you see, running a diet class is a great socially responsible thing to do. But this doesn't replace a strategic approach to social responsibility.

Anyway, there are many more aspects of responsible workplace we need to consider. What time is it? We have another six hours' flying time. I think we can make some good progress in six hours. Unless you want to sit and drool over Brad Pitt?

**Sharon:** Nope. No more distractions. I can drool some other time.

**Arena:** The next area of responsible workplace practices we should talk about relates to **employee recruitment**. Under the heading of recruitment I also include the whole topic of employee diversity and a culture of inclusion, which is much more than a recruitment process, but it starts with recruitment. CSR is a great recruitment tool. More and more research suggests that people looking for jobs, particularly top talent with potential such as MBA graduates are looking for jobs with 'meaning', jobs which give them a sense of contributing to a better world rather than just making money. No coincidence that Wal-Mart changed its company slogan from 'Always Low Prices' to ' Save money. Live better'. People want better lives; they don't just want better jobs. People want to make a difference; their purpose in life is not simply about making shareholders richer.

---

13  hwww.culture-buzz.com/blog/AXE-VS-DOVE-Against-Unilever-1492.html, accessed 2 June 2010.

14  campaignforrealbeauty.com.

People want to feel worthwhile, not just another statistic on the payroll. In a 2008 study by Deloitte and the Aspen Institute,[15] 'the potential to make a contribution to society through one's job is more important to MBA students in 2007 than it was in previous years (26% compared to 15% in 2002)'. Nearly 60% of students said that 'responsible corporate governance and transparent business practices' were very important to them in selecting a job, and nearly 50% said that responsible supply chain management was very important. In another 2008 survey, 'college students continue to demonstrate strong commitment toward the brands they feel are contributing positively to world issues and the environment. A growing 41% (net) of respondents prefer socially responsible brands — compared with the 37% saying so last year. Also, that 41% figure is 24% higher than in '06.'[16] So being a socially responsible company clearly enhances your ability to attract and retain top talent.

How do you ensure a fair and equal opportunity in your recruiting processes? When I ask colleagues why they don't recruit more women or more minorities, they say, 'we are open to all candidates and we treat all applicants on merit'. But this doesn't go far enough. A company that has a monochromic workforce discriminates. That's it. They may not want to discriminate. They may not believe they are discriminating. But, if there is no diversity in the workforce, discrimination is present. That's the hard truth. It's not enough to wait for diverse people to apply. You have to look for them, seek them out and create tailored recruitment programmes to enable them to have a fair chance. You do this by engaging with specialists in the community who have knowledge of different groups in the population who might otherwise have difficulty in applying for jobs or being selected on the basis of standard criteria. Fair opportunity also means opportunities for internal people. In IFC we have an open internal recruitment programme where employees can apply for new positions within the company and have a three-day advantage before the jobs are advertised to the general public. There are many other issues related to recruitment, but I am getting a little tired now and would like a rest. What about you?

**Sharon:** Yes, I think you deserve a break. I understand your point, though. I can't tell you the number of times women candidates have complained to me that a manager asked them how many children they are planning to have and when. A few months ago, a disabled guy who is perfectly able to do programming work wrote a letter to our CEO claiming his 'intelligence was abused' after an interview at Andromex. He wrote that the manager had asked him if being in a wheelchair might affect his programming performance. The manager had also told him, apparently, that the

---

15  www.AspenCBE.org.
16  Alloy Media and Marketing, 'Annual College Explorer Study 2008', www.marketingcharts.com/television/college-students-setting-records-in-spending-civic-engagement-digital-connectivity-5533/alloy-college-company-positive-impact-criteria-2008jpg, accessed 2 June 2010.

Applications Department has a football team and he wouldn't be able to participate and asked if that would that be a problem for him. It sounds ridiculous, I know, but some managers just don't think about what they are saying in interviews. They are embarrassed by difference in people. Actually, that interview could have turned into a legal action, according to the letter the candidate wrote. I understand that it is important to help managers to understand the implications of the way they talk to people in interviews, and more importantly, to view all kinds of people as valuable in their own unique way. Are there any more headlines before we take a break?

**Arena:** Yes, we haven't talked about the way a company trains and develops its employees, or the way a company manages internal communications. We also ought to talk about ethics and effective ethics programmes in the context of a responsible workplace. An ethical culture based on stated values is core to creating the responsibility mind-set and ensuring all employees know what their company stands for and what sort of behaviour is expected from them.

**Sharon:** Yes, we have a code of ethics. It's not been widely published, though.

**Arena:** What are the core elements of the code?

**Sharon:** I haven't memorised it. I can barely remember reading it. I remember it's quite strict about giving and receiving gifts or bribes. I can't really remember anything else.

**Arena:** So maybe your assimilation programme should start with the HR people.

**Sharon:** Now I am quite ashamed of myself. I should have taken more of an interest.

**Arena:** Well, if it helps, I would have answered the same thing a few years ago.

**Sharon:** OK, I think you have earned a break now. I have a lot to think about.

**Arena:** One final bit of data which I often quote. Kaevan Gazdar, in his book Reporting Nonfinancials, wrote: 'Research carried out by the HR consultants Watson Wyatt in 16 European countries shows that companies with strong HR Management deliver almost twice as much shareholder value as their average competitors.'[17]

**Sharon:** Wow!

**Arena:** OK. I want to read a little now. I want to re-read this book I brought with me called Megatrends 2010: The Rise of Conscious Capitalism by

17  Kaevan Gazdar, *Reporting Nonfinancials* (Chichester, UK: Wiley, 2007): 132.

Patricia Aburdene.[18] It's all about social responsibility and spirituality and the way it's affecting businesses. You can read it when I am finished.

**Sharon:** Thanks. I think I have no choice but to become a CSHR manager. Now that I am starting to become aware of these issues, I see that my role is more than just managing the HR function. I think I have a personal responsibility here.

**Arena:** That's great. Let's talk more in a little while.

---

18  Patricia Aburdene, *Megatrends 2010: The Rise of Conscious Capitalism* (Charlottes-ville, VA: Hampton Roads Publishing, 2005).

# 3

# Employee dialogue and engagement

**Sharon:** Arena, put that book down. I want you to talk to me some more.

**Arena:** OK, but it's fascinating. Just look at this on page 23.[1] Jeff Swartz is quoted as saying: 'in a world where a billion people can't read or write, how can anyone say the sole responsibility of business is to shareholders?'

**Sharon:** Arena, you know you are talking to a newcomer to all of this. Before I got on this flight, I thought I was doing pretty well at HR. I thought I knew this profession inside out and back to front. And here I am, after a few hours of you lecturing me, thinking that I have been missing out on half the potential of my role, as though I were doing HR in my own little vacuum. Now don't get me wrong, I am so happy we met up.

**Arena:** They say the teacher turns up when you have a lesson to learn.

## Summary of *Megatrends 2010*

- **The power of spirituality** and the way CEOs have become akin to spiritual leaders, transforming their company's culture
- **The dawn of conscious capitalism** and the growth of stakeholder engagement and corporate social responsibility
- **Leading from the middle** and the power of grassroots and middle management to make waves
- **Spirituality in business** and the growth of spiritual activities in business
- **The values-driven consumer** and the 60 million conscious consumers

1 Patricia Aburdene, *Megatrends 2010*.

who gravitate towards green, organic, natural and values-based products

- **The wave of conscious solutions** and the growing service-provider industry that plays to the spiritual needs of organisations and people
- **The socially responsible investment boom** and the tipping point of investment practices, private and institutional, which are now positively in-screened or negatively out-screened

The overall Megatrend is the Spiritual Transformation of Capitalism.

**Sharon:** Yes, yes, it's that spirituality stuff again, I get it. But no, what I meant was, I am really grateful to you for opening my eyes, for getting me thinking. I can see you are truly passionate about all this. You are quoting your Megatrends book to me as though I am someone who has been doing this for years. HR is not just about people, I know that, it's about creating capability. Suddenly I realise that we have the leverage to create all sorts of new capabilities for our business **and** for our people. But what I meant to say was: Who is Jeff Swartz? What's the big deal about business being responsible to shareholders? Why is that sentence so significant?

**Arena:** OK, Sharon. Let's get to it one by one. Jeff Swartz is an amazing visionary leader. He is the CEO of Timberland.[2] You have heard of Timberland, right? Big outdoor clothing gear manufacturer.

**Sharon:** Yes, Arena. I have heard of Timberland. I am not **that** out of it.

**Arena:** Jeff Swartz has been CEO for over ten years. He is the grandson of the guy that founded the company, but it's really Jeff's doing that has made Timberland one of the leaders in CSR practices in the world. Aburdene mentions in Megatrends 2010 that employees of Timberland get 40 hours paid time off per year to volunteer for community service. I happen to know that their total amounts to something between 70,000 and 80,000 volunteer hours per year. That's equivalent to 40 full-time people. In addition, there are 23 Global Stewards, like local leaders, who ensure the message gets through. They have created dedicated CSR spaces in Timberland offices around the world and drive communication and commitment. There is also the possibility for employees of a six-month paid sabbatical to do something that benefits the community. Again, all of this couldn't happen without the strong support of the HR function. It takes some HR skill to drive a culture that shows such commitment to the community. Timberland is always in the 'Best Companies to Work For' list, and 'Best For Working Mothers' list and more. This is from its website: 'When you join Timberland, we extend an invitation for more than just a job. Through offerings including an employee assistance programme, adoption assistance, pet insurance and elder care programmes, we strive

2 www.timberland.com/home/index.jsp.

to provide support to the **whole** person.'[3] You can't get more spiritual than that, right? What a challenging environment for the HR team, but what a pleasure to be able to work for a company whose leader is committed to driving social and environmental change as part of their very core activities.

**Sharon:** It sounds impressive. It certainly helps, though, to have a CEO who understands all of this. How do I get my CEO to buy into it?

**Timberland values**

- Humanity
- Humility
- Integrity
- Excellence

www.timberland.com

**Arena:** Yes, I agree that is one of our major challenges in HR, not just in the CSR field, but also in many aspects of our work. In the meantime, think of the business benefits — lower turnover, lower sickness rates, new employee skills through volunteer activities, better motivation and commitment — it all comes back to the business.

**Sharon:** Fine, but what about the responsibility of business to its shareholders?

**Arena:** That was a reference to Milton Friedman, the Nobel prize-winning economist who said that the purpose of business is business. He is quoted as saying, 'So the question is, do corporate executives, provided they stay within the law, have responsibilities in their business activities other than to make as much money for their stockholders as possible? And my answer to that is, no, they do not.'[4] These days, the more dominant approach is the one that Swartz subscribes to. That a corporation cannot operate sustainably by focusing only on the amount of money they make, as that is not what most of their stakeholders want. Shareholders may provide the funds, but stakeholders influence the ability of the business to succeed.

**Sharon:** Got it. Down with Milton, right?

**Arena:** Yes, down with Milton. There are some who said they should take back his Nobel prize![5] Look, I need to take a biological break. Here is a short paper I wrote on the subject of stakeholders and stakeholder activism. I wanted to make my CEO aware that he needs to sit up and take stock of this new development. Take a read of this until I get back.

---

3  www.timberland.com/corp/index.jsp?page=workingHere_benefits, accessed 2 June 2010.

4  thinkexist.com/quotes/milton_friedman, accessed 2 June 2010.

5  A reference to a lecture on Ethical Fashion given by CEO of comme il faut fashion house, Sybil Goldfiner, Israel Fashion Conference, 2008.

# Briefing paper on Stakeholder Activism

Arena Dardelle, VP HR, The International Food Company Ltd
June 2009

## Who owns YOUR business?

The concept of business ownership is well laid down in law and subject to a host of regulations around the world. Ownership normally implies the ability to have power or mastery over something.[6] So we would expect that the shareholders of a business would have power, or control, over how the business behaves. However, in these days of stakeholder activism, in all of its various forms, shareholders often find that they have very little power indeed. Let's assume we are talking about stakeholders who are not shareholders. There are many examples of corporations submitting to the will of stakeholders and having to accept the fact that they no longer have power over the way their corporation does business.

## Who owns Starbucks?

One example of this is the capitulation of the Starbucks Corporation in the face of a mass campaign led by Oxfam in 2006.[7] Starbucks, who built their business on the development of specialty coffee blends, sources much of its coffee from Ethiopian coffee farmers. Coffee is Ethiopia's largest export. When coffee farmers tried to register the names of three specialty coffee beans as trademarks, Starbucks is alleged to have wielded its corporate power via the US National Coffee Association (Starbucks is a leading member of this association) to prevent the Ethiopian coffee farmers from receiving the trademark. Oxfam claimed that this would deny the Ethiopians millions of dollars of annual income by providing a fair wage for the local farmers. The UK *Guardian* reported: 'Tadesse Meskela, head of the Oromia coffee farmers cooperative union in Ethiopia, was unimpressed [with Starbucks], however. "Coffee shops can sell Sidamo and Harar coffees for up to £14 a pound because of the beans' specialty status. But Ethiopian coffee farmers only earn between 30p and 59p for their crop, barely enough to cover the cost of production".'[8] Oxfam then launched a mass high-profile public campaign that gained the support of nearly 100,000 activists around the world who faxed letters to the Starbucks CEO, led demonstrations and posted messages of support using the viral power of the Internet. Eventually, Starbucks had no viable alternative option than to back down and support the claims of the Ethiopian coffee farmers and enable them to register their trademarks in the USA, Canada, Japan and Europe,[9] thereby enabling

---

6  www.merriam-webster.com/dictionary/owner.
7  BBC News, 'Starbucks in Ethiopia coffee row', 26 October 2006, news.bbc.co.uk/2/hi/africa/6086330.stm, accessed 2 June 2010.
8  Ashley Seager, 'Starbucks, the coffee beans and the copyright row that cost Ethiopia £47m', *Guardian*, 26 October 2006 , www.guardian.co.uk/world/2006/oct/26/usa.ethicalliving, accessed 2 June 2010.
9  Oxfam International, 'Oxfam celebrates win-win outcome or Ethiopian coffee farmers and Starbucks', press release, 21 June 2007, www.oxfam.org/node/174, accessed 2 June 2010.

them to claim a higher level of prices for coffee bean sales. Significant damage was done to Starbucks' image, enormous amounts of management time was expended in responding to consumer and activist criticisms, and in the period the dispute was live, the Starbucks share price started to plummet.[10] Eventually, trademarks were granted and Starbucks made an agreement with Oxfam and the Ethiopian farmers for continued purchasing at more equitable prices.

Who owns Starbucks? Certainly the shareholders have formal ownership. But in this case, it was the non-profit world and its army of activists who dictated the policy to the coffee giant and caused it to change course.

## Who owns Lafayette?

Lafayette Mining Company is an Australian company that explores and mines metals such as copper and zinc. The company was traded on the Australian Stock Exchange. In 2005, the company engaged in a high-profile mining project at Rapu Rapu, in the Philippines, benefiting from a multi-million $ investment funded by major banks such as ANZ, J.P. Morgan, Standard Chartered and more. Six months after operations commenced, two cyanide-laden waste spills flowed from the mine into waters surrounding Rapu Rapu Island. These spills were linked to fish kills — a disaster with severe implications for the fisheries-dependent people.[11] There were many protests from local residents and activist groups such as Oxfam and Greenpeace, and eventually the mine was forced to shut down. It reopened two years later, to the disgust of many, but by this time the environmentalist pressure had become fierce and Lafayette called in voluntary administration to avoid filing for bankruptcy. Lafayette was delisted from the Australian Stock Exchange, and by mid 2008 had sold its stake in the Rapu Rapu project altogether, leaving much environmental, social and economic disruption in its wake.[12] Who closed the project? This was not a free and voluntary decision of Lafayette's ownership or management. The Chairman of Lafayette 'accused anti-mining groups of what it described as irresponsible and misguided advocacy that is actually anti-poor and economically destructive'.[13] But this criticism was not enough to save the day, in the face of external stakeholder pressure. Stakeholders closed the project.

## Who owns OUR business?

These are two examples of many in which we see the power of global stakeholders to change the way corporations behave. Who owns OUR busi-

---

10  Yahoo Finance shows Starbucks (SBUX) share price in October 2006 was 34.1 while by July 2007 it was 26.4. This was the start of a long drop in its share price; although it cannot be attributed entirely to the Ethiopian affair, this issue did nothing to bolster the ailing share price of this large manufacturer.

11  www.oxfam.org.au/explore/mining/our-work-with-communities/rapu-rapu-the-philippines, accessed 24 August 2010.

12  Bank Track, www.banktrack.org/show/news/strong_criticism_on_reopening_lafayette_rapu_rapu_mine_philippines (9 February 2007), accessed 2 June 2010.

13  www.pmea.com.ph/blog/index.php/2007/06/22/lafayette-criticizes-anti-mining-groups, accessed 18 August 2010.

ness? We must consider how to ensure that we engage the stakeholders who have the power to dictate the way we run our business. We must conduct our business in such a way as to respect their rights and concerns, if we want to achieve our business objectives.

**Stakeholder management is a core element of a corporately responsible and sustainable business.** This requires a culture of listening, engaging and triple-bottom-line thinking. It needs a strong level of participation of all people in the company.

**Sharon:** Interesting. Did your boss take note?

**Arena:** Ah, I haven't given it to him yet. But I know he understands that stakeholder engagement is a core element of corporate responsibility practice and triple-bottom-line thinking.

**Sharon:** Triple bottom line? I have heard that term but I am not quite sure what it means.

**Arena:** Yes, it's quite a common term. It refers to the three kinds of impacts of a company — social, environmental and economic. It means that a business should measure all three kinds of performance and be responsible to all stakeholders, not just the ones interested in the financial bottom line, as the overall sustainability of the business depends on meeting the needs of all stakeholders. It was a thought-leader in CSR called John Elkington who coined the term in the '90s, and he later wrote a book about it called Cannibals with Forks,[14] explaining this triple-bottom-line theory, which was quite influential. Sometimes people call it 3BL. There is even a very prominent CSR communications company in the USA called 3BL Media[15] that specialises in communications on the subject of CSR. They also have what they call a 3BL TV channel where you can view short videos of CSR news and commentary by leading CSR experts. It's worth taking a look when we get back on terra firma. Anyway, let's get back on-topic and stakeholder engagement as far as it concerns our employees. As you now know, CSR-driven businesses engage their employees in their corporate responsibility activities. But now you know that employees won't promote the company's values and practices unless they experience these practices as part of the way the company treats and values them. It's not only a necessity for a CSR business to engage employees, it's an opportunity. CSR needs employees to be engaged and at the same time it helps to engage employees.

I told you a while ago, right, that a core first element of responsible practice is dialoguing with stakeholders so as to understand their needs and aspirations. Let's start there as we talk about employees. The first

14  John Elkington, *Cannibals with Forks: The Triple Bottom Line of 21st Century Business* (Oxford, UK: Capstone, 1997, www.johnelkington.com/pubs-books-business.htm).

15  www.3blmedia.com.

aspect of a responsible workplace is one which understands the aspirations and concerns of its employees, and takes these into account when making business decisions. When did you last do an employee survey? What are the internal communications processes like in your company?

**Sharon:** We issue a monthly news update to all employees, telling them what's going on. We send it out by email, and we print it and send copies to each department. There is an annual managers' meeting where all the managers are updated. There is a company intranet site with a lot of information about marketing and company policies and things. We do an employee survey every two years, analyse the results and take action on things that need to be improved. I think we do well as far as communications are concerned. We also have company notice boards around the offices and factories with updates and information.

**Arena:** That's great. Many companies do much of what you said, but looking through the lens of a CSHR manager, there may be lots more opportunity to really engage employees. Let's zoom in on that employee survey. This is one differentiator between an HR manager and a CSHR manager — the way they design an employee survey. Your employee survey is about satisfaction, right?

**Sharon:** Yes, of course. We want to know that employees are satisfied in their roles, that they enjoy working in the company, that they are getting what they need to do their job correctly and productively. We also want to know what they think about their managers, if they feel they are being managed effectively. If we know all this, we can use the information to retain good people and encourage delivery of desired results.

**Arena:** Fine, but a CSHR manager would want to know more than that. A CSHR manager would want to know if the company values are aligned with company practices, and if employees are positively engaged in a values-based and CSR approach. As in the example of ANZ I told you about. The CSHR manager would want to know what the employees' aspirations focus on, and what the employees expect from the business. The CSHR manager would want to know if the employee feels the company is behaving ethically. So in any survey, the CSHR manager includes a section about values, and the way the employee sees these values in play in the day-to-day business. The survey also includes some open questions about aspirations. Let me switch on my laptop so I can show you some examples from some company CSR reports I have filed on disk.

We talked about Gap Inc. Take a look at their CSR report, which says:

> a strong culture starts with open dialogue, which is why we invest in employee opinion surveys and channels that promote communication. In 2004, we piloted an employee opinion survey, which we expanded in 2005 and 2006. Over the past three years, more than 54,000 employees have participated in the surveys, providing their opinions and ideas. We learned from the survey that we've done well in three key areas: our customer focus, respect for

each other, and our satisfaction in the personal accomplishments of our work. At the same time, employees told us there's room for improvement in several areas, including career development.[16]

Respect is a Gap Inc. core value, and surveys cover not only the degree to which employees are satisfied but also the degree to which they identify with Gap values.

Take another example: Vodafone. I have always admired Vodafone as a company that is very, very strong on stakeholder engagement. In their 2007 Corporate Responsibility report[17] they show the results of their employee engagement surveys over a period of three years.

In their 2007 survey, 81% of their global workforce responded — that's 81% of over 50,000 employees. How good are you at maths?

**Sharon:** That's around 40,000 responses, right?

**Arena:** Well done! Who said HR people can't count?! With that in mind, look at these results:

| Question | 2007 | 2006 | 2005 |
|---|---|---|---|
| (% employees responding positively) | Employee Survey | Pulse Survey | Employee Survey |
| I am proud to work for Vodafone | 78 | 80 | 78 |
| I am rewarded fairly for the work that I do | 46 | 44 | 42 |
| Rate your operating company/Group Function on taking a genuine interest in the well-being of its employees | 57 | 41 | 42 |
| Rate your operating company/Group Function on being ethical in the way it conducts business | 74 | 71 | 75 |
| People in my team are treated fairly regardless of their gender, background, age or beliefs | 81 | – | 71 |

**Arena:** See how they include questions about fairness, diversity and inclusion, employee well-being, and ethics? This is the foundation of internal corporate social responsibility.

16  Gap Inc. CR report, 2006, www.gapinc.com/public/documents/CSR_Report_05_06. pdf: 42, accessed 2 June 2010.

17  Vodafone 'One Strategy Corporate Responsibility Report for the Year Ended 31 March 2008', www.corporateregister.com/a10723/Vodafonegrp08-sus-uk.pdf: 216, accessed 2 June 2010.

## Vodafone values (passions)

- Passion for customers: 'Our customers have chosen to trust us. In return, we must strive to anticipate and understand their needs and delight them with our service.'
- Passion for our people: 'Outstanding people working together make Vodafone exceptionally successful.'
- Passion for results: 'We are action-oriented and driven by a desire to be the best.'
- Passion for the world around us: 'We will help the people of the world to have fuller lives — both through the services we provide and through the impact we have on the world around us.'[18]

**Sharon:** I see. I get the link. So you are saying that in designing employee satisfaction surveys, we in HR should take the lead with a CSR mind-set by creating the link to company values?

**Arena:** Yes, but also CSR values. Questions like:

- Is it important for you to work for a company that invests in the community?

- Is it important for you to work for a company that enables you to volunteer in the community?

- What do you believe our company's contribution to society should be (other than a financial contribution?)?

- Is it important for you to work for a company that protects the environment?

- What is most important to you in your work?

Here's a list of optional employee survey questions that a CSHR manager could try to include in a formal survey. Take a look at it later and maybe you can use it in your next survey.

Arena gave Sharon a long list of employee dialogue survey questions.

18 Vodafone One Strategy Corporate Responsibility Report, www.corporateregister. com/a10723/Vodafonegrp08-sus-uk.pdf: 12, accessed 2 June 2010.

## A selection of employee survey questions designed with a CSR mind-set

### Engagement with company values and ethics

1. Do you find the company values inspiring?
2. What are the most important values you identify with in a work context?
3. Do you uphold the company values when you are not at work?
4. What do you believe our company's contribution to society should be (other than a financial contribution)?
5. What is most important to you in working for this company?
6. Do people in this company treat all fellow employees with respect and dignity at all times?
7. How important do you believe it is important to conduct business in an ethical manner?
8. Are you aware of the company's code of ethics?
9. Does the company code of ethics serve as a guide for you in your role?
10. Is the company effective in ensuring everyone is aware of the company code of ethics?
11. Have you been aware of any breaches of the code of ethics by your co-workers?
12. Does company management provide a personal example of upholding company values?
13. Do you believe a company has a responsibility to society and the environment?
14. Is it important for you to work for a company that practises CSR?

### Marketplace impacts

15. Do you believe that the company treats all customers with respect?
16. Do you believe the company deals fairly and decently with all suppliers?
17. Do you think the company marketing campaigns reflect company values?
18. Do you believe the company pays its suppliers fairly?
19. Do you believe your company upholds principles of human rights in all its dealings?

### Workplace impacts

20. Do you believe the company offers equal opportunity to all, unconditionally?
21. Does the company make sure you know your employee rights at work?
22. Does the company value the differences you bring as an individual to the workplace?
23. Does the company encourage expression of differences in the workplace?

24. Are you shown respect at all times?

25. Do you have feel you have an equal opportunity to advance within the company?

26. Do you feel the company values you as highly as it values its customers?

## Community impacts

27. Does the company management behave with integrity?

28. Are you aware of the ways the company contributes to the community?

29. Is it important for you to work for a company that invests in the community?

30. Has volunteering in the community on behalf of the company provided you with new skills?

31. Have you benefitted from volunteering in the community on behalf of the company?

32. Do you believe your company contribution to the community is serving a real need?

33. Do you talk about your company community activities to your family or friends outside of work?

34. Are you proud of your company's contribution in the community?

## Environment impacts

35. Is it important for you to work for a company that protects the environment?

36. Do you believe it is important for all individuals to reduce their negative effects on the environment?

37. Do you have opportunities to demonstrate your environmental commitment in your work?

38. Do you make an effort to reduce your personal carbon footprint?

39. Have the company programmes helped you to understand your impact on the environment?

40. Do you feel the company has a responsibility to protect the environment?

41. Have you applied positive environmental practices outside of work in other activities?

42. Does management demonstrate a personal example with regard to the environment?

**Arena:** There are many forms of variations on these questions of course. Each company could select the questions most relevant to them. An example of this is the Israeli fashion company, comme il faut.[19] Their business is both owned by women and managed by women. They are strongly supportive of feminist principles. One of the questions in their employee survey is 'Are you a feminist?' enabling them to gauge to what extent employees are influenced by and engaged with the company ideology.

**Sharon:** OK. I am a feminist so I have no problem with that. But I understand. I do a survey and get to know what the employees want from the business. What then? I can't make the boss suddenly change all his plans and do what the employees want. It's not regular stuff like dissatisfaction with pay and benefits, or poor management skills. You're talking about employees expressing things that the company has not committed to providing, or creating values which don't exist.

**Arena:** By and large, I don't believe you will get any major surprises. Surveys tend to be a hard reflection of things we already know but have often not faced up to or openly admitted. We may get some detailed responses that surprise us, but if you know your organisation, in your heart of hearts, you won't be surprised by the headline results. The fact that employees are speaking up in a certain direction may be just the tool you need to help to convince your boss and the management team to sit up and take notice. Remember, this is not just a process to improve CSR. The more you address employee aspirations and concerns, the more they will engage.

Before my current job, I once did a piece of consulting with a small company with fewer than 150 employees. The company operated several community centres, for profit, including one large sports centre. The employees were provided with free passes to the sports centre for themselves and their families. This sounded great, but it was not declared as a taxable benefit, which was against the law. The employees who told me about this knew that it was wrong; they felt rather awkward talking about it, and it became a sort of open and uncomfortable secret. The company management had lived with this situation believing that the cost of paying the tax on this benefit would make it impossible to continue to provide the employees with the benefit. They operated out of the best of intentions, but the bottom line was that they were complicit in illegal behaviour and allowed their employees to understand that it was OK to break the law. I took this up with the management and suggested lower-cost approaches that were entirely legal and enabled employees to retain the benefit. Everyone heaved a sigh of relief! It is only through the survey I conducted and dialogue that I engaged in with employees that this problem came to light and was openly addressed, removing a sensitive point of risk for the company and helping employees to see that ethical conduct is important.

19 www.comme-il-faut.com.

If management is seen to be complicit in unethical behaviour, they have no chance of creating an ethical culture.

Remember that engagement is different from satisfaction. Employees can be satisfied but not truly engaged with core values, principles and culture. They may not even **know** the core values of the business, yet they may be satisfied with their pay, their job and their boss. But if they are not engaged, they will not be able to contribute most effectively because they don't know exactly what the company wants of them. Get that? The best results are achieved when employee are satisfied **and** engaged. CSR requires them to be engaged with the CSR agenda, not just with traditional business objectives.

**Sharon:** I see.

**Arena:** A consultant we use talked about a company they did some work with. It was clear in a very dramatic way that employees were not satisfied with their pay and benefits and felt there were limited career prospects. The company felt that terms and benefits were competitive, and they practised a policy of promotion from within, but the employees felt they were not getting adequate responses on either count. The consultant told the company that its message was not getting through to the employees. It embarked on a programme to understand the underlying issues in more detail, make adjustments where appropriate, though nothing major was required, and communicate to employees much more effectively. The message just wasn't getting through.

The challenge for the CSHR manager is in presenting this to your management team not as an ultimatum but as an opportunity. This is what employees are saying. The management has a choice. It can ignore them and take the risk of their not being fully engaged. What is the cost to the business of this route? Lost business? Quality problems? Poor relationships with customers? Missed deadlines? Lack of innovation? Conflict? Or management can choose to accept that employees are giving them real messages, understand fully, evaluate options and take action. Not everything will be feasible, but research shows that in those cases where there is acknowledgement of the messages, response to employees and action on some of the core issues, engagement is enhanced and results improve over time. This ability to influence the management team is a core HR competency. It was not invented with CSR. The CSHR manager needs to know how to link the two for maximum benefit of the business and the people.

**Sharon:** You have got me wondering how many of our employees are engaged. I know that most of them are satisfied, but we haven't focused on engagement, as we assumed that if they were satisfied, they would be engaged. As we don't yet have a CSR programme, I have never tested their views on CSR either. I am really interested to know if our employees would appreciate some form of CSR activity, and whether this could bring us an advantage in enhancing their contribution. This is so interesting. Do you have any more examples?

**Arena:** There are many different examples. Employee engagement is not just about doing surveys. A survey is a good place to start, so as to understand the measure of identification with and application of corporate responsibility practices, and to understand the aspirations of employees and the messages they are sending. A survey is the first step in creating dialogue with employees — true two-way dialogue. The survey results become a platform on which to have conversations with employees about things that matter.

Arena was interrupted by the pilot announcing a holding pattern prior to touchdown in San Diego. Sharon and Arena listened to the pilot's update and instructions as the plane drew closer to their destination. They put their shoes back on and fastened their seatbelts for landing. As they were breaking through the clouds, Sharon was trying to recall the main points of their conversation so far and decided she would get to her hotel and create a summary for herself so that nothing would get lost. With the faintest of bumps and a slight grating of the airplane wheels, they touched down. Sharon was in the process of thanking Arena for what had been a life-changing flight for her, when Arena interrupted and handed two things. One was a copy of *HRWORLD*,[20] which contained an article called 'Sustainability and Employee Engagement: Which Drives Which?' and another was a case study brief she had written herself on the subject they had been talking about: employee engagement. Sharon knew that she would read both that very evening, jet lag or no jet lag. And then she would write her summary.

The two exchanged details of their hotels in San Diego and business cards for reconnecting back at home. After they picked up their luggage and made for the exit, Sharon heading for the taxi rank, Arena towards the pick-up point where she was being collected by a colleague in the local office of her company, they hugged and wished each other a fun and fruitful stay in San Diego and a productive conference. Arena was feeling she had made a difference, and Sharon's head was buzzing hard with all the new ideas and concepts she had picked up on this memorable flight.

20 A fictional magazine about HR for HR professionals.

# Sustainability and employee engagement:
## Which drives which?

By **Ellen Resnick** and **Carol Casazza Herman**[21]

DOES SUSTAINABILITY DRIVE employee engagement or does employee engagement drive sustainability? It's somewhat of a trick question, because both are true: Sustainability and employee engagement enjoy a synergistic relationship in that they both support and advance one another.

Sustainability is a values-driven topic that motivates employees to get involved in something meaningful and identify with their company. It's about personal responsibility, improving our health, and protecting our legacy to our children.

And while sustainability drives employee engagement, the reverse is also true. Getting employees on board is key to 'making sustainability stick'™. Successful companies create a culture that is focused on the Triple Bottom Line and invite all employees to participate.

### Sustainability: a driver of employee engagement

As HR professionals, you know that employee engagement is important to the success of your company. In fact, you've probably seen research reports that directly correlate employee engagement with business performance. And the link between employee engagement and talent retention is clear: Employees who are connected to their work are more motivated to achieve their best and more likely to stay.

However, did you know that 'reputation for social responsibility' is one of the highest ranking drivers for employee engagement? According to a recent global study by Towers Perrin,* CSR was ranked #3 in the top ten items that drive employee engagement, right below 'senior management's sincere interest in employee well being' and 'the opportunity an employee has to improve skills and capabilities'.

Employees care deeply about their company's social responsibility and sustainability practices. They want to work for an organisation that not only is high performing in its industry, but also has a solid record of performance in environmental stewardship, diversity and community involvement.

So, we know that employee engagement drives business performance and sustainability drives employee engagement. But, what are the implications for HR professionals?

Here are three things you can do to take advantage of your company's sustainability efforts to engage employees:

**1. Communicate early and often to employees about your company's sustainability efforts.** Your employees should be the first to know about your sustainability initiatives; don't neglect them in the rush to reach external stakeholders. And don't

21 An original paper written by the authors especially for this book in November 2009.

rely on your public CSR report or website to inform employees. Make sure your company's leaders are frequently communicating to employees about its sustainability strategy, plans and progress.

**2. Involve as many employees as possible in sustainability initiatives.** Sustainability motivates employees in a powerful way. So the more you involve them in sustainability practices on a day-to-day basis, the more positive and connected they will feel towards the organisation. To encourage accountability, consider including sustainability in job descriptions and your performance management system.

**3. Highlight your company's sustainability focus when recruiting.** Most Millennials want to work for a company that is socially responsible, so promote your sustainability activities and culture to new recruits. As you search for new talent, remember to set new criteria for the competencies, skills and mind-set that align with your increasingly sustainable workplace.

## Employee engagement: a driver of sustainability

Forward-thinking organisations know that sustainability is here to stay. Like quality and safety, it is critical to their future performance and viability. Companies that take a long-term view integrate sustainability into their business strategy and create an engaging triple-bottom-line culture are the ones that will thrive.

At the other end of the spectrum, there are companies who take a short-term approach and use the sustainability halo as a reason to implement some quick cost savings programmes. These organisations fail to articulate a business value proposition for sustainability and employees quickly figure out that it is the 'initiative du jour'.

Employee engagement can be the difference between making sustainability

stick™ and watching an important corporate strategy lose momentum and fizzle out over time.

Here are five ways to engage employees to advance your sustainability strategies.

**1. Communicate to educate and inspire.** Communication helps employees understand:

- What sustainability is and why it is important
- Your organisation's sustainability goals, strategies and plans
- How they will be affected
- How they can get involved

Help your leaders incorporate sustainability concepts in their Town Hall meetings and support managers in communicating with their teams.

Feature inspirational stories about how employees are banding together to recycle, reduce energy and engage in their communities. Show examples of departments and individuals who are making great headway in achieving sustainability goals. In addition to using traditional communication channels, try social media to encourage online conversation about sustainability.

**2. Ask employees to help develop a sustainability value proposition and strategy.** Employees can assist with defining the benefit that sustainability brings to the company, their department and their job — the value proposition. Once sustainability is integrated into your core business strategy, employees will need to translate that into concrete and measurable goals at all levels of the organisation.

**3. Involve employees in planning, implementing and innovating.** Engage employees from the start by including them in your sustainability planning process. When you invite employees to contribute ideas, they experience a greater sense of ownership and offer valuable, innovative solutions. Promote involvement by facilitating engaging face-to-face and virtual meetings, and build online tools that encourage knowledge sharing, problem solving and idea generation across departments and locations.

**4. Incorporate sustainability concepts into training.** Employees need to learn about their role in supporting sustainability in a transformative way that helps them acquire a new mind-set and new skills and behaviours. Create interactive learning events and tools to meet the needs of your organisation and employees' individual learning styles. Use training to develop your employees so they have the competencies and skills to effectively perform their sustainability responsibilities.

**5. Recognise sustainability successes and reward those who excel.** Acknowledge teams and individuals who demonstrate the sustainability behaviours, practices and outcomes that you want. Use informal recognition and formal awards to reinforce new behaviours and motivate employees. To ensure accountability, conduct a thorough review of all your critical HR processes to align rewards and recognition with sustainability performance.

As an HR professional, if you can get sustainability and employee engagement fuelling each other, you will ignite a new kind of 'renewable energy' in your organisation. Help create a sustainability culture that permeates every department and function — that attracts the best and the brightest and encourages them to stay — that motivates every employee regardless of his or her role — and that ultimately helps your organisation achieve triple-bottom-line success.

* Towers Perrin, 2007–2008 Global Workforce Study

---

ABOUT THE AUTHORS

**Ellen Resnick** and **Carol Casazza Herman are partners in a consultancy, Resnick Consulting Sustainability and Employee Engagement. They help organisations engage employees in their sustainability goals and initiatives to drive long-lasting change.** Ellen and Carol offer a powerful blend of experience and expertise in the area of sustainability employee engagement. Ellen, founder of Resnick Consulting, has been providing Fortune 500 companies with effective and innovative employee communication and learning solutions for over ten years.

Carol, former Vice President, EHS at Pfizer Inc. brings deep knowledge of sustainability strategy and implementation. Together, they are a team uniquely equipped to advance their client's sustainability engagement goals to achieve 'sustainability that sticks'™.

# Case study on employee engagement for the HR team

Arena Dardelle, VP HR, The International Food Company Ltd
October 2009

## Case study

This paper describes employee engagement at Eileen Fisher Inc.:[22] Eileen Fisher is a US women's fashion company, employing over 800[23] with a turnover of around $270 million[24] and selling through over 52 own-stores and many additional retail outlets. The company is highly regarded as a leading business for corporate responsibility and demonstrates continuously high levels of employee engagement.

---

**Eileen Fisher: Engage people**

- Excite, motivate, involve
- Embrace each person's energy
- Inspire people to engage their passion, creativity, strengths and skills in the work
- Appreciate and acknowledge everyone's efforts and contributions[25]

---

## Measuring and encouraging employee engagement at Eileen Fisher Inc.

The tool used at Eileen Fisher is the annual Great Place to Work survey, which is distributed and collated by the Great Place to Work Institute and the Society for Human Resources Management (SHRM). This survey is part of the annual Great Place to Work competition, in which Eileen Fisher has been selected as one of the top 25 medium-sized businesses to work for in the US — seven years in a row. The survey (which is completed anonymously by one-third of Eileen Fisher's employee population, selected randomly) uses the Great Place to Work Trust Index and gathers feedback in five areas: credibility, respect, fairness, pride and camaraderie. The feedback comes back to the company segmented by age group, job type, race/ethnicity, sex, tenure and work status (full time/part time). The results are also compared to the other companies in the top 25. Eileen Fisher uses the information to help improve internal practices that impact credibility among leadership, etc. Some examples of the statements employees

22  Many thanks to Amy Hall, Director of Social Consciousness at Eileen Fisher for providing responses to sections on employee engagement.

23  www.eileenfisher.com/media/EFR001/images/static/ourcompany/inthemedia/pdf/jan07_wsj.pdf, accessed 2 June 2010.

24  www.eileenfisher.com/media/EFR001/images/static/ourcompany/inthemedia/pdf/oct08_wwd.pdf, accessed 2 June 2010.

25  www.eileenfisher.com/EileenFisherCompany/CompanyGeneralContentPages/WhoWeAre/Leadership_Practices.jsp, accessed 2 June 2010.

are asked to rate are: I am treated as a full member here regardless of my position; I feel I make a difference here; there is a 'family' or 'team' feeling here; people here are given a lot of responsibility.

One of the key pillars at Eileen Fisher is for people's voices to be heard. The success of the Eileen Fisher business can be attributed, in large part, to a highly engaged, highly valued workforce. Examples of how the company engages employees are: an active Leadership Forum (22 department or initiative leaders that come together on a regular basis to share news, move company priorities forward and discuss important company issues of the moment); open forums (open dialogues between various leaders in the company and the rest of the staff); a variety of committees and task forces, such as the famous Eileen Fisher grant-making committees and the company's diversity and inclusion task force.

The easiest way for Eileen Fisher to know how employee engagement is going is by gauging energy and attendance levels. Managers look at the calibre of discussion that takes place in a collaborative space. Typically, task forces and committees start out strong and then peter out, usually when the goal or purpose of the group becomes unclear. At that point, the facilitator can decide to revive the group and revisit the purpose or to disband the group all together.

In employee performance evaluation conversations, the process includes documenting the values conversation equally alongside the accomplishment and goals conversation. How one 'lives' the mission is just as important as how one carries out the specifics of one's everyday job.

The company has an active diversity and inclusion task force, which explores ways to celebrate diversity and encourage inclusivity throughout the workplace. One outcome of this taskforce has been company-wide education around diversity and inclusion. This includes both wholesale and retail employees.

In terms of recruitment, Eileen Fisher takes a proactive stance on seeking diverse applicants for open positions. Diversity for Eileen Fisher refers to the whole person: diversity of race, ethnicity, gender, personal interests and skills, age, sexual orientation, etc. Eileen Fisher encourages hiring leaders to be open to hiring people not like themselves, as this strengthens the perspectives and richness of the team.

New ways of engaging employees include:

- **EF Voices.** This is an open meeting in which between two and four Leadership Forum members meet up to 20 employees to hear what's on the employees' minds.

- **Ad hoc committees,** such as the 'move committee'. This committee helped ensure that Eileen Fisher's move into a larger space was handled in a respectful, mindful way that honoured the needs of each employee.

- **Company meeting.** At each quarterly (or 3 times/year) company meeting, Eileen Fisher always incorporates an employee engagement exercise. Sometimes, the exercise asks for feedback around a topic raised at the meeting. Sometimes, the exercises encourage people to talk in small groups about ideas or reactions to a topic. It is a quick and powerful way to hear from as many employees as possible.

- **'Idea BOX' online.** Employees are encouraged to submit their ideas about any aspect of the business.

- **Community meetings.** Eileen Fisher holds occasional meetings that gather everyone at a specific location for the purpose of sharing important news and hearing from people at that moment. In 2008/9, there were a series of community meetings related to the company's financial situation and budget cuts. The goal is to convey information and strategies in as transparent a format as possible and discuss implications at all levels.

# 4

# Employee rights

Sharon was feeling rather overwhelmed. Her first ASTD conference, her first major trip to the USA, and around ten hours of flying time during which she had been mind-blown with new concepts that were completely transforming the way she viewed her contribution to the company as an HR manager. She had slept on and off on this first night in San Diego, her head buzzing with new thoughts, after reading the case study on employee engagement and understanding that CSR has a key role to play in the HR approach to engaging employees. She had summarised for herself the key learning points from the conversations with Arena on the flight:

- CSR is the ethical conduct of business, which takes account of the impacts of an organisation on all its stakeholders including the community and the environment, and works to increase positive impacts. This benefits the business and all stakeholders and leads to sustainability

- HR managers must understand the total scope of CSR including its alignment with business strategy in order to perform as a key partner in the development of CSR in business

- HR and CSR must move from 'impacts on employees' to 'positive impacts by employees' — this entails practising CSR internally and ensuring a responsible workplace as an essential element of any CSR programme.

- HR managers need to learn to think with a CSR mind-set and learn the new skills of CSR

- A CSR approach can enhance employee motivation and contribution, and employee engagement is a positive consequence of creating a responsible workplace

- There are many ways of engaging employees to support the development of a sustainability culture

- CSHR manager is the new profession!

Now, thought Sharon, she had better get back to her own agenda and make the most of the conference. She had promised her team a full account of every session and a summary of the material presented. She had better shape up and make sure she proved this trip was value for money for Andromex.

Over breakfast in the hotel, Sharon reviewed once again the intensive conference schedule. Something jumped right off the page at her: a session that she had not even noticed before, right after the opening plenaries. It was called: **Human rights and employee rights — is there a difference?**

This was to be presented by a human rights consultant, with experience in working with the United Nations.

'Employee rights are clear', thought Sharon, 'but human rights? What's that all about?' It sounded suspiciously like something that Arena would have talked about. 'Human rights sounds very close to CSR,' thought Sharon. 'I have to go to this session. Arena would expect me to.' She hadn't a clue what people mean when they talk about human rights, she admitted to herself. It was the sort of thing everyone assumed they knew, but if asked to explain, they found they couldn't. She tried to list her own human rights, but gave up after a few minutes. She wondered what the connection was between human rights and employee rights. Employee rights were much easier to define.

Sharon finished breakfast and made her way to the start of the fascinating ASTD conference. After the first presentations of the morning, at 11.30 she took up a third-row seat in the breakout session on human rights and employee rights. She chuckled to herself: 'Who would have thought that I would choose to come to a session like this? I would never have imagined that this was so important to me as an HR manager.'

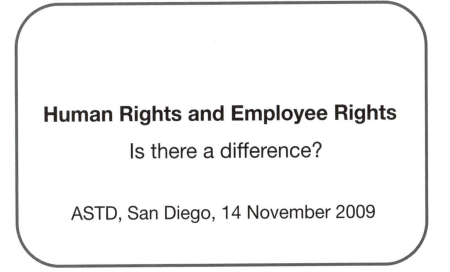

# Human Rights and Employee Rights

## Is there a difference?

ASTD, San Diego, 14 November 2009

The speaker welcomed everyone to the session and began his presentation.

Good morning all! Thank you for attending this session. Never before has the subject of human rights and employee rights received such significant and critical attention.

My name is Ben Parks.[1] I am a consultant to businesses in the field of human rights. I have experience of advising businesses in many parts of the world on how to manage human rights in their supply chains, and, guess what, I was an HR manager in an earlier life, so I understand some of the challenges you face. One of the organisations that has a significant impact on the upholding of human rights is the International Labour Organization,[2] so I wanted to start off by telling you a little about them, to set the context.

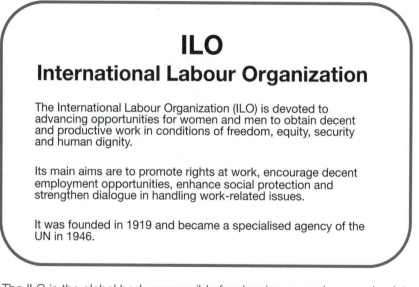

The ILO is the global body responsible for drawing up and overseeing international labour standards. They conduct research into labour practices all over the globe; monitor the application of labour standards; run events and campaigns to enhance awareness and improve practices; issue publications; and run training courses and programmes for a wide range of participants on fundamental principles and rights at work, employment and income opportunities for women and men, social protection for all, social dialogue and much more.

---

1  Ben Parks is a fictional character whose presentation is entirely created by the author. This was not a presentation made at any real live ASTD conference.
2  www.ilo.org/global/lang--en/index.htm.

Human resources managers can no longer plead ignorance. They must be aware of the rights of employees, ensure these are upheld in the business, and act to ensure that each and every employee both understands and actively ensures his or her rights are upheld. Furthermore, they must ensure that all employees have access to solutions to issues relating to abuse of their rights. HR managers must take this into account in all human resources processes. This is both the right thing to do, and the way of all businesses that seek to operate as good corporate citizens. In my presentation today, I would like to explain what we mean by human rights, what we refer to as employee rights and how we should put in place process and training in our organisations to ensure it all happens.

I assume you all know that there is a Special Representative of the United Nations Secretary-General on business and human rights? The current holder of that position is John Ruggie and he has a three-year mandate operative between 2008 and 2011 to develop a framework for business to uphold human rights.

**2008–11 mandate of the UN Secretary-General's Special Representative on business & human rights, John Ruggie**[3]

- Recommend ways to strengthen the fulfilment of the duty of the state to protect all human rights from abuses by or involving transnational corporations and other business enterprises
- Elaborate on the scope of the corporate responsibility to respect all human rights and to provide concrete guidance to business and other stakeholders
- Make recommendations for enhancing access to effective remedies available to those whose human rights are impacted by corporate activities
- Integrate a gender perspective and give special attention to persons belonging to vulnerable groups, in particular children
- Promote best practices in coordination with the efforts of the human rights working group of the Global Compact
- Work with United Nations and consult with all stakeholders, including states, human rights institutions, international and regional organisations, transnational corporations and business enterprises, civil society, academics, employers' organisations, workers' organisations, indigenous communities and non-governmental organisations

You can see this is very clear: protect all from human rights abuses from *corporations*, promote corporate responsibility, ensure people have access to solutions if their human rights are abused, promote gender equality, protect vulnerable groups and so on. Do you get the significance of this? We all need to be *protected* from business interests and activities.

Is business really that bad? Does business make money by abusing people and their rights? Clearly, the view of the United Nations was that this was an issue that was sufficiently important to establish a high-powered office and team of skilled and influential people to rewrite the guidelines and establish new levels of expectation from corporations.

Let me start with two stories, and then we will get down to the nitty gritty of human rights and employee rights, how you establish frameworks in the business and how you train your people.

First, I want to refer to the case of Royal Dutch Shell and Ken Saro-Wiwa. This case was in the public eye in 2009 when Shell made a payout of $15.5 million to compensate the family members of the Ogoni people (an ethnic group of around 500,000 in number) in Nigeria for alleged human rights abuses. That's a lot of money. Let's have a look at that case.

---

3  Information adapted from the Internet portal of the UN Special representative www.business-humanrights.org/SpecialRepPortal/Home/Mandate, accessed 10 June 2010.

> ### Royal Dutch Shell and the case of Ken Saro-Wiwa[4]
>
> - Shell began operations in Nigeria in 1937 and found oil in the 1950s
> - In the late 1980s there were many protests about Shell's operations due to environmental issues and continuing poverty in the region
> - The Ogoni people were especially affected and vocal in their, often violent, protests
> - Shell reportedly asked the commissioner of police for security protection
> - In 1994, following mob killings of Ogoni leaders, Ken Saro-Wiwa, a leading activist, was arrested
> - He was subsequently executed along with eight other activists in 1995
> - Shell was implicated in this execution, by having encouraged tough security measures against activists
> - Shell denied all implied involvement but was widely criticised and boycotted
> - In 1996, a lawsuit was brought against Shell for human rights violations against the Saro-Wiwa family and the Ogoni people
> - In 2009, 13 years later, Shell agreed to pay $15.5 million in a settlement

As you can see, Shell was operating in the Niger Delta region. The circumstances were very complex — rule of the military junta, many opposing political, financial and social interests, escalating levels of protest and violence. Shell was in Nigeria to do business. Extract oil and make money. But in the pursuit of making money, corporations must assess the way their actions impact on the rights of indigenous peoples, among other things. In this particular case, the key group of locals affected by Shell's continuing operations were the Ogoni people. On the one hand, there were several environmental issues that affected the quality of life and health for the Ogoni people as a result of oil spills and flaring practices, and, on the other hand, there were large protests at the inequitable distribution of wealth, as Shell and the military government got richer and richer, and the Ogoni people got poorer and poorer.

To cut a very long story short, Ken Saro-Wiwa was a leading activist who was executed by the military government of the time, together with eight other Ogoni activists. Many said that Shell were indirectly involved in these killings and that Shell officials had helped the government execute these men by 'furnishing the Nigerian police with weapons, participating in security sweeps of the area, and asking government troops to shoot villagers protesting the construction of a pipeline that later leaked oil'. Later, relatives of the late Ken Saro-Wiwa took Shell to court for their alleged part in the killing of Saro-Wiwa. Eventually, after several years in and out of the courtrooms, Royal Dutch Shell voluntarily agreed to make this multi-million-dollar payout. The Guardian.co.uk reports that Jennie Green, a lawyer with the Centre for Constitutional Rights who initiated the

---

4  Sources: David Vogel, *The Market for Virtue: The Potential and Limits of Corporate Social Responsibility* (Washington, DC: Brookings Institution, 2005); Ed Pilkington, 'Shell pays out $15.5m over Saro-Wiwa killing', *Guardian*, 8 June 2009, www. guardian.co.uk/world/2009/jun/08/nigeria-usa, accessed 2 June 2010.

lawsuit in 1996, said: 'This was one of the first cases to charge a multinational corporation with human rights violations, and this settlement confirms that multinational corporations can no longer act with the impunity they once enjoyed.'[5]

What's the point here? This was nothing to do with Shell's employment practices or application of international labour standards. This was nothing to do with Shell being an employer. This was nothing to do with the Shell Human Resources Department. Or was it?

We cannot know precisely what was the nature of Shell's activities. Much has been written and much has been debated, but it there seems to be a consensus that Shell's people on the ground in Nigeria had at least some involvement in issues which were beyond 'business as usual' and were implicated in some way with regard to the unfortunate events in this area. The consensus is that large corporations must operate with regard to their interactions with local communities and have respect for the human rights of all.

How is this related to the human resources manager? First and foremost, human rights abuses are not committed by corporations or companies or departments. They are committed by people working in those departments or corporations. They are committed by people who need to know the framework of acceptable conduct within the business. They need to understand the implications of their actions and need to take personal responsibility for everything they do in the name of the business they work for. They need to be trained in the specifics of human rights, as well as employee rights, and they need to be able to identify potentially explosive or sensitive situations. And they need to be personally accountable for their actions. Not knowing, not understanding or not receiving specific instructions from the C-suite is no excuse.

The HR function in any business has an important role to play. While in some businesses human rights may be seen and dealt with as a legal issue, the basic culture of respect, ethical behaviour, dialogue and personal accountability are things that the HR department has a role in ensuring. The HR department often defines the training programmes that need to be put in place to ensure human rights awareness. The HR department is responsible for a system that links personal accountability and ethical behaviour to reward systems and remuneration. The HR manager cannot turn a blind eye to the issue of human rights, because it is the people in the business who are faced with maintaining appropriate conduct. The people are the faces of the corporation, and they are the ones who have to take decisions on the front line. In the case of Shell, people on the ground clearly had some complex issues to deal with — keep the business going, navigate a politically explosive environment, respond to the demands of the Ogoni activists, protect their own people and property from violence. How could the HR department of this company have helped create a better outcome? We will never know the answer to this question, but you,

5  Ed Pilkington, 'Shell pays out $15.5m over Saro-Wiwa killing', *Guardian*, 8 June 2009, www.guardian.co.uk/world/2009/jun/08/nigeria-usa, accessed 2 June 2010.

as HR managers, should be concerned with understanding the impacts of the activities of your colleagues and your role in creating an ethical, respectful, accountable culture.

And now, another insight relating to human rights.

During the month of September 2009, Ben & Jerry's renamed its Chubby Hubby ice cream flavour to Hubby Hubby, in celebration and support of the new law in the State of Vermont that permitted the issue of marriage licences to same-sex couples. The ice cream company, based in Vermont, explained that this was consistent with their social values and support for equal rights for all people. Sounds good, right? Unless you are violently opposed to same-sex marriage, or the involvement of business in social issues in such an obvious way. The issue of this ice cream flavour created quite a controversy. There was a significant backlash against Ben & Jerry's. An article by James Delingpole in the Telegraph.co.uk entitled 'I don't need my ice cream to "educate" me about the glories of gay marriage or wind farms'[6] received 101 comments, most of which were against gay marriage, and most against Ben & Jerry's promoting it with its ice cream. One comment, just to illustrate my point, goes like this: 'I can take my custom elsewhere — there are many good ice cream producers. I certainly don't need to put up with funding social engineers like Ben & Jerry's.'

Now just to be clear, Ben & Jerry's has a history of positive social practices and was one of the first companies to produce a social report — you can find

6  blogs.telegraph.co.uk/news/jamesdelingpole/100008205/i-dont-need-my-ice-cream-to-educate-me-about-the-glories-of-gay-marriage-or-wind-farms, accessed 2 June 2010.

the report for 2008 and previous ones on its website.[7] I personally believe that gay marriage is a basic human right and I believe that this company did a positive thing. But my point is, how does this relate to the human resources function? Here again, human resources do not necessarily play a role in deciding how to promote ice cream, but they do play a role in how employees of Ben & Jerry's — over 500 of them — relate to this approach. How do they respond to calls from the general public complaining about this campaign? How do they respond to positive feedback? How do they relate to gay colleagues in the workplace? It wouldn't look too good if Ben & Jerry's was supporting gay marriage in a marketing campaign but practised discrimination in its own company. What do HR managers need to be aware of? How should they address these issues in the company culture and internal communications? How can they create a culture that is consistent with the external face of the company? How can human rights be on the internal agenda, not just the external agenda?

I hope that these two different human-rights-related insights have demonstrated that the HR function has a role to play in upholding human rights, educating, training and ensuring corporate internal and external integrity.

Back to John Ruggie. His conclusions, published in his 2008 'Ruggie Report', were that the state needs to protect against corporate human rights abuses, the corporation needs to respect human rights and effective grievance mechanisms must be put in place for victims of human rights abuses.

# The 2008 Ruggie Report[8]

## *protect, respect, remedy*

- **Government** efforts to protect against human rights abuses by businesses
- The **corporate responsibility** to respect human rights
- The need for more effective **access to remedies** for human rights abuses by victims of corporate abuses

'Corporate human rights responsibilities
go beyond legal compliance'

7 www.benjerry.com/company/sear.
8 Anthony Ewing, 'The Ruggie Report on Business and Human Rights: Lessons for Leading Companies', Logos Institute, logosinstitute.net/blog/2008/05/29/the-ruggie-report-on-business-and-human-rights-lessons-for-leading-companies, accessed 10 June 2010.

After this long introduction to this broad topic, I will now talk a little about human rights, and about employee rights and some internationally accepted labour standards that the ILO is active in promoting.

Human rights. How many of you have read the Universal Declaration of Human Rights? How many of you know what your rights as individuals are under this globally ratified convention? How many rights can you name? I will spare you a test on this subject. The Universal Declaration of Human Rights was adopted by the General Assembly of the United Nations in 1948. There are 30 articles, or rights, which the Declaration refers to. I won't list them all here, but I do advise you to take a look on the UN website and read the Declaration.[9]

A nice summary of the key rights in the Declaration is provided in a book about *Social Responsibility in the Global Apparel Industry* by Dickson, Loker and Eckman.[10] They organise the 30 separate articles into four main areas as I show you on this slide:

## The Universal Declaration of Human Rights

**Article 1: All human beings are born free and equal in dignity and rights**

**Equality**
Prohibition of discrimination on the basis of race, color, sex, language, religion, political beliefs or affiliations, national or social origin, property or birth.
**Life and security**
Rights to life, liberty, security, and the right to be free from slavery or torture, a just legal system and equal protection under the law.
**Personal freedom**
Rights protecting personal privacy for family, home, thought, religion, opinion and property ownership.
**Economic, social and cultural freedoms**
Right to social security, to work, equal pay, to form and join unions, to rest and leisure, and to adequate health care and well being.

You can see the implications here for businesses; I won't elaborate on that now. Suffice it to say that many of what we consider today to be employee rights stem from this base document that addresses our rights first and foremost as equal human beings on this planet, regardless of who we do or don't work for.

In terms of employees and labour standards, some of these rights are encompassed in the **Labour Principles of the United Nations Global Compact**, and are derived from ILO conventions and recommendations, including the

---

9  www.un.org/en/documents/udhr/index.shtml#a1, accessed 2 June 2010.
10  Marsha A. Dickson, Suzanne Loker and Molly Eckman, *Social Responsibility in the Global Apparel Industry* (New York: Fairchild Books, 2009).

1998 ILO Declaration on Fundamental Principles and Rights at Work, which are used to set global labour standards.

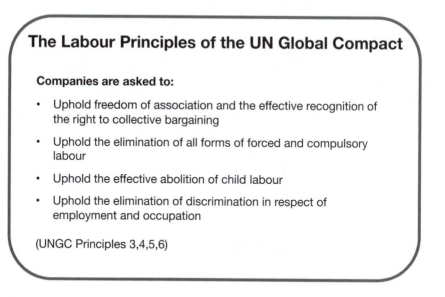

### The Labour Principles of the UN Global Compact

**Companies are asked to:**

• Uphold freedom of association and the effective recognition of the right to collective bargaining

• Uphold the elimination of all forms of forced and compulsory labour

• Uphold the effective abolition of child labour

• Uphold the elimination of discrimination in respect of employment and occupation

(UNGC Principles 3,4,5,6)

These four core elements — freedom of association, non-forced labour, no child labour and no discrimination — form the basic fundamental protection of workers' rights. These principles are based on core labour conventions that are ratified by governments and have the status of law in the ratifying states. The conventions on which these four core principles are based have been almost universally ratified by governments globally.

I will address each core principle in turn and show how the HR manager needs to be a proactive advocate and protector of these principles in his or her organisation. Then I will talk about a few more employee rights, and how they can go beyond compliance in the context of these core elements, and thereafter I will talk about effective training models for human rights and employee rights. After that, I am sure you will be ready for lunch! Though I will be happy to take questions from those who are interested.

Much of the information I will share with you is taken from the ILO publication *The Labour Principles of the United Nations Global Compact: A Guide for Business*, 2008.[11]

---

11  International Labour Office, *Labour Principles of the United Nations Global Compact: A Reference for Business* (Geneva: ILO, 2008, www.ilo.org/empent/Whatwedo/Publications/lang--en/docName--WCMS_101246/index.htm, accessed 2 June 2010).

# Freedom of association

Respect for the rights of all employees and workers to freely and voluntarily establish and join groups for the promotion and defence of their occupational interests.

## Freedom of association

You probably all know what this means. It is important to emphasise that freedom of association *must* include the freedom to negotiate collectively, and the freedom of discrimination as a result of participating in or supporting collective bargaining activities or joining a union. Employers must not interfere with the running of such employee organisations.

Normally it rests with the HR department to interact with and manage collective negotiations. Similarly, a request to form a workers' association would normally land on the HR manager's desk. It is important for HR managers to understand their responsibilities towards such workers' associations and respond appropriately. All must be familiar with the local regulations in their own states or countries in which they operate. A recent article on the Oxfam website[12] recounts a series of incidents involving the firing of employee representatives and firing of workers participating in a legal strike at factories producing for Adidas. The sport footwear producer Puma disclosed in their 2008–2009 CSR report[13] that over 30% of instances in factories who failed social and environmental performance standards were related to freedom of association and industrial relations issues. Many companies have been accused of union-busting, including Wal-Mart. An article that appeared in the *Guardian*[14] describes how some employers hire consultants to disrupt union activities and

12 www.oxfam.org.au/explore/workers-rights/adidas/looking-in-side-adidas-indonesian-factories, accessed 2 June 2010.
13 ir2.flife.de/data/puma_csr/igb_html/index.php?bericht_id=1000001, accessed 18 August 2010.
14 Laura Smith and agencies, 'Union-busting Tactics on the Increase, Warns TUC', *Guardian*, 12 February 2008, www.guardian.co.uk/politics/2008/feb/12/tradeunions, accessed 2 June 2010.

prevent freedom of association. These are the most obvious of labour standards breaches. There are many other subtle forms.

Why would employers wish to avoid freedom of association and collective bargaining? The obvious reasons, I am sure you can list them as well as I can — fear of loss of management control, management time involved in negotiations, fear of higher costs, expectation of having to fund higher employee benefits, etc. However, you can probably also list the benefits of maintaining a positive collective relationship with employees — certainly this is the sustainable approach. In any event, as HR managers, this is definitely in your patch. Part of your role is to create the conditions in your organisation under which respect for workers organisations and collective dialogue is maintained.

# Elimination of forced labour

Forced or compulsory labour is any work or service that is extracted from any person under the threat of penalty, and for which that person has not offered him or herself voluntarily.

### Elimination of forced or compulsory labour

Forced labour — getting people to work against their will. The fact that you pay them is not relevant. If they have not agreed explicitly to work for you, then this is considered forced labour. The ILO estimates that there are over 12 million people in forced labour worldwide. Again, forced labour can and does come in many forms. There are frequent occurrences of documents being confiscated in factories in China and other Asian countries thereby preventing workers from leaving of their own free will. The use of prisoners for work activities also constitutes forced labour as they are often not free to refuse to work. One of the most horrific forms of forced labour is human trafficking, which we see in the sex, drugs and smuggling industries. But closer to home, perhaps, are the allegations of forced labour in the sugar industry in the Dominican Republic, which supplies companies such as Tate & Lyle.[15] How many of you think of that when

15  www.reuters.com/article/pressRelease/idUS99073+17-Sep-2009+PRN20090917, accessed 2 June 2010.

you add a spoonful of sugar to your morning coffee? The HR manager must be aware of these issues so that he or she can provide the right awareness education and training for all the people involved in the business — whether it be in local subsidiaries in countries where there are higher instances of forced labour, or whether it be with company decision-makers responsible for selecting outsourcing operations. Even withholding payment or non-payment of wages constitutes a violation of rights under the forced labour concept.

---

# Elimination of child labour

Child labour relates to national laws that prescribe the minimum age for admission to employment of persons below the age for completing compulsory schooling and in any case not less than 15 years of age.

Lower ages are permitted for transitional periods—generally in developing countries where economic and educational facilities are less well developed. In such cases the minimum age is 14, or 12 where 'light work' is concerned. The minimum age for hazardous work is 18 years for all countries.

---

## Elimination of child labour

Don't get child labour confused with youth employment or having your kids come into the office for pocket money during the summer. Child labour is the use of children of school age in any form of work that prevents them from gaining an education and that is likely to harm their health, safety or morals. Morals, of course, because one of the most widespread forms of child labour is the trafficking of children in the pornography or prostitution industry. However, even in regular, so-called 'respectable' businesses — agriculture, textile and apparel manufacture, manufacture of toys and others — the level of child labour is frightening. There are over 200 million children illegally employed throughout the world. And more often than not, the fact that they are children is only one issue; many of their other basic rights are violated as well. In 2009, we witnessed a boycott by governments of cotton harvested in Uzbekistan because of the widespread use of child labour. Schools are closed down for three months during the harvesting period and children (and many adults as well) are forced to work in the fields. More than 25 major brands and retailers joined a campaign to end forced child labour in Uzbekistan, including Gap Inc., JC Penney, Levi Strauss & Co., Nike, Nordstrom, Timberland and Wal-Mart.[16]

---

16  Tom Harkin, 'Hard Truths About Uzbek Cotton', *Los Angeles Times*, 25 Septem-

Companies have instructed their suppliers not to buy Uzbek cotton until the government takes meaningful steps to restore basic human rights in its cotton sector. So think about that when you are next buying a cotton T-shirt. I could go on with many more examples of child labour abuses, but I think you get the picture. As with the issue of forced labour, this one is clearly one for HR managers to be aware of. Another aspect of creating awareness might relate to those who manage the financial investments of the company, for example. Are these fund managers aware of child labour issues in companies they are investing in? Do they apply any form of social screening before making investments?

## Elimination of discrimination

Discrimination in employment and occupation occurs when a potential candidate is treated differently or less favourably because of characteristics that are not related to his or her merit or the inherent requirements of the job.

These characteristics commonly include in national law: race, colour, sex, religion, political opinion, national extraction or social origin. They may extend be extended in law to include sexual orientation and HIV or AIDS.

### Elimination of discrimination

And the fourth core principle relating to basic labour rights is about discrimination. I think this is the one that you as HR managers are probably most familiar with. No company wants to discriminate. No company has a stated objective of discrimination. But whenever you see a company where there is little or no diversity among the employee population, then you know that discrimination exists. Unlike child labour or forced labour or freedom of association, discrimination is more difficult to identify and address, because it can emerge in very subtle ways. I am not going to give you my lecture on diversity and inclusion here today, as we don't have time, but eliminating discrimination is something that goes to the very core of the culture of the business and behaviour of every single employee. Eliminating all forms of discrimination needs continued awareness and attention to potential pitfalls and risks. Discrimination occurs in all processes — recruitment, remuneration, maternity provisions, performance

---

ber 2009, www.latimes.com/news/opinion/commentary/la-oe-harkin25-2009-sep25,0,3490812.story, accessed 2 June 2010.

evaluation and promotion opportunities, training and development, occupational health issues and more. There are many ways to address discrimination and to ensure respect for all individual differences in the workplace. Of course, this is where HR managers can shine. There are significant competitive advantages to be gained by maintaining a diverse workforce, though I won't go into this in detail here.

In conclusion of this section, you can see that the four basic employee rights relating to freedom of association and elimination of forced labour, child labour and discrimination in the workplace are all issues which HR managers must be aware of and provide the tools and processes in their organisations to ensure rights are respected.

There are many other rights that employees are entitled to, usually framed in local employment laws and regulations, and those contained in employment contracts between employers and employees. HR managers are usually familiar with these and mostly have systems in place to observe the law in these matters, such as payment of salary in line with the terms and conditions of employment, although there are many instances of non-adherence to law.

What I want to do now is turn our attention to the way a company can uphold human rights and employee rights and the role that HR managers must play.

## Human resources managers should:

1. Ensure existence of policies and systems that maintain human and employee rights in the business and its supply chain
2. Ensure awareness and training for all employees in company policies on human rights
3. Proactively inform employees and assist them to understand and realise all of their rights

- Does your company have a human rights policy?

- Does your company have a systematic programme of training for all employees in human rights and employee rights?

- Does your company have a mechanism for dealing with grievances related to violation of rights such as discrimination?

- Does your company regularly perform audits in relevant parts of the business?

- Does your company audit your suppliers in your supply chain for human rights-related issues?

- Does your company screen for human rights in investment and acquisition activities?

- Does your company act with transparency — is your policy posted on your website for all to see, and do you report about the way controls are exercised in your in-house operations and with your suppliers?

If you can answer 'yes' to all the above questions, then you could probably be giving this lecture instead of me. If you answer 'no' to a couple or more, it is time your HR function became more proactive in promoting human rights.

---

# Human/employee rights training

- *Everyone* in the business
- In the context of local countries
- In the local language
- Using specific examples related to day-to-day decisions and consideration of human/employee rights implications
- Repeated annually or at least every two years

---

Training in human rights is recommended for every single employee in your business. There are many forms of training, ranging from courses and workshops through to computerised self-learning modules. The ILO conducts a wide range of training and can come to your company to deliver training programmes. You will find many different resources and publications on the ILO website. And you are free to write to me for guidance on any related topic.

The thing about training in human rights and employee rights is that it must be specific. These subjects should be taught within the context of a local country and perhaps even an industry sector. The first time around, you should probably involve an external expert to assess how these principles are most relevant for your business, and construct a training framework that is feasible for the different categories of employees. Each employee must be made to think about the risks related to his or her activities with the company and how these principles should apply. You should ensure that human rights training is delivered in the local language so that everyone can truly understand all the nuances.

I hope I haven't bored you too much — human rights is not a particularly 'sexy' subject, but it is one that no HR manager can afford to ignore. Thank you for your attention. I am happy to take questions now.

Sharon decided not to stay for the questions. So many issues she had not thought about at all in the course of her work or in regard to her role as an HR manager. She had heard the term 'human rights', of course, but if anyone had asked her to explain this before today, she wouldn't have known where to start, and she certainly would not have been able to say how it related to her role. Sharon's head was reeling with all this new information and her shoulders were heavy with this new-found set of responsibilities. She felt a little ashamed. How could all this have passed her by? She made her way slowly to the lunch area, determined to establish a framework for dealing with human and employee rights in a comprehensive way at Andromex. She thought about her employee handbook — how much of that related to employee rights? Nothing. It was all about the company and the expectations of employees. Not a thing about what the employee was entitled to by law, or over and above the law as was determined by company policy. She made a plan to research human rights policies and make it happen at Andromex.

# A sample human rights policy for a business[17]

## Human rights principles

Our company is committed to corporate socially responsible business practices and works actively to address human rights issues in our own operations, our commercial relationships with suppliers and the communities and societies in which we operate.

We respect local, cultural and political differences, and all our business activities adhere to basic human rights, in line with the Universal Declaration for Human Rights. We assess our business activities to determine where we have direct or indirect impacts, ensure compliance with human rights legislation and strive to have a positive impact on our stakeholders and on society at large. We use measurable standards that reflect internationally recognised human rights standards and conventions.

## Our commitments:

- Integrating human rights standards in our business practices
- Sharing best practice and developing collaborative solutions with other leading companies
- Benchmarking our employee policies to ensure that we provide good working conditions that comply with international human rights standards
- Continuously reviewing our strategic initiatives, such as product development or new markets, to address human rights implications
- Requiring that all suppliers adhere to all relevant international human rights standards in areas such as working conditions, appropriate use of security staff and protection of privacy
- Engaging with stakeholders to identify opportunities to promote human rights in areas relevant to our business activities
- Monitoring our impacts and reporting on our performance to ensure continuous improvement

17 Inspired by The Body Shop policy on human rights, www.thebodyshop.com/_en/_ ww/services/pdfs/AboutUs/Humanrightsprinciples.pdf, accessed 2 June 2010.

# 5

# Employee reward and recognition

Sharon was enjoying the ASTD conference. She had picked up new perspectives on learning technologies, improved training impact, Web 2.0 learning, more of the usual theories on talent management, facilitating organisational change, training trainers and a host of other topics that regularly find their way onto human resources conference agendas.

She had made several notes and had met many interesting people. Many of these were HR managers from companies around the world. Given her new interest in corporate responsibility, Sharon made a point of asking the HR managers she met what role they played in the CSR practices. The responses she received were mixed, ranging from those who were not very aware of CSR (much like herself before she had boarded her flight to San Diego), to those who felt it was an integral part of their role (much like Arena). The latter were often employed by large multinationals, the companies that have been issuing CSR reports for several years. Sharon thought she ought to take a look at some of these reports. These HR managers were very aware of the roles their companies played in making the world a better place, even to the point of evangelism. Is that what Sharon was becoming? A CSR evangelist? That's the term they give to those who think they have 'seen the light' of CSR and believe there is no alternative, and don't hesitate to tell others about it, repeatedly. Sharon didn't like to think in those terms, it sounded rather extreme to her. Though she did feel she had 'seen the light' a little and could no longer consider her role in terms of traditional human resources.

It was now the end of the second day of the conference, and Sharon was alone for the evening. She thought of giving Arena a call, but didn't want to disturb her. Arena had given her almost ten hours of free consulting time, after all, on the flight. She decided to call home to her family. Her eight-year-old daughter, Michelle, picked up:

**Michelle:** Hello, this is Michelle Black. Who do you want to speak to?

**Sharon:** Hello, Michelle Black, this is mummy.

**Michelle:** M – u – m – m – y !!! Mummy, mummy, mummy – today we made kites in school and I flew mine and it flew for ages, and it was yellow, it was the only yellow one, all the other children chose other colours, and mine flew for ages, and Daddy told me that we could go to the park on Saturday and fly my kite. Did you buy me any presents, mommy?

**Sharon:** Hello Mummy, how are you Mummy, how is your trip Mummy, I am happy you called Mummy.

**Michelle:** Hello Mummy, how are you Mummy, how is your trip Mummy, I am happy you called Mummy.

**Sharon:** Michelle, sweetiepie, I am fine. How are you managing with Daddy and Darren and Julia? Are you having fun?

**Michelle:** Yes Mummy, everything's fine. Did you buy me any presents, Mummy?

'Typical,' Sharon thought. 'What values did I bring my kids up with? What would they think of corporate responsibility? What about personal responsibility? Do we really instil a sense of ethics and creating a better world into their consciousness? The future generation. After all, sustainability, it's all about them, right?' She thought this was a little complicated to discuss over the phone, so she spent a few minutes talking with her other two children and her husband, Robert, promised to be home in another four days, and replaced the phone, pensive. She thought to herself: 'Just look at me! I learn a new way of thinking related to my work, and I immediately start applying it to my personal and family life. Is that it? Is the power of corporate social responsibility so strong because it engages employees outside of the workplace in all facets of their life, and adds value? I must talk to Arena about this.' Sharon continued to wonder about the way she demonstrated values to her children, and what sort of a role model she was, as a mother. She asked herself if she could name the values that she tried to live by and found herself listing a number of generic values that almost anyone could aspire to — honesty, respect, decency, integrity, caring for others. She wondered about the environment. Was that one of her values? In the corporate responsibility context, caring for the environment is just as important as social values. She wondered if she demonstrated these values to her children? It was the kids who were coming home from school these days telling her she should do more for the environment — recycle paper, plastics and batteries, put their morning snack in a reusable box and not the plastic sandwich bags she was used to. Every day another suggestion. The kids asked her if she bought organic eggs. Her son, Darren, even asked why she didn't drive a hybrid car. Hybrid car. It had never entered her mind. She came to the conclusion that she probably didn't demonstrate enough of a commitment to the environment. Her thoughts turned back to her work and the impact of social and environmental responsibility in the workplace. She tried to make a quick mental assessment of how she was demonstrating CSR values at work and came to the conclusion that she still had much to do. 'Organisations,' she thought to herself, 'are basically a bunch of people. You can't have corporate responsibility until everyone has personal responsibility for corporate responsibility. She began to realise the enormity of the task she had ahead of her. A whole new corporate culture.

Faced with the rest of the evening alone in the hotel room, Sharon flipped open her laptop and dealt with a few urgent emails. Nothing about the environment, she mused. No one from the office asked her how much carbon dioxide she had emitted today. No mail related to the environmental impacts of Andromex Ltd. Her thoughts drifted back to all those companies who voluntarily issue CSR reports. She wanted to know more. That afternoon, she had heard an interesting presentation about reward mechanisms that drive management performance. Interesting, but not mind-blowing. The concept of allowing managers to select their own salary and benefits package from a menu of options was not new, though the presenting company appeared to have gained good results after they introduced this system. Reward and recognition. What would that mean in the context of CSR? Sharon decided to investigate what companies were saying about reward mechanisms and recognition and CSR on their websites and in their CSR reports. She did a web-search for the words: 'CSR reward and recognition'. The first reference on the list of links was to the Reward and Recognition programme at Serco Sodexo Defence Services (SSDS), a joint venture company providing services to the Australian Defence Organisation.[1] Sharon surfed to the link and read that their programme is called 'Star Performers', and it awards quarterly cash bonuses for individuals or teams.

## SSDS Star Performers programme

Employees can be nominated for their achievements in four categories.

### Customer Service

- Consistent high quality service
- Going above and beyond everyday service

### Innovation & Initiative

- New ideas that save time and money
- Initiatives that improve the work environment

---

1 www.ssds.com.au/reward-and-recognition1.html, accessed 2 June 2010.

**Community & Environment**

- Outstanding work in the community
- Fundraising
- Initiatives that benefit the wider community

**Health & Safety**

- Improvements in the health and well being of employees and the customer
- Safety initiatives in the workplace

In addition, Serco, one of the joint venture parent companies, has a programme called the Pulse Awards. All quarterly Star Performers are eligible to be nominated for this reward and recognition programme. Serco Pulse Awards are based on Serco's Governing Principles,[2] which includes a reference to social responsibility.

# The Serco Governing Principles

We foster an entrepreneurial culture
*We are passionate about building innovative and successful businesses.*
We enable our people to excel
*Our success comes from our commitment and energy to go the extra mile.*
We deliver our promises
*We do what we say we will do to meet expectations*
We build trust and respect
*We build trust and respect by operating in a safe, socially responsible, consistent and honest manner.*

The Pulse Awards[3] are made to individuals who go beyond expectations in living up to these governing principles. There are two levels of recognition: divisional and global. Winners' names are published on the Serco website. Global award recipients are invited to an Awards gala dinner in London, and a cash donation is made to a charitable cause selected by the winners.

Sharon thought this was incredible. A reward and recognition programme that relates to company values and includes reference to social responsibility, working in the community, supporting health and safety and more. 'This is clearly aligned with a CSR mind-set,' she thought. 'Sounds like the sort of policy a CSHR manager would develop. How on earth can I get something like this moving in our company? They will think I am off on another HR jolly, more nice-to-haves that don't generate revenue. Generate revenue. Why are the revenue generators the only ones that are valued in the business? I have enough

2  www.serco.com/pulse/principles/index.aspx, accessed 2 June 2010.
3  www.serco.com/pulse/work/index.aspx, accessed 2 June 2010.

of a hard time convincing my boss, and my friends on the Exec team, to invest in people and training and organisation development. Now I have to ask them to invest in people investing in the community. It seems to me that CSR has to overcome quite a lot of ingrained paradigms of traditional ways of doing business. What a pleasure it must be to have a CEO who understands and buys into CSR. I understand that CSR is not something that can be driven by HR, but I am beginning to understand how the HR manager can partner with the CEO and the Exec team in supporting the CSR objectives of the company.'

Sharon reverted to her thoughts about remuneration and benefits and Serco Sodexo. Does this company pay a decent wage and offer attractive terms of employment? This is surely more important than rewarding for values, important though values may be. Sharon continued to search through the SSDS website and saw that their corporate policy states 'We employ people under fair, reasonable and market competitive terms and conditions.'[4] In addition, Serco Sodexo employees are offered a range of personal benefits through a corporate programme that gives employees access to discounted goods and services from over 4,000 suppliers.[5] This includes travel and accommodation (car hire, travel insurance, holidays, hotels), leisure and entertainment (movie tickets, magazine subscriptions, concert tickets, golf memberships), shopping (shoes, clothing, jewellery, discounted vouchers and gift cards), home and lifestyle (linen, flowers, phones), and health and beauty items. 'This is very, very impressive,' thought Sharon. 'Competitive salary, extensive benefits and recognition programme for acting in line with company values. This seems a holistic approach to reward and recognition that takes into account the business aspects of HR management as well as the strategic elements of CSR. I am beginning to understand how these are related in terms of reward and remuneration. It all fits together quite well.'

Sharon surfed back to the web search page which had led her to the Serco Sodexo website. She noticed that several of the references were to CSR reports. 'The night is still young,' she thought, as she opened a bottle of cola from the mini-bar and settled in for a few more hours of research in her hotel room in San Diego on this, the second evening of her long-awaited conference. She decided to tackle some CSR reports.

Sharon thought she would start with global multinationals as they appeared to be the most advanced in the CSR context. She opened up a new document on her computer and recorded her findings as she progressed with her review of reward and recognition based on CSR principles. She thought she might email this paper to Arena and get her observations. Arena would be pleased to see she had been doing some self-study.

---

4  www.ssds.com.au/employee-relations-policy.html, accessed 2 June 2010.
5  www.ssds.com.au/Employee-Benefits.html, accessed 2 June 2010.

# Reward and recognition in CSR and sustainability reports for 2008

## Reports

Procter & Gamble Sustainability Report 2008[6]
Unilever Sustainable Development Report 2008[7]
Wal-Mart Global Sustainability Report 2009[8]
Intel Corporation Corporate Responsibility Report 2008[9]

## Reward

The coverage of reward systems and benefits to employees in most CSR and sustainability reports is not extensive. In most cases, the reporting companies content themselves with a generic statement of policy or approach — for example, Procter & Gamble says the principles for compensating company employees are 'Support the business strategy; Pay for performance; Pay competitively.'[10] It also says: 'P&G supports paying employees a competitive wage, as benchmarked against other leading companies. Consistent with our principle of valuing personal mastery, we reward employees for improving their skills and capabilities.'[11] Wal-Mart says: 'We want to make sure that we give our associates the pay, benefits and opportunities they need to make a career at Wal-Mart.[12] The Unilever report contains nothing at all about reward. Intel provides detailed coverage of employee compensation, describing its system which is called T-Comp, and says: 'T-Comp is based on five guiding principles that support our philosophy of rewarding both individual performance and corporate success: meritocracy, market competitiveness, alignment with business performance, promotion of health and welfare, and balance between employee and stockholder needs.'[13] The section is highly detailed and describes Intel's policy of paying above market averages.

## Benefits

The Wal-Mart report focuses on health benefits provided to employees: 'We believe that when we can provide comprehensive, affordable benefits for our associates, we are giving them and their families the ability to both save money and live better, healthier lives.'[14] Unilever states: 'The Company's benefits have been developed to help protect the financial security of

6  www.pandg.com/company/our_commitment/pdfs/PG_2008_Sustainability_ Report.pdf, accessed 2 June 2010.
7  www.unilever.com/sustainability, accessed 2 June 2010.
8  www.corporateregister.com/a10723/26536-09Su-5997136H4502946912U-Gl.pdf, accessed 2 June 2010.
9  www.corporateregister.com/a10723/26211-09Su-7024548M5786733525L-Gl.pdf, accessed 2 June 2010.
10  P&G report 2008: 35.
11  P&G report 2008: 75.
12  Wal-Mart report 2009: 4.
13  Intel report 2008: 58.
14  Wal-Mart report 2009: 83.

employees. These benefits include comprehensive coverage for health care, generous vacation and holiday time, and other work/family balance benefits, including flextime, child care leave and less-than-full-time schedules.'[15] Intel reports on health benefits, retirement benefits and a range of other programmes. This includes a sabbatical programme for employees in the USA and Canada: an eight-week paid sabbatical upon completion of each seven years of service in addition to annual vacation time.

## Recognition

Although most reports refer to employees as the ones driving sustainability, and as most critical to the business, there is surprisingly little about recognition mechanisms for employees. Intel includes a whole section on employee recognition, saying: 'From everyday "thank-yous" to banquets, several forms of recognition reward employees for their accomplishments. Recognition includes corporate-wide programs as well as local programs created by individual business groups to address specific goals.'[16] Their practices include four different types of recognition programme, including one that rewards demonstration of Intel Values,[17] and recognition for community volunteering and environmental practices.

**Intel values**
- Customer orientation
- Discipline
- Quality
- Risk taking
- Great place to work
- Results orientation

## Conclusions

Reward and recognition with a CSR mind-set is critical to a business that wishes to succeed with corporate social responsibility. Effective reward and recognition demonstrate a company's intention to reward employees fairly, care for their well-being and appreciate their contribution. When aligned with a holistic approach to human resources, reward and recognition practices support the CSR approach of the company and are designed with the interest of employees, stakeholders, in mind.

Despite this, the details provided in CSR reports are not extensive. The key themes seem to be:

- Establishing levels of pay that are competitive

- Providing a level of additional benefits, especially health benefits, for employee well-being

Intel shows up as a clear leader, both in the transparency of their reporting, and in the policies they adopt.

Human resources managers should consider the way they develop reward and recognition programmes because linking these to the CSR objectives of the business could improve corporate sustainability performance.

15  Unilever report 2008: 75.
16  Intel report 2008: 56.
17  www.intel.com/lifeatintel/values, accessed 2 June 2010.

Sharon thought to herself that she would have expected companies to say more about this in their CSR reports. She remembered seeing something about employee perks as part of total remuneration packages, so she searched and surfed to the Forbes 100 Best Companies to Work For 2008 list of companies in the USA with 'unusual perks'.[18] She noted some of the companies on the list:

- **Chesapeake Energy Corp** offers free instruction and certification in scuba-diving for employees

- **eBay** offers specially adapted prayer and meditation rooms for employees

- **Genentech** offers employees a payment of $4 per day if they come to work by bicycle, on foot, via public transportation, or in a carpool

- **EOG Resources** matches employee contributions to charity dollar-for-dollar, up to $60,000

- **MITRE** offers higher learning with tuition reimbursement up to $20,000 per year

- **KPMG** offers most employees a full five weeks of paid time off in their first year of service

- **Google** offers employees $1,000 towards the purchase of a hybrid or electric car, and a discount programme for certain employees who install solar panels in their homes

- **Microsoft** offers perks such as dry cleaning and postal services at the Redmond campus, free grocery delivery and a dollar-for-dollar match of employee charitable contributions up to $12,000

Sharon noticed that some of these perks were related to social and environmental issues such as charitable contributions and environmental good practice. She thought that this was a very good way to give benefits to employees while reinforcing the company's CSR message. She came across another website offering 'Customized Lifestyle Incentive Programs'[19] to enrich employees' lifestyles — including limo rides to Niagara Falls, days on the golf course, a Ginger Rogers and Fred Astaire special, a cardio-salsa fitness programme, winery tours and more. 'Fat chance!' she chuckled to herself.

'Of course, there is the living wage question that Arena talked to me about and the amazing project that Novo Nordisk undertook to identify and implement a living wage.' Timberland did something similar, she had noticed on the web. She had downloaded Timberland's 2009 corporate responsibility report.[20]

---

18  money.cnn.com/galleries/2008/fortune/0801/gallery.BestCo_unusual_perks. fortune/index.html, accessed 2 June 2010.

19  www.lifestyleincentives.ca/rewards and recognition.htm, accessed 2 June 2010.

20  Timberland Company, *Responsibility Beyond Factory Walls: Engaging Factory*

In this report, Timberland explained its approach not just to 'living wage' but also to 'sustainable living environments'. She re-read the introduction to this section:[21]

> Ensuring workers are paid a wage that at least allows them to meet basic needs is a complex subject, especially given the local economies in which they live. Timberland upholds all minimum wages in countries where we operate, but we also recognize that minimum wage in many places is not sufficient to meet workers' basic needs or opportunities for betterment. We believe that higher wages alone do not necessarily create improved living conditions. It is within this context that we have defined our approach to support and facilitate sustainable living by addressing the environment (societal infrastructure) that workers live within rather than focus on wages alone.

In Timberland's factory in the Dominican Republic, Sharon read, Timberland realised that left to their own devices, employees would not necessarily spend money in a way that would guarantee them a better future. Therefore, while maintaining a decent level of pay, Timberland sought to provide them with life-skills, a literacy programme and access to nutritious food, drugs and home appliances, etc. 'An interesting perspective,' thought Sharon. 'This is really corporate social responsibility beyond the letter of the law, and clearly something that will benefit the company in the long term because employees will be more motivated, more loyal and less troubled by health problems, family issues and general subsistence concerns. It's smart, but why doesn't every business behave in this way, if it's such a good thing? The phenomenon of the "working poor" has been growing in intensity in many countries around the world.'

Sharon noted that a report released in October 2008[22] by the Working Poor Families Project revealed that more than 28% of American families with one or both parents employed are living in poverty. The report also found that 9.6 million households could be described as low-income or 'working poor': that is, families earning less than 200% of the official poverty level. There were 350,000 more such families in 2006 than in 2002. More than 21 million children lived in low-income working families in 2008, an increase of 800,000 in four years.

'How can this be?' thought Sharon. 'And what is the responsibility of a business to pay people enough so they can live a decent life with access to the necessities for good health and self-development? Businesses fix wage levels

---

*Workers & Strengthening Communities 2009 Report* (Stratham, NH: Timberland Company, 2009, www.earthkeeper.com/Resource_/PageResource/Beyond-Factory-Walls-2009_Timberland-Report.pdf, accessed 2 June 2010).

21 Timberland, *Responsibility Beyond Factory Walls*, www.earthkeeper.com/Resource_/PageResource/Beyond-Factory-Walls-2009_Timberland-Report.pdf: 13.

22 Tom Eley, ' "Working Poor" Report: Nearly 30 Percent of US Families Subsist on Poverty Wages', Global Research.ca, 10 August 2009, www.globalresearch.ca/index.php?context=va&aid=14715, accessed 2 June 2010.

based on competitive forces, supply and demand, within a framework that enables the business to be profitable and grow. Within this, people are paid according to their level of responsibility and in some cases, their potential to grow into roles with higher levels of responsibility.' Sharon had never considered this question of living wage or the role of the HR manager in addressing the problem of the working poor. It just hadn't occurred to her that this was an issue for the HR function. Why on earth should this be her problem? Everyone at Sharon's company, Andromex, was paid according to the law as a minimum, and there was a structured and equitable policy of determining wage levels, bonuses and social benefits, and a remuneration strategy that rewarded the best performers and the high potential talent. 'Isn't that good enough?' she said to herself. Sharon thought her compensation and benefits policy was pretty good, and certainly very competitive. To go as far as to consider whether people can live decently on the amount in their monthly pay-check was a new concept for Sharon. She thought it was rather ridiculous. 'There are so many factors which determine how people live — the size of their family, their backgrounds, the way they spend and save — surely companies cannot be held responsible for all of this. How on earth can anyone suggest that companies build their pay packages on this basis? It's just not economical.'

This was getting too far-fetched, she thought: it was depressing. HR is not social work. Responsibility is one thing, but meeting everybody's different and unique personal finance and development needs, well, that was just stretching the concept too far. She felt a little let down — as though the demands of a corporate responsibility programme were just too intensive for her to deal with and totally outside the scope of her role as an HR manager and business partner. And, frankly, completely irrelevant to meeting the needs of shareholders. Maybe it was just starting to sound like a big waste of time. She decided to call it a day and go to bed.

Sharon was just about to shut down her computer, rather confused and disappointed, when it dawned on her. Why shouldn't a company take such factors into account when fixing remuneration levels? Why focus only on the immediate business factors, such as competitive wage levels and the need to retain good talent. Typically, these issues were not ones that affected the managers or high-skilled population. It was primarily the unskilled or low-skilled employees in a business who were receiving the lowest wage levels and whose alternative personal resources were limited. It affected those who lived from month to month, with no reserves and no financial advantage to take them beyond their current position in life. The ones who just survived from day to day and were wholly dependent on their monthly income. Sharon began to think about this. She recalled some examples of companies taking responsibility for their employees' entire well-being, even before it became popular to talk about social responsibility:

- In 1888, Lord Lever, the founder of Lever Brothers created the large estate at Port Sunlight in the north of England to house all the employees of the big soap factory[23]

- In the USA, Henry Ford built houses or housing complexes in many cities to house Ford company employees out of concern for his employees living conditions

- The Tata Steel business in India continues to provide free housing and a range of facilities for its employees[24]

Why did companies do this? Because they had a need to attract and retain a stable workforce. And this was the most cost-efficient way to do it. Perhaps they also had a natural concern for the living conditions of people, but whether this is true or not, the fact remains that going beyond the letter of the law by providing holistic benefits for employees was also a kind of corporate social responsibility. Apparently this approach was in the long-term interests of these companies. And all of them succeeded in developing their businesses into global enterprises. Including social considerations in the way businesses build remuneration and benefits policies is not new, but today, it has a name. It's called corporate responsibility, thought Sharon.

'Next exercise,' Sharon mumbled to herself, pleased with her progress working through this dilemma. 'My next exercise has to be to work out what constitutes a corporately responsible approach to reward and recognition. Perhaps I will write an action plan for our company, for next year, or the year after. It will probably take me a year to get my boss to approve it,' she sighed. But, diligently, she opened a new document and wrote an ambitious heading, took a bite of an apple (she always had one in her bag) and set to work. She started to write a policy, while continuing to dip in and out of relevant websites, CSR reports and e-book previews. First, she took a look at her current remuneration policy at Andromex.

'The purpose of this remuneration policy is to support the company in delivering its business objectives, by providing the company with a competitive advantage in attracting, hiring and retaining high-quality employees, and serving to motivate them to deliver outstanding performance. The key principles of the remuneration policy are:

- **Competitiveness.** A competitive salary and benefits package compared to the local markets in which we operate

- **Excellence.** Providing incentives to drive superior performance

---

23  en.wikipedia.org/wiki/William_Lever,_1st_Viscount_Leverhulme, accessed 2 June 2010.
24  www.tatasteel.com/corporatesustainability/emp_gen.asp, accessed 2 June 2010.

- **Alignment with business results.** Providing special rewards linked to the financial performance of the company and the delivery of shareholder value

- **Performance-oriented.** Developed in a professional manner, in line with a defined procedure, which rewards for performance and delivery of results. In some cases, additional rewards will be provided for future performance, i.e. for those individuals who demonstrate high potential to make stronger contributions in the future

Having reread this a few times, Sharon realised it was focused on one thing: money. Money for performance, money for results, money for shareholders. Money, money, money. She almost burst into song, thinking of Liza Minelli in *Cabaret,* but held herself back as she realised that this was actually quite sad. She thought how inadequate money was as a driver of performance, and how unsustainable this was for the business. Unsustainable. 'I've got the jargon,' she thought. She wondered when money had ever been the most important thing in her motivation to do a good job. There was one occasion, she remembered, when she felt she had been treated unfairly, after colleagues all received pay rises and she hadn't . 'But it wasn't about the money', she said to herself, 'it was about the injustice. A key principle of any remuneration policy has to be fairness and equality. I now realise that our remuneration policy says absolutely nothing about that.' She drafted the principles of a new policy.

## Corporate social responsibility and remuneration policy

### Driving principles

This remuneration policy is designed to provide employees with legal, fair, equitable, supportive, engaging, attractive, flexible, proactive and transparent remuneration and reward packages, in the belief that employees who are able to live decently and provide for their future will be free to devote their maximum energies to producing their best performance on the job. While this might mean, in some cases, providing remuneration above average competitive levels, it is our belief that this will serve the company's financial interests over the long term, as employees will be loyal, long-serving and motivated to do well. This policy also reflects the company's belief that we have a duty to contribute to the development of society in which we live and do business, through providing employees with remuneration that enables them to better themselves and contribute to the fabric of the community around them. Our remuneration policy is:

**Legal.** The company observes all laws and regulations, local and internationally relevant, with regard to remuneration and reward for employees, at all times, with no exception. This is our minimum position, and all the following principles have been developed to enhance this minimum position in ways which the company believes best serves the business and employee interests.

**Fair and equitable.** This remuneration policy rewards managers and employees in line with their contribution in a fair and equitable way, without discrimination based on gender or other elements of diversity. All employees should have the opportunity to earn equal levels of reward, compatible with their role in the company, their support for the company's mission and values, their performance, and their overall contribution to the business, to stakeholder satisfaction and to society. The remuneration amounts applying to different levels of management and non-management in the company reflect different levels of responsibility and expertise, within a framework that is fair and equitable, as determined by external advisers.

**Supportive.** Remuneration levels should take into consideration both local standards of living and competitive market forces for different types of role. This principle means that we do not blindly pay the legal minimum wage, but aspire to provide base remuneration packages that enable employees to achieve a reasonable standard of living and to develop themselves and their families over time. In addition, in fixing absolute remuneration packages, we will take into account the competitive market rates and create such differentiation as is necessary to reflect the requirements of roles of different levels of responsibility, expertise and functional scope.

**Engaging.** It is our belief that employees are more engaged when they are treated as partners in the achievement of business objectives. Therefore, our remuneration policy includes an element of profit-sharing for all employees, distributed in an equitable way.

**Attractive.** As a business operating in a competitive market environment, we offer a competitive remuneration package to ensure that the company is at no disadvantage when competing to attract and retain employees. While we know that remuneration is not the sole driver of employee motivation, we recognise that remuneration is one factor in the total assessment that a potential employee makes before deciding to join a company, or deciding to stay. An attractive remuneration package reflects the high value the company places on its employees and their contribution, and is therefore an essential element of this policy, contributing to the company's achievement of its business objectives.

**Flexible.** This remuneration policy takes into account the individual needs of different employees and allows flexibility of choice for employees. The total remuneration and reward cost can be personalised for employees, within a guiding framework, to ensure benefits that are relevant to different stages of life and lifestyle needs, such as pension plans, health plans, housing needs, family development, investment in education and more, in order to provide the optimum package for each employee. The company provides qualified consultants with different areas of expertise to advise employees on making the best choices for them.

**Proactive.** This remuneration policy prescribes an annual review of remuneration levels against all the principles contained in this policy, external factors and employee performance and contribution. The company does not wait for employees to ask for a pay rise or change in remuneration package. The company proactively updates remuneration packages in the light of aforementioned annual assessments.

**Transparent.** This remuneration policy is transparent and is designed so that every employee can understand how his or her remuneration package is calculated, and how it may develop in the future. Every employee is provided with training on the principles and practice of his or her remuneration package calculation, and how the employee may influence his or her own remuneration and reward levels.

Sharon reread her list and smiled. She wondered if this trip to San Diego was causing her to get a little giddy. Perhaps when she landed back home, to the stark realities of the daily fight for survival in the competitive jungle, this would all seem like a pipe dream. But for now, she felt this seemed like a very corporate-responsible HR approach.

The key elements of the remuneration package would include:

- Base pay for a standard working week
- Overtime pay
- Annual bonus based on achievement of personal and team targets — business results and promoting company values
- Annual profit sharing element
- A benefit package including elements related to pension, healthcare, education, housing and childcare, with flexible choice elements for employees

In addition, she would include a recognition award for employees making some form of outstanding contribution, the details of which she would work out at a later stage.

The screen began to blur, and Sharon felt her eyelids start to close. She realised she was completely exhausted. She looked at her watch: it was 2.30 a.m. 'Enough', she said out loud. 'Enough remuneration. No amount of money in the world would stop me crashing on those soft pillows right now this minute.'

Switch off computer. Head on pillow. Sleep.

# 6
# Employee well-being, health and safety

Sharon awoke reluctantly to the harsh sound of the alarm clock, which was showing the time 07:00. It was quite persistent. She realised she had no choice but to shut it off, and force her heavy limbs out of the warm bed she had slept in for the last four and a half hours, drag them into the bathroom and get them under the shower, preferably with the rest of her body. While she regretted staying up so late the night before, she still felt a buzz about what she had accomplished. A muted sort of buzz, as she realised that waking up, on this third day of the conference, would be a slow process. Nonetheless, she showered, dressed, towel-dried her cropped hair, dabbed on a little make-up, gathered her laptop, mobile phone, cables and adaptors, notebook and conference file, and by 7.30 was ready for another day of listening, learning and new insight. Just as she was leaving the hotel room, en route to breakfast, her mobile rang. It was Arena.

**Arena:** Hey, Sharon, how are you? I have been looking out for you at the conference, but there are so many people here and so many sessions that everyone gets lost in the crowd. How are you doing? Surviving?

**Sharon:** Good morning! How great of you to call. Thanks, I am having a fabulous time. It's all so interesting. I am so glad I came. I have to say that your brainwashing me on CSR on the flight over has made a real difference to the way I am listening and thinking about HR. I attended a session yesterday on human rights, something I would never even had noticed before. Arena, you have a lot to answer for.

**Arena** (laughing): That's funny. I will be happy to brainwash you some more whenever you like. In fact, I was wondering if you want to join us for dinner this evening. Some of the HR and CSR team from IFC, and a few of our friends, are getting together at Ecoveg Café.[1] It's on 5th Avenue in the city. It's vegetarian. It'll be fun. Want to come? You have to be prepared to be brainwashed, though.

**Sharon:** Hey, sure. That's me. Brainwashing candidate numero uno. Thanks for thinking of me. Sounds great. What time?

**Arena:** Six thirty, OK? We'll see you there. Just follow the noise.

**Sharon:** Fantastic. Thanks. I'll be there. Have a great day.

**Arena:** You too, bye.

**Sharon:** Bye.

'That was really nice of Arena to call', thought Sharon. 'She is such a nice person. I can see why see has succeeded being an HR manager. Oops! A CSHR manager. Funny. I will have to get used to calling myself that. Eventually, when I do something to deserve that title. It will be great to get out of this hotel for the evening and have a little fun. Vegetarian, huh? Can't remember the last time I had a real vegetarian meal. Oh well, I can always order a steak via room service when I get back, if I need to,' she chuckled to herself. She made her way to the breakfast room, which was rather crowded with ASTD-tagged people, nodded good morning to a few, acknowledged a few nods back, ate a quick breakfast and stretched tall with anticipation of another energising day. On her personal schedule for this third morning of the conference was the General Session — the opening plenary, for which she would be a little late — it started at 08:00, followed by:

- 10:00: A session on e-learning and lowering delivery costs of training, presented by a leading e-learning consultant

- 11:30: A learning lab (facilitated discussion) for HR managers from the manufacturing industry

- 13:00: A stretch break — an experiential session about re-energising

- 13:45: A session on work–life balance

- 16:00: A session on reading and sorting resumes for the discerning recruiter

Sharon thought that was a good programme — training, recruiting, best practices, a quick stretch in the middle to make sure she didn't drop from exhaustion, and the work–life balance session, another session she would probably have skipped had she not met Arena two days before. Again, Sharon marvelled at the power of that in-flight conversation to cause her to change her priorities. She realised that she had been too internally focused for too long. Getting out and about to conferences and meetings, especially ones on such a massive

---

1 The Ecoveg Café in San Diego is fictional.

scale, was not just about reinforcing learning and picking up new tools, she pondered, it was about the people you met along the way, and their experiences, more powerful than most of what you hear in the conference sessions themselves. 'Networking,' Sharon said to herself, 'this is the value of networking. As of now, I am going to become a much better networker.'

Sooner than she had anticipated, and after having enjoyed stretching and de-stretching in the lunchtime session, it was 13:45 and she was settling herself in to her seat on the third row of the Work–Life Balance Session.

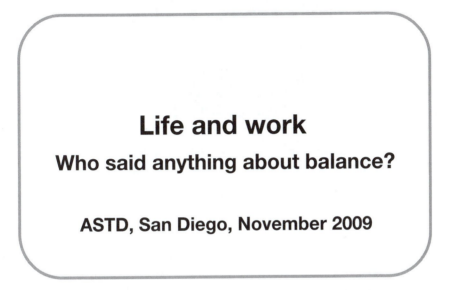

# Life and work

## Who said anything about balance?

### ASTD, San Diego, November 2009

Good afternoon. My name is Jan Marley,[2] and I make a living advising companies and individuals on work–life balance. Actually, there is no such thing as work–life balance. Funny, really. People pay me to advise them on something that doesn't exist. And now, here are all of you, expecting me to lecture to you on something that doesn't exist. Well, forget it.

---

2  Jan Marley is a fictional character and all of her presentation is the original work of the author.

Perhaps I am a fake? An imposter? Let's do a little test. How many of you participated in the lunch-time stretch session? Hands up, let's count.

(Of the 123 people in the session, 14 raised a hand. Jan made a quick count.)

Good: 14 people. Thanks. Made you feel good, right? Gave you energy to come to this session, right? You did something to get your yin and your yang back into harmony. Or your chakras. Whatever. You recharged your batteries. You made time in the day to invest in your own well-being. Why would you do that? Well, so you wouldn't fall asleep in this session for a start, correct? You invested in your own well-being so that you could be alert and productive for the rest of the afternoon. Feel more balanced out now? Well, I've got news for you. That's not balance. Look at it this way.

Not much balance there, right? But maybe one hour of stretching is enough. One hour of exercise, or meditation or relaxation is worth an extra 45% productivity boost. That's my figure. I didn't quote it from anyone. But in my experience, it's true. Give people options to create enough space to do what they need to do to meet the different obligations they have to others and to themselves, and they suddenly become much more productive in their work lives and their private lives. And that's the essence of work–life balance. More overall productivity, for many reasons. Maybe I should call myself a productivity consultant. I would probably make more money that way! Anyway, joking aside, for a while anyway, what I wanted to do in this session was make you aware of the things that pull us and push us in different directions in our daily lives, that potentially conflict, cause us to experience at best a sense of loss of control and at worse, disorientation, stress, even depression and potentially suicidal tendencies.

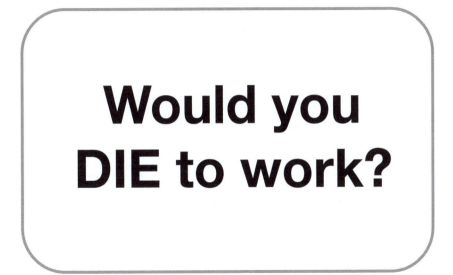

# Would you DIE to work?

This may sound a little far-fetched, but in 2008 and 2009, 25 employees at a company called France Telecom committed suicide.[3] The main reason that is cited in the surprisingly few reports we could retrieve on this subject was the fact that their work stressed them out. They were under pressure to deliver more and more, under tighter and tighter deadlines, and, it seems, had to do this in a fairly unsupportive working environment that didn't give them room for building positive relationships. And not only that, aside from the devastation of their families when their husband, father, brother, mother, sister, aunt or whoever killed themselves, just think what family life must have been like prior to that point. The families of people under extreme stress at work are among the first to suffer. Now, I am not going to quote statistics to you here, or even a

3 www.watoday.com.au/breaking-news-world/suicide-toll-at-france-telecom-hits-25 -20091016-gzkk.html, accessed 18 August 2010.

scientific correlation of stress factors and family impacts. I think you get what I am talking about. We love our work but we don't want to die for it. Dr Stephen Covey, author of the famous *The Seven Habits of Highly Effective People*,[4] said, I think, that no-one gets to the end of their life wishing they had spent more time at work. And I suspect he is right.

There are many reasons we might be stressed out at work. Take a look at this slide:

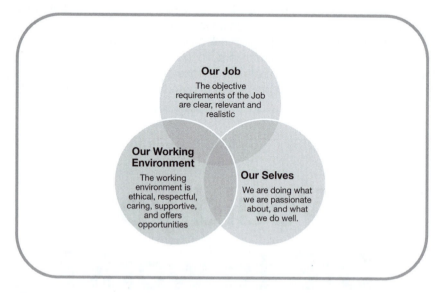

Ever heard of people bring promoted to their level of incompetence? That's a great cause of stress. Ever heard of people being asked to tell lies to customers? Ever heard of people having to work in roles they are clearly not suited to? Ever heard of people whose colleagues leave them off the Christmas Party list? What about people who are punished for taking time off to care for a sick child? Or people who sit in an open-plan office and just can't concentrate. Or people who work in an office job and never get any exercise? All of these factors are stress drivers. And we haven't even scratched the surface yet. Our job, our workplace environment and ourselves must be working in harmony at work to prevent such stress factors turning us into obnoxious people, or even dead people.

First, we must be in a job that makes reasonable demands of us. It's OK if we have challenging and stretching goals, in fact, that's a good thing. But if the challenge and the stretch become immobilising, we have a problem which will soon throw us off balance in all areas of our life, not just work. Part of this is about knowing exactly what performance expectations we are measured against.

Second, we must have a working environment which cares about us and

4  https://www.stephencovey.com/7habits/7habits.php, accessed 25 August 2010.

is flexible enough to adapt to our changing needs. We must feel we are more than a statistic, that we count, because our working environment treats us with respect, listens to what we have to say, and provides opportunities for development or promotion, as far as is possible in the organisational context. More often than not, the prime element of the working environment is the boss. Gallup did a lot of research on this and some of you may be familiar with the Gallup 12 questions.[5]

The third, and arguably most important of all, is you. Your natural aptitudes and what you are passionate about. If you are doing work that you love, and it plays to your strengths, then that will energise you and make you more productive in all of the different roles in your life.

So what we are aiming for is **harmony**. Harmony between the different roles each of us chooses to perform in our lives, blending in with our work role in a way which energises us to do and be all that we want. Given the predominant amount of time we spend at work, a stressful situation at work can have a singularly negative effect on everything else that we do in our lives.

But work–life balance — I call it balance because it's easier because it's a term that everyone is familiar with, but what I really mean is work–life harmony — is not only about managing stressful situations. There are many more aspects to work–life balance.

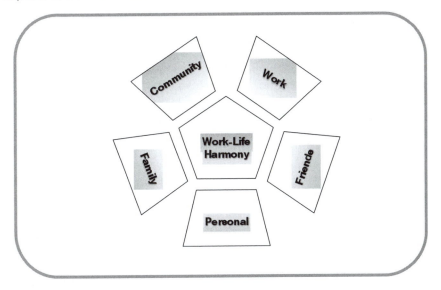

We all need to consider each different facet of our lives and how things hang together. Imbalance in any one of these may affect the others — sometimes in

---

5  The Gallup 12 questions were referred to in Marcus Buckingham and Curt Coffman, *First, Break All the Rules: What the World's Greatest Managers Do Differently* (New York: Simon & Schuster, 1999). See an overview at gmj.gallup.com/content/1144/First-Break-All-Rules-Book-Center.aspx, accessed 2 June 2010.

big ways that we can't help noticing. Such as stress at work, or family matters. Sometimes in more subtle ways, like not having the time to see old friends or go to the gym — these things tend to catch up with us over the long term.

What are the areas in which a workplace can contribute to creating a positive environment in which everyone can strive, with no unnecessary stress?

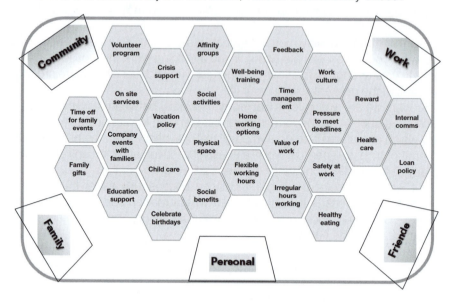

As you can see, there are many things to think about. Some impact more on how we feel at work and how effective we can be. Some impact more at the interface between ourselves and our family and friends — the amount and quality of time we have outside work. How many times do you get home in an evening and just crash out on the sofa because you don't have the energy to do anything else? Some things impact more on our personal well-being and health. Sitting all day in front of a computer screen, for example, can give you neck-ache or back-ache. Believe me, I am talking from experience! Some things impact on how we take our place in our community, such as if we have an opportunity to volunteer at a local charity. The headlines in this chart are just a few of the areas you might consider in terms of work–life effectiveness impact. There are many more. Let me touch on a few of these to give you a taste of what I mean, and then we will look at some company examples of programmes that assist employees in managing conflicting responsibilities and priorities more effectively.

There is clearly something about the work culture that impacts on our effectiveness at work, and the mood we take home with us. If the culture is open, supportive, enables the development of positive relationships, if conflicts are resolved fairly and amicably, if the bosses listen and enable true dialogue and feedback, we are more likely to be more productive at work and finish up our working day feeling satisfied. If the culture is long hours and expectation that you will answer your mobile phone and email at any time of the day, night or weekend, then tensions will start to emerge. And your daughter will probably throw your phone out of the car window at some stage.

There is something about the way we are rewarded that impacts on our effectiveness; while reward is not a key motivator, it is a basic necessity for the maintenance of a reasonable standard of living. If my salary is inadequate to support my basic needs, then my life will not be in harmony. If I don't have a pension plan, I may not be able to support myself once I retire.

There is something about the way the workplace enables me to work safely, free from physical hazards, and free from any form of violence and abuse, including harassment. If I trip over a loose computer cord and break my leg, this has a big impact on my work–life harmony. If I am the victim of sexual harassment in the workplace, this could affect my whole outlook on life whether I am at my desk in the office or not. If I am a victim of verbal abuse, this could erode my self-esteem and make me less productive in my home life.

If I am a young parent, or a single parent and, while this mostly applies to mothers, it applies more and more these days to fathers as well, I may need support in childcare, either in finding a suitable facility for my child or in financing the most suitable option. If I have just given birth, I may want a little more time at home with my new baby than the legal minimum and be stressed at the possibility of raising this with my employer for fear of losing my job. If I have young children at home, an early start in the office may be difficult for me because I must take my children to kindergarten. Alternatively, I need to pick them up at four o'clock, just when the department head has scheduled a meeting. And to top it all, I don't have time to pick up the dry cleaning, go to the bank or post office, or get my hair cut at the hairdressers. All of these things require us to make choices about what we will give priority to in our lives. Inevitably, in a rigid work structure, we have to make either/or choices and one element in our lives — our work, our family, our sense of personal duty or well-being, suffers. I could go on. And on. And on. And on. And I could tell you so many stories of people who have made so many sacrifices in order to retain their job, or develop their career, that we would be here till the next conference. So I am going to move on to look at the key ways in which the more enlightened companies are starting to address the establishment of a workplace which encourages the harmonious management of work and the rest of what there is.

Before I do, a question.

# Who is responsible for your work–life balance ?

How many times do we blame the company? How many times do we say we can't leave the office before 7 p.m. because no one else does? How many times do we hear people say that they spend so much time at work that they have neglected their friends? This is not a company policy. It's just a culture that has developed. We feel awkward about leaving 'early' (though it might actually be quite late) because people might think we are not working hard enough or that we might not be as committed as they are. We don't want to appear as someone who is not committed enough to be promoted or eligible for a bonus. So we stay, feeling we are trapped. There are several outcomes to this scenario: We stay late and remain conflicted at home, causing stress in the home environment. Or we leave at a reasonable time and feel guilty, causing internal stress, which leads to lower productivity. Or we eventually feel we cannot maintain the pressure and leave to find another job. Or we talk to our manager or human resources manager and agree on a solution. Believe it or not, the simple solution of talking to a manager about a straightforward issue such as this is the one that happens least in most organisations. This is because this perception that by looking after ourselves we are in some way negating our commitment to our company, or not fulfilling expectations of us, is so strong. How many employee performance reviews count the hours you stayed at work or state the time you left the office? I haven't seen any that do. But many include benchmarks on achievement, performance, results, output and productivity. By coupling an association of commitment with time in the office, we are making an assumption that delivers the worst of all worlds. Who is responsible for this? The company? Our colleagues? The system? Ourselves?

# Don't blame the system. Change the system.

Bottom line, folks, is that everybody owns their individual and personal responsibility for deciding where to draw the line. Everybody must understand their own limits, their own biology, their own priorities and their own values, and act accordingly. Everybody needs to decide what's right for themselves. I know that if I have computer work to do, I need to do it in the morning or late at night, because between the hours of 2 and 4 p.m. I fall asleep at the screen. I know that if my 8-year-old son is sick, I have to stay home. I know that if I have a lot of Internet work to catch up with, I do it best at 10 p.m., at home, when the house is quiet. I know that if I am asked to attend a meeting at 8 a.m., no matter how important, I decline, as I take my children to school and I am not prepared to give that up. I go to the gym three times a week at 6 p.m., otherwise I wouldn't be able to function. I arrange my work schedule around these and other priorities. In some ways, it might be easier for me because I am independent. But even so, my choices sometimes conflict with the service I can give to clients, which has the potential to impact my income and reputation. However, I have learned to stand my ground, and my clients now respect this and, frankly, are even a little envious. I remember talking to one guy, called Gerald,[6] in a company I was working with. He said that he left the office twice a week at 4 p.m. to collect his children from school. He just left. He said that after a while, people started coming up to him and saying how wonderful they thought it was that a father took the time to be with his children like that. Instead of becoming the outcast, he became the hero. He wasn't punished, he was promoted. Even then, he still collected his children from school twice a week.

I maintain that everyone has individual and personal responsibility for their

---

6  Gerald is a fictional name but his story is based on a real person, who was an employee at the time the author served as Human Resources Director.

own lives and must decide where to allocate their time and their energy in order to achieve harmony between work and other priorities. Hah! Easily said, right? Just decide your priorities and act accordingly. Wouldn't it be nice if the world were so simple? The plain fact is that most people need help in dealing with this, because the collective peer and top-down pressure in organisations can be too overwhelming for one individual to deal with. I am talking to you not as employees in your organisations but as managers with a vested interest in recruitment, retention, productivity, performance and a culture which enables people to do their best work. Changing the system is part of the core role of human resources managers. I maintain that the development of a culture in which individuals can achieve work–life harmony is a *shared* responsibility between individuals and organisations. I maintain that the human resources function must identify the opportunities that arise for the *business* when individuals work in harmony with themselves.

# Human resources managers have a responsibility to change the system.

So, all of you human resources managers out there. It's your responsibility too. You are charged with partnering the business to deliver better performance. You are skilled at developing processes and tools which support a performance culture. Helping employees to achieve work–life harmony is part of this culture. There is a business case for this:

- Companies that support flexible work arrangements had **3.5% higher market value** than companies without: Watson Wyatt Human Capital Index
- Workers who believe they have flexibility are able to **work eight hours more a week** and still feel they have work–life balance: IBM
- Pepsico's fitness programme produced a **300% ROI** ($3.00 for every $1.00 invested)
- A nine-year study of the corporate wellness programme **saved $225 per employee** per year in reduced hospital admissions, mental health visits and outpatient services, even after deducting the cost of paying employees to participate: Johnson & Johnson
- Emergency back-up childcare programme yielded a **125% ROI within 6 months** of implementation; steadily ramping up to a 521% ROI by the fourth year: KPMG
- Approximately **$1 million saved** annually by extending the job guarantee for new mothers on maternity leave to six months: Aetna
- Fitness centre participants had medical payments one-fifth lower, accident-related disability costs a third lower and workers' comp costs per claim **79% lower** than non-participants: Applied Materials[7]

Need more? Go to the Alliance for Work-Life Progress website[8] and you will find many more examples of how implementing work–life programmes contributes to improved business results. Take a look at this too:

Amid soaring health spending, there is growing interest in workplace disease prevention and wellness programs to improve health and lower costs . . . we found **that medical costs fall by about $3.27 for every dollar spent on wellness programs** and that **absenteeism costs fall by about $2.73 for every dollar spent.**[9]

7  Data source: www.awlp.org/awlp/library/html/businessimpact.jsp, accessed 8 June 2010.
8  www.awlp.org.
9  According to research at Harvard University and Harvard Medical School, Boston, MA: Katherine Baicker, David Cutler and Zirui Song, 'Workplace Wellness

While there are many more studies and papers on this, the actual measurement of such programme effectiveness is still not widely performed. Nonetheless, no one can deny the benefits for individuals, organisations and society as a whole. For this reason, work–life balance is often quoted as a key element of corporate social responsibility practices and included in corporate CSR reports. Even US President Obama and First Lady Michelle Obama see the need for greater flexibility in workplace practices to enable people to manage all their conflicting priorities. In March 2010, they held a summit to discuss modernising the workplace to meet the needs of workforces and families and making workplaces more humane in moral terms, believing this to be instrumental in delivering greater productivity.[10]

The key elements of work–life balance practices adopted by companies fall into six categories:

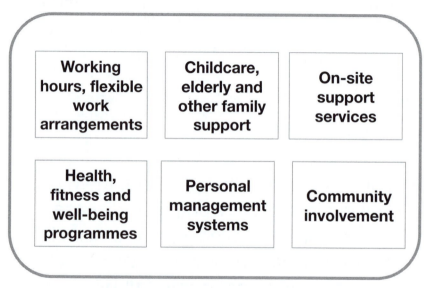

We don't have a lot of time left, so I will say a few words about each of these just to give you a flavour of what could be involved. Those interested in more information are invited to contact me after this session.

**Working hours and flexible working arrangements** cover the entire gamut of working arrangements ranging from relatively simple programmes to complex work structures which need detailed planning. All of these must be checked of course against local regulations in your own countries. This category includes:

---

Programs Can Generate Savings' (2009), content.healthaffairs.org/cgi/reprint/hlthaff.2009.0626v1, accessed 8 June 2010.

10 Dan Froomkin, 'White House Launches Push for Workplace Flexibility', *Huffington Post*, 31 March 2010, www.huffingtonpost.com/2010/03/31/white-house-launches-push_n_520909.html, accessed 4 June 2010.

- Reduced number of hours in a working week (total hours counted as a full-time position)

- Compressed working week (four long days rather than five average days)

- Job-sharing

- Flexitime arrangements to start and finish work within a flexible schedule range

- Working from home arrangements — teleworking or telecommuting

- Extended unpaid leave

- Extended maternity or paternity leave

- Paid leave for special family events

- Sabbaticals

**Childcare and other family support arrangements** cover the ways in which companies can support employees by sharing some of the family burden and even involving families in understanding the workplace environment. This covers things such as:

- Child care allowances for employees

- Education funding for children of employees

- Emergency childcare service or babysitting service

- On-site childcare arrangements

- Open family day at work

- Subsidised weekends or trips including families

- Support for employees with elderly or sick parents — time off or subsidised care plans

- Gifts to family when new employees join the company

- Newsletter designed for children or families of employees

- Home loans or car loans

- Emergency funds for employees experiencing hard times for different reasons

- Special aid for one-parent families

- Loans or grants to employees who adopt children

- Movie club for employees and families

**On-site support services** are those that save employees time by enabling them to handle some of their personal and family duties without leaving the office. This includes contracting with various service providers to deliver their services to the company offices or factories:

- On-site grocery or general store

- Mobile post office

- Mobile dry-cleaning or laundry service

- On-site gym or local gym subscription

- On-site cash dispensing machine or other mobile banking services

- On-site workshops for developing hobbies such as photography or Internet skills or organic cookery, or support groups for single parents, weight-loss, home finances, etc.

- Mobile hairdressing services

- In-site dining facilities

- Mobile travel agency services

- Collective purchasing programmes for electronics, theatre or concert tickets and more

- Employee hot-line for advice on different subjects

**Health, fitness and well-being programmes** are possibly the most widespread, and include a wide range of options that a company can adopt to support employees in caring for their own health and well-being. I am not referring here to the company responsibility to maintain a safe and healthy working environment as stated by law. These are requirements and responsibilities of the company. Here I relate to examples of how companies go beyond the letter of the Health and Safety laws to provide additional support for employees. These may include:

- Workshops on health, fitness, diet, nutrition, stopping smoking, low-calorie cooking and many more

- Sports programmes including leagues for different sports and sponsored sports days

- Subsidy for sports clubs or fitness programmes

- Programmes for learning a new sport activity

- Programmes for groups or individuals to adopt healthier lifestyles

- Ergonomics checks for all employee work stations and modifications to space and furniture

- On-site medical services or mobile clinic or doctors/nurses

- Extended health insurance and/or dental insurance

- Musical and other cultural events

- Stress management counselling in groups or individually

- On-site social workers to help employees in crisis situations

**Personal management systems** include ways for employees to manage their time most efficiently in line with their values and needs. This could include:

- Personal finances management workshops

- Personal time management programmes

- Partnering in family leadership for couples

- Personal effectiveness management programmes

- Email and social media time management

- Skill-building workshops such as mediation skills, learning a foreign language, computer skills or more

And finally, **community involvement**. This doesn't seem as obviously connected as some of the other things we have mentioned to improve employee productivity or engagement. So I prepared a special chart on this just for you. There is rather a lot of data. Which is good, right?

**Outcomes of effective volunteering programmes include:**

- **An improved rating among employees for their employer as a place to work** compared to other companies (63% saying above average or one of the best, compared to 57% before the programme)
- **Increased job satisfaction levels** (64% fairly or very satisfied among all employees, compared to 62% before; satisfaction among volunteer programme participants rose to 67%)
- **Increased positive word of mouth among employees about their employer** (54% saying they would speak highly of their employer, compared to 49% before the programme; among volunteer programme participants, the rate rose to 57%)
- **Higher retention rates for employees who participated in volunteer activities** than for those employees who did not. Employees who volunteered appeared to be more prone to pursue promotion and development activities in the months following the participation in the volunteer programmes
- **Approximately 62% of workers 18–26 years old would prefer to work for a company that provides opportunities for them to apply their skills to benefit non-profit organizsations**
- **About 76% of young workers said that volunteering helps them hone their leadership skills**
- **75% said volunteering lets them develop skills they can use at work** (Deloitte 2007)
- **70% of young workers feel companies should use volunteering as a professional development tool**
- **91% of Fortune 500 HR managers surveyed** believe that contributing business skills or expertise to a non-profit organisation in a volunteer capacity can further develop an employee's business skills
- **56% of Fortune 500 HR managers say volunteering is encouraged as part of their company's development and training programme** (Deloitte 2008)[11]

11  Data in this chart was sourced from Junior Achievement, *The Benefits of Employee*

As you can see, community involvement is a factor in developing employee engagement, and in enabling managers to achieve a certain level of harmony with the way they perceive their work and their contribution to society. Work–life programmes tend to have a tangible and high payoff for the business. In particular, where employees volunteer in causes which they believe in, or are connected to the community in which they live, they become better employees, happier at work and happier with themselves. This is also part of achieving work–life balance and delivers a measurable contribution to the business in terms of attraction, retention, turnover rates, absenteeism, conflict management, skill development, team building and productivity.

The point is that the human resources function must drive the establishment of a culture in which community involvement can take place, because work–life balance is mission-critical for organisations and will become more so in the future. It's not about balance but about helping employees achieve harmony, supporting employees in the way they make choices and providing tangible frameworks in which they can increase their awareness and make better choices for themselves. Note that I have not covered other things that also impact on employee engagement or working culture because, of course, work–life balance cannot be a stand-alone — remember what we said earlier:

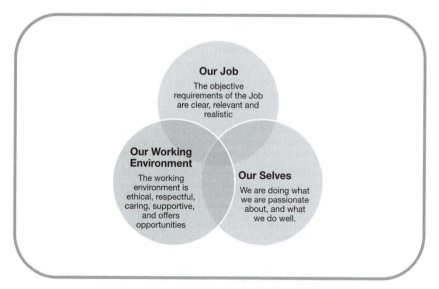

In a company where there is a basically positive approach to the workplace culture and framework, with clear job requirements and the people suited to the jobs they are doing, and a basic level of ethical, open, inclusive and supportive management approach, a company's attention to work–life balance issues can

*Volunteer Programs* (Colorado Springs, CO: Junior Achievement Worldwide, 2009, www.ja.org/files/BenefitsofEmployeeVolunteerPrograms.pdf, accessed 1 June 2010).

tip the scales and turn a good company into a great company, which makes a contribution far beyond that of delivering profit for shareholders. I would recommend you to review the work–life harmony checklist of programmes I just discussed and see how you are doing as human resource managers in supporting your business in this way. My advice is to target to have at least one programme in each of the six focus areas, and develop from there.

# Life and work

## Who said anything about balance?

## *We did!*

# Thank you and good luck !

Thank you all for listening and I hope that I have provided some new insights. That's all we have time for today, except for a few questions.

**Participant:** Jan, thank you. That was very interesting. But in my company, most of our employees are shift workers on a production line. We can't do flexitime or job-sharing, as the jobs require specific training and start and finish times that are dependent on a team, not on one individual. We can't do telecommuting for obvious reasons. We can't even allow the employees time off for volunteering as this would affect the production line teams and schedules. I have tried to think about how we might help employees and be more flexible, especially as we would like to offer more jobs to women, but so far I have not come up with a solution. What would you suggest?

**Jan:** Thank you for that question. Yes, some work situations make flexible work arrangements more difficult to achieve. I can certainly understand shift times and the fact that they must be respected. However, job-sharing could offer a solution. In many companies I know they maintain several shift floaters whose main purpose is to release people on a recurring basis or on an ad hoc basic to allow them to attend to personal matters without using up all of their vacation days. The additional cost of extra floater hours is well compensated for by the increase in productivity and employee motivation and loyalty as a result of the flexibility. Ultimately, if this is quite impossible, there are many other things in the other focus areas that you could consider to assist employees in achieving the balance that is right for them.

**Participant:** Jan, I also found your talk very interesting. I work for a small company; we are just 180 employees. Everyone has to do everything and pitch in, and I can't see us implementing major processes such as the ones you mentioned. How does everything you mentioned apply to small businesses?

**Jan:** Thank you for your question. You will be surprised at this, but I spend a lot of my time working with small businesses of below 300 people. Precisely because of the lack of process in many small businesses, work–life harmony becomes more important. In many small businesses there is no human resources manager, for example, and no set of human resources policies, jobs aren't well defined, and employees have to take on responsibilities that are unrelated to their core job. I see this time and time again. This in itself places people under great stress. You have to manage this. You cannot keep stressing people out without paying for the consequences. In a small business, this is even more essential because the cost of recruitment and replacement is very high.

On the other hand, communication in small companies is more direct and easier to gather. In the small companies I have assisted, we have carried out a survey of employees to assess where they stand on work–life balance issues and what's important to them. In some cases, very individual solutions were applied, such as one accounting clerk who needed to leave her office at lunchtime to provide lunch for her elderly mother who lived alone, or a single-parent father, a factory shift leader, who was given use of a company car on workday evenings to pick up his two young children from school in order to gain an hour at work each day by not travelling by bus. These are unique and individual solutions that, if established with the right sort of expectations and in a transparent way in the organisation, can actually deliver benefit and even become something that other employees admire and appreciate. Other employees, for example, were very supportive of Jed, that's the single-parent father, using a company car that would otherwise sit in the car park overnight. They saw it as the company truly caring about employees.

What I am saying is that with small companies, there may be a little more scope for the application of individual solutions, rather than broad-scale collective solutions. There are also many things that small companies can implement without massive resources either money-wise or time-wise — on-site workshops, a hot-line for employee issues, time off to handle personal or family business and more. My advice is to understand what is problematic or causing dissonance for your employees and that will define your opportunity.

The next question from the audience was from Sharon.

**Sharon:** Hello Jan. My name is Sharon and I am the HR Manager for

Andromex. Andromex is a privately owned company with around 2,500 employees. We haven't considered any of these work–life balance programmes seriously up until now and I can't say that we have any sort of policy or programmes beyond providing extended medical insurance coverage, employee loans and options for extended unpaid leave. I was wondering. If I were to start today, what should be the first thing I should do?

**Jan:** Thank you, Sharon. Of course, the first step in any change process is to understand what is. You should do some research in your organisation to find out what people are feeling. You could do this in a written survey, but I would recommend a series of focus group discussions with a range of different types of employee to hear things first hand. Using this, you could extrapolate some assumptions about what might work best and make an assessment of the cost–benefit. As I mentioned previously, one initiative in each focus area would be a good way to start, even if these are small initiatives.

**Sharon:** Thank you.

**Jan:** Thank you too, and thank you all. Please do be in touch if I can serve you in any way. I will leave you a handout [see overleaf] which is a selection of themes you could use in a survey to understand where the employees in your company are having balance problems. Thank you and enjoy the remainder of the conference.

Sharon took a look at the handout and began answering the questions silently in her mind. She realised that, on the whole, she had managed to achieve a certain level of harmony, but not without having gone through some personal stress and pain. She certainly identified with the statements about late meetings, email overload and difficulties in family relationships. She recalled the problems last year when she was developing the new global recruitment model and had to work late almost consistently for several weeks. She frequently didn't get home in time to put the children to bed, let alone make meals for them all. When she came home she didn't have the energy to do anything very much other than stare at the TV. Twice, she had had to spend most of her weekend in the office. She had missed Darren's first concert with his guitar band and Michelle's Easter Parade party. Her husband, Robert, who was usually so patient, became so frustrated that they had had a major fight and didn't talk to each other for two days. The children were unsettled and Julie, the 11-year-old, had asked if they were going to get divorced. Michelle had heard her parents fighting and spent the whole evening crying into her pillow and wouldn't respond to anyone. Even Sharon's best friend, Lyndsey, told her that she was losing it and had better get her priorities right. Sharon had been jerked into reality by this incident. She had never been under so much pressure at work before that she had neglected almost everyone else. The fight with Robert made her realise that she had to make a change. Even though she was still in the middle of the recruitment model, she set limits and decided that she would work

**A selection of employee questionnaire themes: work–life balance (Agree/Disagree statements)**

**Effectiveness on the job**
- I feel happy with the amount of time I spend at work
- I have control over my time at work
- I am subject to continuous interruptions in my working day
- I often respond to emails and/or calls outside working hours
- I often have to take work home even though I don't want to
- I never seem to be able to get to the end of my task list
- My workload is unreasonably heavy
- I leave my desk for a few hours and come back to a long list of emails I have to answer
- I am required to attend meetings which end late in the evening

**Work trade-offs**
- I have the ability to manage my time at work to ensure I meet my personal or family commitments outside work
- I refrain from taking holidays because of work overload
- I use my entire annual holiday every year
- I work at weekends because I have to keep up with my workload
- I go into work even though I am sick, though I know I shouldn't
- I stay late at the office because that is what is expected of me

**Company support**
- I feel the company cares about my personal well-being
- If I had a personal or health problem, I feel the company would help
- I feel that if I don't spend long hours at work, the company will not value me
- I would like to be able to work flexible hours
- I would like to have the option of doing part of my work from home

**Effectiveness outside work**
- I feel happy with the amount of time I have for my family
- I feel happy with the amount of time I spend with my friends
- I have enough time to maintain hobbies or personal interests outside work
- I would like to do (more) volunteer work in the community but cannot because of work commitments
- I get home from work and have no energy to do other things
- Travelling to and from work takes a long time

**Family commitments**
- I am a single parent and have difficulty balancing working and looking after my children
- I have a partner who works and expects me to help at home, but I don't have time
- I have dependants who rely on me to support them
- My family understands my work and the hours I spend at work
- My commitment to work has caused difficulties in my family relationships
- I never seem to have enough time to spend with my children

**Community**
- I don't have time to volunteer in the community, though I would like to
- I don't have any contact with my neighbours

**Overall well-being**
- I feel pressured by the number of commitments I have in my life
- I never feel I am coping well with everything I have to do
- I wish I had more time for myself
- I don't have time to go to the gym or practise any form of sport
- I never thought this job would take up so much of my time and energy
- I feel the amount of stress in my life is more than I would like

very late three nights a week, no weekends except for some emails on Saturday, and no talking about work when she got home. She managed to submit the recruitment model on time and have it agreed by the management team, without any noticeable reduction in quality. However, she had realised that she had come close to creating a major family crisis, which, actually, she had brought on herself. The lecture on work–life balance made her realise that there are many employees who don't have the ability to recognise when they are heading for such a crash, or the ability to set the right limits.

For Sharon, this was a short-term problem, but for others, it's a way of life. She recognised some of the signs in her company. She saw how the Finance and the Marketing Departments never left the office before 7 p.m., sometimes later. Everyone stayed late. She had occasionally wondered if there was actually so much work that everybody had no choice but to work such long hours, but, frankly, she hadn't felt she needed to get involved. After all, if no one was complaining, it couldn't be that serious. Now, after this lecture, she was beginning to think that the head-in-the-sand approach was a lack of responsibility on behalf of her HR function. The role of HR is to actively and proactively seek out the issues, not wait until someone complains. Work–life balance issues are sensitive and not easy for people to raise because, as the lecturer had said, people are worried that they might be seen as less committed, or that they might jeopardise chances for promotion or advancement. 'This', Sharon thought, 'is something else I have to deal with.'

Sharon packed away the questionnaire into her conference folder and made her way to her hotel. She decided not to stay for the closing plenary, in order to have a little time to rest before meeting Arena and her friends that evening. All in all, she felt that she had gained her money's worth from this conference. And in a different way than she could ever have imagined before she had alighted that fateful plane to San Diego.

At six thirty the same evening, Sharon was sitting in Ecoveg Café. Arena came through the glass doors together with three other people — one woman and two men. She saw Sharon and immediately approached and gave her a big hug.

**Arena:** Hey Sharon, you're here. That's great. I am so glad you could make it. Here, meet John from ICF, he's HR Manager for our US Operations. Meet also Liam from our plant in the Midwest. He is our Environment Officer. And meet Maria from Italy, who is the HR Manager for an Italian company, Autoricambi,[12] which makes vehicle parts, right Maria?

Maria nodded and smiled. Everyone shook hands, exchanged business cards and sat at their designated table. They started chatting about the conference, their impressions, the people they had met, their families, what they had been reading recently and what seemed to Sharon like just about everything else

---

12 Autoricambi is an entirely fictional company.

including the weather. They all ordered — Arena recommended the tofu and spinach risotto to Sharon and ordered the same for herself — and they all raised their glasses to San Diego and great conferences. Throughout dinner and dessert the conversation flowed in many different directions and Sharon thought that she hadn't had such an interesting evening for quite some time. However, at the back of her mind were still many thoughts about CSR and the revelations of the last few days. She couldn't help herself. She had to solicit the opinions of the others around the table.

**Sharon:** Liam, what brings an environment officer to the ASTD Conference? I don't see the connection.

**Liam:** Yes, I asked the same question, Sharon. But when the boss says fly to San Diego, you fly. John here and Arena both asked me to come and co-present the work we have been doing on G teams. We presented our case study on this today after two years of work.

**Sharon:** G teams? Should I know what that means?

**Liam:** Green teams, Sharon. Sorry, I am so used to IFC-speak. We have set up employee green teams in different departments and locations at IFC. These are teams that promote the assimilation of green thinking and behaviour in the workplace. It takes the concept of corporate environmental responsibility right to the level of individual employees and makes it very real for them in their daily jobs. Employees also come up with great solutions for things that reduce cost in the business and improve product environmental attractiveness, such as in packaging. What we have found in the last few months is that employees are also taking in what they learn on the job and applying it off the job, at home. They are recycling more at home, using less electricity, consuming less. We are looking at ways to measure this so as to understand the entire indirect effect of the G team activity.

**Sharon:** That sounds amazing, Liam. Would that work in any company, or would it have to be a food company like IFC. At Andromex, we work on software solutions, not tangible products that you can eat. We don't have issues with production plants and packaging. What would G teams do at Andromex?

**Liam:** I've never worked in a software company but I imagine the principles are the same. Every company, of every size, no matter what the business sector or activity, has an environmental impact both in direct terms, based on the way people use, re-use, recycle or reduce consumption of energy and other resources, and in indirect terms, through the products it sells and the ultimate impact on lifestyles, business processes or the behaviour of people outside the company. Every single employee plays a part in creating this impact. Every single employee can play a part in reducing their individual impact within the context of their job. I will bet you that G teams in your company would deliver an ROI within 12–18 months of their establishment. That's what we found at IFC.

**Sharon:** I understand. And I would certainly like to hear more. I would love to be in touch once I return to the office, and get some suggestions on what we might do with G teams at Andromex. Would that be OK, Arena? John ?

**John:** Uh oh, Sharon. Be careful with this guy. He may not be a human resources man at heart, but he knows how to energise people about the environment. He is the best environmental officer around. You should see him run a workshop on waste in the workplace. He spends the day before collecting people's office waste and brings it in this massive sack and starts sorting through it in front of all these people who have this horrified look on their faces and scrunched up noses, as though they expect it to smell like the local sewage farm. It's not usually all that smelly but people find the subject of waste rather distasteful at first. But believe me, Liam makes them understand that waste can be one of their most valuable resources. They say that people can tell a lot about you from what you throw away. It's true in the office too. You can tell a lot about the sustainability of the business by what's in people's trash cans under their desks. Though we try to stay clear of things that might embarrass them!

**Liam:** Yes, I sort through the waste first and if someone has been doing things in the office that I feel they might not want disclosed in public, I spare them!

**John:** Feel free to be in touch, though. We would be happy to help if we can.

**Liam:** Of course we would be happy to help.

**Arena:** Sharon, Liam has done a great job working with HR to develop green teams and it has made a big difference to our use of resources — electricity bills, water usage, paper — you name it. Some of our employees have suggested packaging solutions that even the most experienced technical guys hadn't come up with. But as Liam mentioned, the most rewarding thing for me is the evidence that we have engaged people beyond the workplace. They are changing behaviour at home, saving money on their home electricity and fuel expenses and more. It has taken us nearly two years to reach this level of penetration of the programme. We have trained up G team leaders in every department and we now have a league where each team is measuring its own environmental impacts improvement. We call it GTL — the Green Team League — and we run it as a global programme. Each G team has a GTEB — a Green Team Environmental Benefit. And once a quarter we update the league table and award all the leading G team members a trophy and a cash prize, which represents part of the savings they are making for the company. Once a year, our CEO awards the top five G teams an eco-vacation, together with their families. This builds environmental awareness, team relationships, engagement, you name it. And the programme, after two years, pays for itself. My secretary is on the HR G Team and she says she's cut her paper usage by over 40% in 18 months, for example, through double-sided printing, using half pages instead of full pages, re-using paper and envelopes, etc. Anyway, I strongly recommend you having a discussion with Liam about this; I am sure that he can help. But I didn't bring you all here to do business, we are supposed to be having fun. This isn't an extra conference session!

**Sharon:** Yes, I know. But I still have a lot to understand about CSR. For example, today I attended a work–life balance session. It was very interesting. It made some very clear connections between the way a company considers all aspects of well-being of employees and actual health and safety issues. The presenter put up a slide saying 'Would you DIE to work?' and talked about a spate of suicides in a French company, driven apparently by an awful work culture. She also quoted some fantastic numbers about how much both a company and a government saves if companies take proactive measures to care for the health of their employees. It was convincing, I can tell you that. I found myself thinking more about workplace impacts on employees.

**Maria:** We are looking to develop our CSR programmes also. The main thing we have focused on in our workplace activities so far is the physical working environment and safety. Our CEO said that that is our first responsibility, to create a workplace free from harm and safety risks. He said that compliance with legislation is important, of course, but the real difference in safety results comes from changing people's mind-sets about safety working. In our plants, there is a lot of heavy machinery and metallurgy work, and many safety hazards. Our CEO said he would not consider doing more on social responsibility activities until we could demonstrate to ourselves that we are number one in safety. He made the Safety Manager in the Operations Department, and myself, as Human Resources Manager for Operations, jointly responsible. He said it is not just about implementing procedures, it is creating a safety culture. Whenever he uses the word culture, the next words he utters are human resources. He says that anything to do with changing the culture must be supported by HR. Both the Safety Manager and I and my team have safety targets in our annual work-plan, and our bonus is determined on how we deliver against these targets. I had to make a big shift in my thinking, I can tell you. I didn't consider safety to be part of my brief as HR manager, I thought it was something that operations people handle. Aside from arranging safety training sessions from time to time, I did not see it as part of the culture, and certainly not as a key part of HR responsibility. Now, believe me, I am well versed in issues relating to employee safety and ways of assimilating a safety culture.

**Sharon:** What things have you done with regard to employee safety, Maria?

**Maria:** Over and above the formal safety training that every employee must complete, which is the Safety Manager's responsibility, some of the main actions that relate to changing the culture, or go beyond the minimum requirements of the law, include a major study that we completed this year on ergonomics and the evaluation of every workstation in the company for ergonomic risk: we made changes where appropriate, replacing some workstations, seating, workspace design and so on. We have made safety a core part of our internal communications. We have nominated additional safety leaders in each department and trained them in assessing safety risk. We hold an annual Safety Week in which all employees, including the senior management, identify safety risks and raise issues. The Safety Management team commit to investigating and responding to all these issues within 48 hours. They work round the clock during Safety Week, but people feel it is worthwhile because they know they will get quick responses, and they feel good about making a difference. We have made safety performance part of the annual employee evaluation, and any employee who does not behave in a safe manner does not receive an annual bonus, no matter how well he or she performs. On the other hand, employees who identify safety risks that our qualified auditors didn't pick up, either during Safety Week or at any other time, receive a special bonus.

Our CEO always talks about safety. In every HR training programme there is a short introduction that covers key messages for employees, and one is always relating to safety. A little like the safety announcement on a flight. Every time you go into a training session, you fasten your seat-belt and listen to the safety message. We regularly send Safe-Tweets to all our employees. This is a short tweet-style message on our internal direct messaging system where we remind them to check for safety risks in all they do. All this is on the job. We also do a lot to instil safe driving practices for those who drive company trucks or have company cars, and drivers in general. Company car drivers, for example, are called in for a discussion with their manager and the Safety Manager if they have been involved in more than one car accident per year.

There are many more things that we do. It's all about making this an important basic mind-set of people, in the same way as quality or ethical behaviour should be part of the basic mind-set. The results speak for themselves. Last year we went the longest time ever in the history of the company without a lost-time accident, and we recorded the fewest number of accidents ever. In a survey we did among new hires, they said that safety was one of the most important aspects of working in the company and they felt the company was investing in employee safety to a high degree.

After last year's results, my boss, the CEO, said he felt we had laid a good foundation and that we should start looking at how we develop our CSR programme. Now we have started working on employee diversity, which is another cultural and mind-set shift that my boss believes is crucial for long term success.

**Sharon:** That's really something. It sounds like you have made tremendous progress. But can you explain to me what this meant for you as an HR manager. I mean, there is only so much cultural change you can drive in a company at any given time. There is only so much that people can assimilate. Culture change isn't overnight. What did you have to stop doing in HR in order to give safety this sort of priority? And CSR is fine, but surely your first commitment should be to HR and developing the skills and capabilities of the people?

**Arena:** Hah, Sharon, I was wondering when you would raise that. I saw the way you looked when Liam was talking about G teams and now Maria is talking about S teams.

**Sharon:** What?

**Arena:** Safety teams. I could see it all over your face. Where on earth will I find the time and the resources to do all of this? It's like adding another job on top of my HR job. Right? Isn't that what you were thinking?

**Sharon:** Yes. I just don't see how I can set up G teams, S teams, D teams.

**Arena:** What?

**Sharon:** Diversity teams.

The others all laughed.

**Sharon:** How can I set up all these teams that are not core HR priorities and still do my job? Come on, you guys, you must have endless resources or CEOs who never look at the bottom line and just keep investing in more HR processes. I have never heard of a boss like that.

**Maria:** Sharon, remember, my boss said to focus on safety before doing everything else. He said S teams before G teams and D teams. For me, it wasn't such a stretch. There was a clear focus.

**John:** I understand you, Sharon. But the thing you have to remember is that CSR is a way of doing business. It's about doing what you do today in a more responsible manner. So with G teams, for example, we tried to incorporate the G team activity into current ways of working without burdening everyone with a whole new set of activities. Aside from a short meeting once a month, and with the more established teams, once every two months, the other things that happen are integrated with existing team activities as far as possible. If we are writing a newsletter, then we find a way to include something from a G team. We don't create a newsletter especially for this, except once a year when we support our annual CSR reporting process and publish a G team annual report. If we are holding a team-building event, we use green as a theme to use in the process. If we are approving a new product launch event, we make sure that one of the marketing people, who is a G team member, ensures that the launch event is planned along G principles — environmental principles. If we are planning a trip abroad, we look at the carbon footprint of the flight for alternative routes, alongside other costs and considerations. We can't always choose the greenest alternative, but G teams mean that everyone is so aware of green themes that they are always considered. Liam has helped us a lot with this — he has produced many sets of guidelines for us, such as Green Events, Green Meetings, Green Travel, which apply specifically for our business, not just the generic guides you can download from the Internet. In any role, there are a number of basic conditions you have to meet and priorities you have to juggle. Some things need more initial focus as you establish an infrastructure, but by integrating CSR themes into our existing HR process, we have found that the net additional work is not significantly increased. It works together quite synergistically.

**Arena:** I agree with John, but I am sure that you will need to make some trade-offs in the early days of developing your programme, just as we did, though John might not recall. Once you have a basic level of awareness and commitment in the business, all incremental change requires fewer resources. But I have no doubt that in the first major mind-set shift you will have to make some hard decisions about priorities for use of HR resources.

**Sharon:** Perhaps I will just go into hibernation for the rest of the year. Either that, or I am going to be so overworked and stressed out that my work–life harmony will shoot off the scale, and I don't mean in a positive way.

**Arena:** You just have to pace yourself and the organisation.

**Sharon:** You are always so optimistic, Arena.

**John:** Oh yes, she believes in rainbows, all right.

**Arena:** Right, that's enough about HR and CSR and G teams and D, S and any other teams. We are here to relax. Sharon, start relaxing. Now!

With that, everyone relaxed. They spent the rest of the evening, which wasn't all that long, tasting a mix of desserts, talking about sports, strange people they had met at the conference, holiday destinations, fashion, their children and the new iPad. Around 11.30 p.m. they all took their leave, promised to stay in touch, wished Sharon good luck with her CSR headaches, and returned to their respective hotels for their last night in San Diego.

# 7

# Recruitment, diversity and inclusion

Sharon was feeling more and more pleased with herself. The conversation last night with the group that Arena had put together had really contributed to her understanding of workplace practices. So many thoughts, so many ideas to digest. Slowly but surely, Sharon felt it was all coming together and making some sort of sense, even though the scale of CSR was beginning to unsettle her.

She made her way to the fourth and final day of the conference. She skipped breakfast, still feeling rather 'heavy' after all she had consumed the evening before. She had made a point of tasting everyone's meal, and she hadn't left a grain or crumb on her own plate. Perhaps she should ensure there were more vegetarian, or even vegan, options, in the company canteen than just the usual one rather tired dish. 'This CSR thing gets just about everywhere,' she thought to herself.

She arrived at the conference lobby and made a beeline for the coffee counter, believing a double shot of caffeine would equip her for this, her final day at the conference. Just as she was about to help herself to coffee, she noticed a woman to her right, and, as tends to happen at conferences, Sharon's eyes went straight to her name tag: 'Ilana Atlas, Group Executive, People & Performance, Westpac Banking Group, Australia'.[1] Sharon, determined to make the most of

---

1  Ilana Atlas kindly agreed to provide her insights for this book. She is not a fictional character like Sharon. Ilana Atlas, BJur (Hons), LLB (Hons), LLM, was appointed Group Executive, People & Performance for Westpac Banking Group in 2003. Before retiring in January 2010, Ilana was responsible for all human resources strategy and management, including reward and recognition, learning and development,

every opportunity for networking now she realised she must adopt it in a more concerted way, raised her eyes and smiled at Ilana Atlas.

**Sharon:** Hello, I see you are at Westpac. I am pleased to meet you. My name is Sharon Black, I lead HR at Andromex, a software solutions manufacturer based in Bristol in the UK. It's quite a way for you to travel from Australia for this conference.

**Ilana:** Hello, Sharon, pleased to meet you too. Yes, it is a way to travel, but you know, there are always opportunities to combine conferences with other business meetings that I have been putting off for a while. After I speak today at the HR training session, I will fly out to Boston.

**Sharon:** Oh. When is your session?

**Ilana:** I am the 9.30 plenary. Then I have a couple of hours before I leave for Boston. I haven't made up my mind what to attend. I am a little conference-fatigued, I must admit. I tend to hear much of the same things, nothing terribly innovative. I am considering using the time in between to catch up on some correspondence.

BOOM! Sharon almost reeled over. Here was a senior leader of Human Resources, saying she had two hours to spare. 'How many times does that happen?' thought Sharon 'Dare I ask her to spend some time with me? Dare I? Go for it!' Sharon urged herself on. 'She can only say no. What have you got to lose?'

**Sharon:** Ilana, you will probably think this is terribly forward of me, but I have to ask. If you have some time spare before you leave, would you consider spending it with me? I would greatly appreciate your thoughts on different aspects of human resources and on corporate social responsibility from an HR perspective. This trip has been an eye-opener for me. I have been learning about many aspects of HR and CSR, and I would absolutely love to hear what you have to say. I have seen the Westpac CSR report for 2009, so I know that Westpac is a leader in CSR. I would be so grateful to have some time with you, to talk about your perspectives on all of that.

---

careers and talent, employee relations and employment policy. She was also responsible for Corporate Affairs and Sustainability including internal and external communications, government relations and Westpac's strategy in relation to corporate affairs and sustainability. Ilana joined Westpac in 2000 as Group Secretary and General Counsel. Prior to joining Westpac, Ilana was a partner at Mallesons Stephen Jaques. She practised as a corporate lawyer and held a number of managerial roles in the firm including Managing Partner and Executive Partner, People & Information. The author is very grateful to the Senior Sustainability Advisor at Westpac, Alison Ewings, for making the connection to Ilana Atlas and obtaining her feedback and insights.

The introduction and close of the conversation, where the two meet and take leave of each other, are the fabrication of the author, but all Ilana's other comments in this fictional dialogue with Sharon are real quotations from Ilana Atlas and not modified in any way by the author.

**Ilana** (smiling): Well, Sharon, it looks like I won't be catching up on correspondence after all. I would be happy to help. In my role, I am responsible also for corporate responsibility, so I imagine I will be able to answer all your questions. Why don't we meet here at eleven? And we can find a quiet corner to talk.

**Sharon:** Oh, thank you so, so much! I will take some time now to prepare myself and come with some specific questions.

**Ilana:** Yes, fine. I must admit that it will be quite a refreshing change for me too.

Sharon was over the moon. A group executive of such an impressive business. Someone who was already a CSHR manager. And just approaching her like that, living in the moment, being forward, asking for what you want. Sharon was over the moon. She felt so proud of herself, as though she had won an Olympic Gold. She couldn't wait to tell Arena. More importantly, this was a way for her to get a second opinion. Everything she had heard from Arena made sense, and the more she heard, the deeper she delved, the longer she thought, the more she recognised the clear opportunity ahead of her. But, even so, even though she valued the vast experience that Arena appeared to have, getting the inside view from another expert would set her mind at rest that she was moving in the right direction. Moreover, it would lend greater credibility to her recommendations to her boss, and her Management Team colleagues back home in the office. She imagined herself quoting to them, 'The HR Director of Westpac said . . .'. It sounded very convincing.

At eleven precisely, Sharon was by the coffee counter, waiting for Ilana. Here she came. They greeted each other with smiles and a few words about Ilana's HR training session, and then they moved to the lounge on the lower floor, which was spacious and reasonably empty.

**Sharon:** I have prepared several questions for you, Ilana. I had a look at your profile on the Westpac website, and I now realise that you have responsibility for corporate affairs and sustainability including internal and external communications. That's wonderful, because most of my questions relate to the interaction between human resources and corporate responsibility and sustainability. I am trying to work out exactly what the role of the HR manager is in relation to corporate responsibility. This is something I have become aware of, I am ashamed to say, only recently, and I am doing my best to work it all out. It's such a broad subject.

**Ilana:** That sounds fine, Sharon. Let's get started. We have 90 minutes, and then I need to move on to the airport to catch my flight. Ask away!

**Sharon:** Thank you so much again, Ilana. First of all, what does managing corporate responsibility and sustainability mean for you personally?

**Ilana:** Ultimately it's about being values-led and focusing on the impacts of the organisation on a range of stakeholders. It continues to be a fascinating and rewarding journey, not just for me personally, but for the organisation.

**Sharon:** What, for you, have been the highlights of your achievements in CSR practices at Westpac?

**Ilana:** Overall, I think a key highlight has been the move to a more intuitive leadership style by the entire leadership team and a real embedding of sustainability within the organisation. Our decision-making is guided by what is the right thing to do, even if all the benefits aren't spelt out from the outset. This is true not only for senior managers but has also been a real 'grassroots' movement within the organisation. Sustainability has become a very real part of the fabric of our business. This values-based approach has seen us take early action on a range of sustainability issues, of which climate change is probably the one for which we are best known. More recently, it has seen us put into place responsible lending practices and support services for customers well before the downturn. Of course, for me, it has also been about the progress of our people policies and practices away from command and control to reflect generational changes in our workforce and provide greater workplace flexibility and autonomy.

**Sharon:** What was the logic in combining the role of human resources management and corporate responsibility and sustainability in Westpac? How do these roles fit together in your view and what are the key areas of interface and synergy?

**Ilana:** When our employees come to work they don't leave their values and beliefs at the door. Rather, they expect to find that our norms approximate their own. Today, in our company, we run an economic system and a social system. Our values bind these two parts of the company together – they make the culture gel. I think we are just coming to realise that the most important values for a company – if not the only ones – are those aligned with social values. So the links between people and sustainability are strong ones. While a number of our people activities are considered part of the broader sustainability agenda – diversity, health and safety and so on – much of sustainability is about change management, about the way we think about our business and the types of group we engage with. Given this strong cultural overlay there are obvious areas of synergy. Of course, a number of sustainability mega-trends are also critical to HR: war for talent, ageing populations, changing attitudes to work – particularly between generations. People are also key to delivering on many aspects of our sustainability strategy – customer service and centricity, for instance, means thinking differently about the way we do things.

**Sharon:** What do you believe are the key skills HR managers need to support responsible business? Is this different from the widely understood role of the HR manager in supporting business strategy where CSR is not a key driver?

**Ilana:** At the Westpac Group it has been about encouraging a culture of 'doing the right thing'. While you could argue that the fundamentals are the same, such as incorporating behavioural elements into performance review systems, it is also about encouraging people to think more broadly about the impact of their decision-making. The cultural dimension and empowering people to live their values at work is key.

**Sharon:** What do HR managers need to do differently to create a culture of corporate responsibility in the business? And how has this been developed at Westpac?

**Ilana:** Ultimately embedding sustainable business practices is about making them simply part of the way we do business. This needs to be reflected in all of our business processes and HR is no exception. But it is also about the intangibles and providing scope for intuitive and values-led decision-making. A recent example has been the introduction of an organisational mentoring programme that matches high performing employees with community organisations to assist on major change programmes. It not only brings about measurable change to our community partners but also exposes our employees to different types of organisation and to a range of social issues while providing great development opportunities for the individuals themselves. Training is also key and will only increase in importance. There are skills that specific job families will require around things such as assessing climate risk or understanding the needs of community organisations. But also there are the more generic skills of being able to adapt to an ever-changing world and to think beyond traditional organisational responses.

**Sharon:** Employees are key stakeholders in your business. What are the most effective mechanisms for listening to and dialoguing with employees that you apply at Westpac? How has employee feedback influenced your HR policies and practices?

**Ilana:** We use a range of tools to better understand the views of our employees. This includes a formal annual survey of all employees across the Group. This survey consistently rates sustainability-related activities as a key driver of employee satisfaction. We monitor whether employees have seen progress on issues identified on previous surveys and it has shaped our training and policy development. We also undertake specific focus groups and consultation on policy development, involving both internal and external stakeholders. More recently has been the introduction of blogs and employee-driven content through our communication channels. However, such mechanisms are never a replacement for face-to-face engagement. Our leadership team is committed to regular updates which give them an opportunity to speak face to face with employees across the country. I'm always pleased at the frankness of the questions asked at these forums and the transparent nature of these discussions. Our culture of transparent communication is led from the top but evidenced throughout, as is our CSR approach, which has been driven by our employees as much as by our senior leaders.

**Sharon:** What are your key HR practices relating to employee well-being? To what extent have these been influenced by CSR strategy?

**Ilana:** Many of the drivers of sustainability are also drivers of our overall business strategy, including our people strategy and over time become more and more difficult to separate. So much so that it becomes increasingly difficult to speak of one without the others. Employee well-being is a great example of this and can be equally viewed through a people, business or sustainability strategy lens. Our strategy focuses on three target areas: healthy lifestyle promotion, including fitness, nutrition and sleep, early detection and prevention of serious illness and disease; the creation of a supportive environment for mental health; and building resilience in all. Our response is tailored to each of our geographies but includes heath and well-being expos, influenza vaccinations, the introduction of Westpac Assist, which supports customers facing financial difficulty, a suite of support services we offer to help employees and access to independent counselling services to employees and their families. These structured programmes are supported by locally driven initiatives. Participation in the Global Corporate Challenge, weight-loss programmes and yoga classes are just some examples of these. There are also strong synergies with our focus on community involvement. For example, in Australia, hundreds of employees participate in the annual Walk to Cure Diabetes event. In the Pacific Islands we also recognise that there are specific and significant areas of health need where we can play a major role. In 2008, our operations in Papua New Guinea released an HIV/AIDS Management Policy, supported by Papua New Guinea's Business Against HIV and AIDS organisation. The policy incorporates activities tailored to meet the needs of our people, their families and local communities, focusing on education and practical initiatives to reduce the spread of HIV/AIDS in the region.

**Sharon:** What elements of Westpac employee performance, reward and recognition programmes support or link with CSR strategy?

**Ilana:** It is important that our formal and informal reward and recognition programmes reinforce our sustainability strategy. Each of our executive team members shared our 2009 emissions-reduction target in their personal performance scorecards to help marshal organisational effort behind this activity and build support for our climate-change programmes. More broadly, each employee has a corporate responsibility component to their scorecard, the specifics of which are agreed with their manager, as well as behavioural based measures that reinforce our values. Less formal are a range of awards programmes, most notably our annual CEO awards, which include categories for both community and environment for individual and team activities. Employees are also entitled to paid volunteering leave and we will match their charitable donations up to the value of $10,000 (AUD) each year.

**Sharon:** Westpac is a seasoned CSR reporter. I read your 2009 report just now before our talk, and I have to say, it's very impressive. I learnt so much. Is your CSR report used within the business to engage employees? If so, how? And how effective is this? Do you have a measure of how many employees read your CSR report?

**Ilana:** More than 80 people across the organisation are involved in the development of the report each year, either by participating in interviews as part of the organisational assurance component or in providing data and information. So in this sense the engagement is very direct and occurs across all levels of the organisation. Of course, our employees are also directly responsible for delivering our performance targets so communicating them publicly certainly lifts the profile and the resolve to achieve them. We know that employees are interested in our reporting, although over time our internal engagement activities have meant that much of the information in the report is also communicated internally via other channels. We do know that employees are increasingly using the report with their customers to assist them in talking about our sustainability performance and commitments. In combining our sustainability report with our Annual Review, many employees will also receive the report as part of the information they receive as shareholders reinforcing the significance of our sustainability activities to the organisation.

**Sharon:** Gender equality is a significant element within CSR practice. As a woman in a senior position in a prominent business, what has been your position on advancing women at Westpac? What have been the challenges and successes?

**Ilana:** Even before I joined Westpac, there were a number of initiatives aimed at helping women advance through the organisation. Over the past few years we have expanded them and I have been a proud supporter of these programmes as well as the more broadly based ones to assist our emerging leaders. Important to this have been initiatives promoting flexible work practices, not just for female employees, but for all employees. Opportunities for extended leave and flexible hours are enjoyed by a range of employees for a range of reasons.

**Sharon:** How does Westpac use CSR in recruiting programmes? Have you noticed any shift in potential employee interest on CSR aspects of Westpac's business over the past few years? In what ways does Westpac gain advantage in recruitment talent as a result of your CSR focus?

**Ilana:** Following our first public sustainability report we saw a dramatic increase in the number of graduate applications, and we know that it is an area of increasing interest to graduates. What is perhaps more important is that this is reflected in employees' experience of the organisation once they join. Fostering an understanding of our sustainability commitments is an important component of our induction programme. More specifically for graduates we have run over the last few years a Graduate Sustainability Program which provides graduates with an opportunity to work on sustainability questions faced by the organisation while helping them develop communication and influencing skills. A number of the projects worked on have since been implemented and the programme has been important in making sustainability real for this group of employees. Our internal research has shown that employees that are engaged in sustainability are also engaged in Westpac's business strategy and that sustainability plays a role in employee satisfaction and we would also expect retention as well.

**Sharon:** I am conscious of time, and our 90 minutes are nearly up. This has been absolutely fascinating for me, Ilana. You have given me perspectives and insights I couldn't have hoped to gain from any textbook or any conference. I really want to thank you again and again for spending your valuable time with me. I can't express how grateful I am. It seems to me that your approach to CSR and HR is a very harmonious and synergetic one, very inspirational while being very practical and down to earth. I am sure this conversation will remain in my mind for a long time to come and guide me as I develop my own position on CSR and try to drive change in my company.

**Ilana:** I am pleased to have been able to help, Sharon. That's another element of a corporate responsibility mind-set — helping others understand and develop their own corporate responsibility. I want to emphasise that our employees right across the organisation have driven our CSR practices as much as our senior leaders. It is in our culture — the people we hire and what we value. Guided by our values and our commitment to doing the right thing they really bring our CSR commitments to life.

And now, with your permission, I will gather my bags and see if my car has arrived. Here is my card, don't hesitate to be in touch and let me know how you have been getting on. And if you are passing through Sydney, come and visit.

'Fat chance of me passing through Sydney,' Sharon thought. But she didn't say that. Instead, she responded more politely.

**Sharon:** Thank you, Ilana. Have a good flight and remainder of your trip. I am very, very grateful to you.

The insights Sharon gained from Ilana were rich and rewarding. She remembered that Ilana said that following the publication of Westpac's first sustainability report there was a dramatic increase in the number of graduate applications. This was proof that reporting makes a difference. More employees were using the sustainability report with customers to assist them in talking about their sustainability performance and commitments. More proof. More than 80 people across the organisation involved in the development of the annual sustainability report. Significant critical mass. Sharon felt that there was a strong theme of transparency and reporting in what Ilana had told her.

Sharon had liked what Ilana had said about values. 'When employees come to work they don't leave their values at the door.' Sharon stopped to think. It's true, she felt, that people don't metamorphose when they clock in to work in the morning, but at the same time, she wondered if it didn't depend on whom you recruit and how you create the right culture in which the right values can be displayed. Sharon felt that not everyone had their own set of clearly articulated values that guide them in every personal and professional decision. And values are so diverse. If all employees brought their own values to the workplace, there would be so many, conflicting values that no one would be able to collaborate on anything, she thought. Every person you talk to in the business would have a different set of values. She remembered that quote by Anita Roddick that Arena mentioned. 'We were searching for employees but people turned up instead.'[2] She also remembered reading an article about Eileen Fisher, who said 'We don't hire someone if they are not kind.'[3] An indication that people are inevitably diverse and, by definition, so are their values. Kindness, Sharon thought to herself, how many times do we put that in the job description, or in the candidate profile when we are recruiting? Everyone knows right from wrong, more or less, but embedding a common set of values in a large organisation, when everyone has different perspectives, life experiences, backgrounds, views and paradigms is not something to be sneezed at. 'The question is,' Sharon thought, 'to what extent does it all start with the people you recruit?'

Sharon looked at the final sessions of the final day of the conference. It was already 12.30. There was nothing that she felt particularly inspired to go and listen to. Her flight out of San Diego was at 9 p.m. and she wondered what the best use of her time would be. She decided to take the afternoon to visit a bookshop and see if she could pick up some good books on the subject of CSR. She would also be able to pick up some gifts for the children and Robert. Airport buying was always so expensive and the selection was never quite appropriate. In any case, she felt she would be so tired when she got to the airport that the last thing she would want to be doing was gift-hunting. She went back to her room, packed up all her things and brought her bags down and checked out, leaving her suitcase in the storage room. Then, she caught a taxi straight to the University of San Diego campus bookstore.

Sharon was pleased that there was a whole section assigned to CSR and sustainability. She wished she had asked Arena for recommendations, but she didn't want to disturb her by calling her. Looking at the heavily stocked shelves, she was astounded to see so many titles and didn't know where to begin looking. She decided to limit herself to four books. She could always buy more later on. She noticed a young man browsing the section and asked him what books he would recommend for someone who wanted to get a general understanding of CSR and sustainability and its practical application in business. She told him she would like him to recommend three books. The young man was more than helpful and pointed her in the direction of four books which he said were outstanding, explaining that he could easily recommend at least 25 books, but he would remain with four, one more than she requested. He selected each book one by one and gave her a brief run-down on each one.

2  Anita Roddick, *Business as Unusual*: 55.
3  Beth Wilson, 'Fisher Reveals Her Feminine Approach" ', *Women's Wear Daily*, 9 October 2008, www.eileenfisher.com/media/EFR001/images/static/ourcompany/inthemedia/pdf/oct08_wwd.pdf, accessed 5 June 2010.

# Four recommended books on CSR

## The High-Purpose Company: The Truly Responsible (and Highly Profitable) Firms That Are Changing Business Now
by Christine Arena (New York: Harper Collins, 2007)

This book introduces a new approach to assessing the corporate social responsibility of a range of companies. Essentially, after a long period of research and in-depth assessment of 75 companies, the research team led by Christine Arena used 'The Litmus Test' to determine whether these companies were demonstrating their 'Higher Purpose', which was the sum of their corporate values put into action. Of the companies analysed, only 16 passed the test, including Eileen Fisher, Tom's of Maine, General Electric Company, Wegmans Food Markets and DuPont. The book describes the different stages in achieving a higher purpose and continual cycle of self-improvement and responsiveness to stakeholders. It is a great overview of many different aspects of what is, and what isn't, corporate social responsibility.

## Strategy for Sustainability: A Business Manifesto
by Adam Werbach (Cambridge, MA: Harvard Business Press, 2009)

This is an interesting book that is mainly about the leadership of CSR and sustainability. It draws much from the author's personal experience and insight and proposes some interesting tools for organisations that would like to manage their sustainability programmes in a more strategic way. One of the most interesting insights is the way the author, as part of his role as CEO of Saatchi and Saatchi S, developed the Personal Sustainability Project for the engagement of Wal-Mart employees in sustainability efforts. The book also gives some interesting examples of best practices from other companies such as Method, Dell, Nike and Xerox.

## Supercorp: How Vanguard Companies Create Innovation, Profits, Growth and Social Good
by Rosabeth Moss Kanter (New York: Crown Business, 2009)

This book is the outcome of three years of research into a number of global corporations and their business practices. The focus is mainly on organisational culture and people practices and how these support business growth, as well as making a positive contribution to society. The companies highlighted in great detail in the book, those that are called vanguard companies, are Procter & Gamble, IBM, Banco Real, Publicis Groupe, Cemex, Diageo, Omron and Shinhan Financial Group. Mainly a good-news book, highlighting the most positive aspects of these businesses, it gives a good overview of how culture, values, caring for people and society can deliver improved innovation and other business benefits that lead to sustainable profitability.

> ### Making Sustainability Work: Best Practices in Managing and Measuring Corporate Social, Environmental and Economic Impacts
>
> by Marc Epstein (Sheffield, UK: Greenleaf Publishing, 2008)
>
> This is a very comprehensive book about the ways in which companies manage CSR. It proposes a framework for implementing corporate sustainability, identifying stakeholders and developing strategy. It is packed with many examples from businesses all over the world, operating in different sectors. It's full of models and analyses and one of the most comprehensive books you can find on this subject. It's not a bedtime read, like some of the others; it's more of a textbook, but it is certainly one that should be in your collection if you want to deepen your specific knowledge of CSR and sustainability subjects.

Sharon was thrilled. Each book sounded wonderful. She decided to take them and not waste time looking further during the limited time she had left. She made a mental note to scour sites for other books, once she was back home and, she promised herself, not before she had read the four she was about to purchase. Sharon loved reading and was especially happy to contemplate reading these new books that would advance her self-education programme in CSR. Sharon paid for the books and left the University store. She spent another couple of hours in downtown San Diego selecting gifts for her children and two shirts for Robert and, pleased with her afternoon, returned to the hotel just in time to collect her bags, freshen up and take a taxi out to the airport for her flight back to London.

~

Sharon was sitting in the lounge waiting to board her flight, wondering whom she would meet this time around. It would be just incredible if she would be seated next to another CSHR manager, she thought. Two flights with CSR educators would be a little too much to comprehend. After boarding and making herself comfortable in her window seat, selecting Christine Arena's *High-Purpose Company* to begin with, she thought it was strange that this author's surname was the same as her new CSHR friend's first name. She thought it was just one more of those uncanny coincidences. Looking around at other passengers boarding and stuffing as much as possible into the overhead lockers, her curiosity was finally satisfied when a young man in jeans and a Timberland sweatshirt sat in the seat next to her. He smiled and introduced himself as Malcolm.[4]

**Sharon:** Hello, Malcolm. I'm Sharon.

**Malcolm:** Have you been to the ASTD?

---

4 Malcolm is an entirely fictional character and not based on any known individual.

**Sharon:** Yes. I assume you have too.

**Malcolm:** Yes, this is my third time now. It's a great gathering. I'm in recruiting, how about you?

**Sharon:** I manage HR at Andromex Software Company.

**Malcolm:** Oh yes, I've heard of Andromex. You had a big recruiting drive a few months back — programmers and support technicians, I think, right?

**Sharon:** Yes, we won a large contract in Eastern Europe and needed to bring in another 40 people in the UK. It was quite a stretch. Who do you work for?

**Malcolm:** I work for a recruitment and executive search company called PeoplePower. We're based in London. We specialise in management recruitment and specialised functions. We had a stand at the conference. Fortunately the rest of the team are packing up and leaving tomorrow. They let me duck out early, as it's my wife's birthday tomorrow and I don't want to miss it. It's that birthday when you have to start calling yourself thirty-something and not twenty-something, so it's quite an important event.

Sharon laughed. They talked a little about the conference, exchanging impressions, and sooner than they knew it, dinner was being served. As they ate, Sharon asked him about socially responsible recruitment.

**Sharon:** Malcolm, let me ask you something. I have been getting more interested recently in the concept of CSR — corporate social responsibility. I am trying to work out its relevance for my role as an HR manager and to understand the implications for me and my work. I have looked at many aspects of the way CSR is developed in a business and how it changes the approach to what we do. What I was wondering is, given that your clients, I suspect, are primarily HR managers, whether any of them introduce recruitment requirements which relate to different aspects of CSR as part of the recruitment brief? Is it something that you're noticing more these days?

**Malcolm:** It's funny you should ask that. I attended a conference on CSR in London a few months ago; in fact we took a stand there as well, as we are definitely seeing a rise in the number of jobs for CSR people, although there was a dip in 2008/2009 with the global financial crisis. Things have picked up since then, and we think it's a market we should tap into and develop as an area of expertise. The market for CSR people has become very competitive indeed. There are many boutique placement firms that are focusing on CSR or sustainability jobs. In a recent article I read on the Internet, CSR was number five in the fastest growing employment trends.[5]

5  'Job Search Site Indeed Reveals Top Job Trends for 2009', www.sdhinteractive.com/blog/2009/12/job-search-site-indeed-reveals-top-job-trends-for-2009, accessed 5 June 2010.

The range of CSR-type jobs is increasing — there are several hundreds of positions advertised each year. And there is starting to be some specialisation within the field — environmental-type roles, which might be relating to waste management or energy consumption or other related roles, carbon traders, social auditing and supply chain monitoring roles, CSR communications, diversity officers, ethics officers, governance roles and of course, the overall CRO-type role

**Sharon:** CRO?

**Malcolm:** The corporate responsibility officer, the most senior person in charge of sustainability and corporate responsibility programmes in the business. The growth in this type of role alone is incredible. CSR is becoming more of a profession and less of a non-standard recruitment requirement. The industry is changing and the amount of green jobs, sustainable jobs, value-based careers is growing all the time. Acre Resources, a leading CSR recruitment firm says that over half a million green jobs will be created in the next five years in the UK alone.[6] Our team at PeoplePower believe we can gain a share of this market because we have a very strong position in management placement in industry and other sectors.

**Sharon:** I see. That is interesting. But what I was wondering is whether you are seeing employers asking for CSR-type requirements when recruiting for non-CSR type positions — regular professions such as marketing, IT, sales and HR. Is there anything different about the way companies are recruiting all roles today, as a result of CSR?

**Malcolm:** I would be exaggerating if I said that anyone is talking to us about CSR unless if it for a specific CSR opportunity. A few companies who we support on an ongoing basis for all their recruitment needs have updated their code of ethics and recruitment procedures to make an assessment of values of candidates and whether they match the company values. But this is still very minor. We see the beginning of what might become mainstream, which is another reason we need to be in this market. If we do not demonstrate CSR expertise and understanding, we will lose ground because companies want us to align our recruiting methodologies with their sustainability programmes. What tends to be more prominent, and perhaps more important for you to understand as an HR manager, is the desire for diversity in general recruiting. Companies are now starting to demand that we supply candidates for positions that represent diversity, rather than just the standard run-of-the-mill candidates. We now have to think about women, minorities, older people and some even specify disabled people, and present a range of candidates for selection.

6  UK Parliament, 'Memorandum Submitted to the Environmental Audit Commons Select Committee by Acre Resources Ltd.', 27 May 2009, www.publications. parliament.uk/pa/cm200809/cmselect/cmenvaud/memo/greenjobs/uc2602.htm, accessed 5 June 2010.

This makes our job harder, actually, because this is another parameter that we must take into account. Not only must we focus on the personal qualifications and attributes, we must ensure we review and select a diverse mix for the HR people to consider.

**Sharon:** Ah yes. So there are two aspects that I need to think about in my recruiting programmes. One is the recruitment of CSR professionals and the other is the diversity of general recruitment. Thanks, Malcolm. That's something I hadn't thought about. I will have to start considering this. I don't see us recruiting a CSR person in the near future. I expect I will be the one to fulfil that role in the meantime. But the diversity question is certainly relevant. I must say that we have never created these sorts of criteria in our job searches before.

**Malcolm:** I was talking recently to Ellen Weinreb,[7] one of the most well-known professional sustainability recruiters based in the US. She has one of the highest successful placement rates in the business for CSR people and a vast knowledge of the industry. She says that companies are using CSR to sell themselves to candidates in terms of their overall positioning. She's been tracking CSR jobs for years. She scours CSR jobs that are posted on the Business for Social Responsibility website[8] and has analysed the growth and changing nature of CSR jobs over a six-year period. In March 2010, Ellen published her fifth CSR jobs report; the first was in 2004, and the new one covers 819 jobs during the period 2004 to 2009.[9] The number of jobs posted in 2009 dropped by 57% over 2008, showing the effects of the financial crisis, but in the last quarter of 2009, things started to pick up again quite seriously. In 2008, 210 jobs were posted but in 2009, only 91 jobs overall.

Ellen's analysis covers three types of CSR employers. The first are

---

7   Ellen Weinreb is not a fictional person! She founded Sustainability Recruiting to fulfil the hiring needs of socially responsible businesses. She brings more than a decade of experience as a consultant with organisations ranging from large multinational corporations — such as Levi Strauss, Hewlett Packard and Clorox — to start-ups and mid-sized enterprises — such as New Leaf Paper and Calvert Investments. Ellen has gained a deep understanding of the skills and expertise that are needed to develop a successful sustainability strategy. Ellen's knowledge and commitment to the field dates back to the early 1990s when she served as a Peace Corps volunteer in Cameroon and supported coffee farmers in developing a sustainable business model. In 1997, during the course of obtaining her MBA, Ellen gained first-hand CSR experience at L.L.Bean where she was responsible for assessing their nascent labour practices programme. For more information about Ellen, visit her website at www.ellenweinreb.com. The author interviewed Ellen Weinreb via telephone in February 2010.

8   Business for Social Responsibility (BSR): www.bsr.org/resources/jobs/index.cfm, accessed 5 June 2010.

9   Ellen Weinreib, 'CSR Jobs Report. The State of the CSR Job Market: Key Findings and Trends. An Analysis of 819 CSR Jobs: 2004–2009', www.ellenweinreb.com/docs/CSR_Jobs_Report_2009.pdf, accessed 5 June 2010.

companies — multinational and smaller companies who hire in-house CSR managers or specialists. Examples will be global corporations such as Disney or Hewlett Packard, or smaller companies such as Seventh Generation. The second type of CSR employers are service organisations who are under contract to provide a form of CSR service — this would include CSR associations such as BSR itself, who offer support services, consulting firms and compliance organisations who provide auditing or environmental risk assessment services. The third type of CSR employers are what Ellen calls independent organisations who look at CSR from the outside — NGOs such as Oxfam or CERES, public organisations such as the World Bank or the ILO, research or academic organisations or socially responsible investing organisations that make assessments about the level of CSR in businesses on behalf of investors. In 2009, the jobs advertised were fairly evenly split across all three types of CSR employer. I do remember that the Walt Disney Company was the biggest hiring corporation with 28 jobs over the six years, and the non-profit organisation BSR advertised a whopping 69 jobs during the same period. Ellen's report shows that the seniority of CSR jobs has been increasing — instead of recruiting for managers, companies are more and more recruiting for directors, VPs and global corporate positions. Ellen told me that she is seeing movement of CSR professionals between companies — those who have been successful in one company and are being headhunted to other companies to lead similar programmes. Also, what is absolutely fascinating is the Wal-Mart effect. Ellen said that the Wal-Mart sustainability programme,[10] launched in 2009, has had a massive impact on the entire Wal-Mart supplier base, and caused many Wal-Mart suppliers to realise they need to get themselves in shape on sustainability, and many have started recruiting sustainability professionals in the packaging field, life-cycle analysis of products, carbon management and a whole range of specialist areas. Most of these jobs can't be filled internally, though some of the less specialised jobs are being filled internally by candidates who learn the role on the job. Those jobs tend not to get posted publicly, of course. Ellen says that the UK is the biggest market for CSR and sustainability professionals, with more jobs than the USA, which surprised me, actually. So, you see, this is something we can't ignore.

**Sharon:** That's very interesting, Malcolm.

**Malcolm:** Even HR Jobs are now starting to include references to CSR. I noticed a job advertised just last week where the job description said the HR manager would be involved in projects across HR including Investors

---

10  In 2009, Wal-Mart launched the first phase of their Sustainability programme in its supply chain at the Wal-Mart Live Better Sustainability Summit, in which it announced it would require sustainability data from 100,000 of their first-tier suppliers in order to be able to measure the sustainability of every produce they sell. For more information see: Wal-Mart, 'Sustainability Index', walmartstores.com/Sustainability/9292.aspx, accessed 5 June 2010.

in People, CSR and community issues.[11] Look Sharon, I have a file of CSR-type jobs in my briefcase that have been published recently. Want to take a look? I really need to get some sleep.

**Sharon:** That would be great. Thanks.

Malcolm unstuffed his briefcase from out of the overhead locker and pulled out a file called CSR Recruitment. He handed it to Sharon. Despite feeling rather tired and knowing she ought to get some sleep as well, Sharon started to thumb through the jobs, thinking there was a whole field of recruitment that had passed her by. A whole sub-profession of the HR recruiting role that was now populated by specialists, as Malcolm said, but would most likely become more common in the future. As she looked through the documents, she was amazed at the titles of roles she had never heard of before.[13] The selection that caught her eye included:

- Climate Director
- Ethical Supply Chain Manager
- CR Strategy Team, Senior Analyst
- Director of Corporate Responsibility
- Sustainability Strategist
- Code of Conduct Auditor
- Manager Global Community Involvement
- Business Leader, Corporate Responsibility
- Energy Efficiency and Solar Energy Engineer
- Director of Investor Programmes
- Energy Engineer

11  This was a job advertised in www.PersonnelTodayJobs.com, accessed on 12 February 2010, for an HR manager in a company in Hemel Hempsted in the UK. However, a search of HR jobs sites shows few HR roles that include reference to CSR, sustainability or community programmes.

12  walmartstores.com/AboutUs/321.aspx, accessed 5 June 2010.

13  While there are now tens of sites on the Internet posting CSR and sustainability jobs, one of the leading sites is Business for Social Responsibility in the USA, www.bsr.org/resources/jobs/index.cfm, and Acre Resources in the UK and the US, www.acre-resources.com/csr-and-sustainability-jobs. The jobs referenced in this section were taken from these sites during February 2010.

- Responsible Procurement Manager

- Sustainability Programmes Coordinator

- Director, Sustainability and Corporate Responsibility

- Business Development Manager — Wind

- Director of Compliance

- Director of Corporate Responsibility Communications

- Environmental Affairs Marketing and Engagement Manager

- VP of Social Innovation

- CSR Director

- Global Sustainability Manager

- Ethical Trade Executive

- Climate Change and Energy Director

- Carbon Reduction Commitment Coordinator

- Regulatory Lawyer

- Head of Sustainability — Biofuels

Sharon thought that this range of new roles, which didn't exist ten years ago, was just incredible. She noted that these positions included many senior positions at director and VP level, as Malcolm had said, and covered the spectrum of sustainability fields. She saw that many of these roles were for leading companies such as Nike, Danisco, Walt Disney, Twinings, Starbucks, Coca Cola Enterprises, GlaxoSmithKline, and wondered if this was appropriate for large companies but still irrelevant for smaller businesses. Then she remembered the Wal-Mart programme, and the fact that so many smaller businesses that supply Wal-Mart were gearing up to manage sustainability in a more professional way.

Sharon took a look at the CSR director-type roles and tried to understand what sort of profile was sought. She looked through a few of the roles in more detail and noticed that three things stood out:

- Experience in a relevant CSR field

- Excellent analytical skills

- Outstanding communications skills and communications management

In addition, there were a range of other personal competencies and skills required, including: project management, external relations, knowledge of the non-profit sector and leadership qualities. Interestingly, she thought, two of the small sample of jobs she reviewed indicated the need for someone with the ability to influence senior management. As though part of the CSR role was to create its own legitimacy. She reflected on the way HR had had to confront this issue over the years. CSR, like HR, is a long-term approach to doing business, which requires an upfront investment in resources in order to deliver long-term returns. The deliverables of HR are not always easily or immediately quantifiable, which requires the HR manager to be in constant pursuit of the 'business case for HR', and has resulted in recent years in HR managers being called 'HR business partners' rather than just HR managers. This reflects the need for HR people to understand the business and align themselves with business direction and to ensure the HR strategy and processes support strategy and help the organisation develop capabilities to execute the strategy. She wondered if CSR was in a similar trap. At one level, the organisation knows intuitively that it must adopt a CSR approach, but at another level, it is not really convinced of the value, especially in the short term. The cost of good HR management is significant to a business, though, Sharon thought. Everyone knows that this is a net gain over time, even though proving it might be tough. HR managers spend hours in executive meetings justifying their own existence. She had had her fair share of this experience herself, too. Perhaps this was what was expected of senior CSR people — to create legitimacy in the eyes of senior managers. Sharon certainly knew that at Andromex this whole area was new and not something that would be accepted easily, because she wasn't sure that her boss, despite being a visionary and committed to strong people processes, would fully accept this direction. At least, he had not initiated any discussion himself on this topic so far, nor asked Sharon to do so.

The other thing that Sharon noted was that there wasn't a role called CSHR manager. She wondered if that would ever be identified as a specific role, or whether the CSR elements of the HR role would just be seen as part of that HR role and not something that deserved special attention. Despite the massive exposure during her trip to certain people who had taken CSR on board as part of the HR function, she did still not get the sense that CSR was something very high on the HR agenda.

Sharon also noticed a meeting summary in Malcolm's file about a global chemicals company whose CSR director he had apparently recently met.

**File Memo**

**Notes from a meeting with ChemCo Global CSR Director, 2009**[14]

- ChemCo is committed to maintaining a working environment in which every single employee can contribute to the success of the business, each with his or her own unique expertise.
- ChemCo's recruitment policy is a global policy and applies to every ChemCo operational location throughout the world. The policy is based on an individual's suitability for the intended role, his or her skills, competencies, professional experience and relevant academic qualifications.
- In the UK, ChemCo is one of the leading employers, hiring around 1,000 individuals each year.

ChemCo makes significant efforts to recruit from diverse population groups, based on ChemCo's commitment to the communities in which the company operates. ChemCo proactively seeks diversity in the recruitment process, with special focus on the following groups:

**Women.** ChemCo makes special efforts to ensure there is a strong pipeline of women in the recruitment channels, and never starts shortlist interviewing for any position unless there is at least 40% compatible female representation. This has required significant reach-out to women via universities, and friends/relatives of employees, local community connections (occasionally developed through volunteer work in local communities) and partnerships with NGOs that support women's economic empowerment. In some cases, the company has invested in vocational training for women to ensure there is a pool of available women for certain skilled jobs over time. The company has significantly increased its intake of women at staff levels, first-line manager levels and graduate trainees.

**Individuals who have lost their jobs with other companies.** ChemCo has a structured process for approaching companies who have downsized or restructured, resulting in groups of unemployed. ChemCo approaches such companies, and, with their agreement, conducts recruitment days for laid-off employees, with the intention of hiring those deemed suitable for work at ChemCo.

**Unemployed individuals.** ChemCo maintains a close relationship with the governmental Department for Work and Pensions and Jobcentre Plus,[15] in order to offer unemployed people, including many with special needs who might otherwise not get through regular recruitment filters, the chance of a new job with the company. Hundreds of employees have been recruited via this channel.

---

14  ChemCo is a fictional company, though some of the processes described were inspired by a real company for whom the author has consulted, but which requested not to be quoted in this publication.

15  www.dwp.gov.uk/about-dwp/customer-delivery/jobcentre-plus, accessed 5 June 2010.

**Ethnic minorities and special groups.** ChemCo maintains a range of initiatives with NGOs who promote the interests of certain groups within the general population. These include ethnic minority groups of African, Caribbean, Asian and Chinese origin and people with disabilities. Through intensive work in partnership with support groups for these minorities, ChemCo has succeeded in designing special recruitment processes and now recruits at least 200 such individuals per year.

**Social networks recruitment.** ChemCo has developed expertise in recruitment via social networks such as Facebook, LinkedIn and other sites. This is now a strong recruitment channel and attracts people of all ages and backgrounds and not only young people. ChemCo has a full-time Internet Recruitment Manager, who conducts all the online recruitment processes, and manages the company's recruitment website, adding interesting content attractive to potential new recruits.

- All these measures have significantly expanded ChemCo's resourcing channels in the UK and enabled the company to recruit not only a diverse population but also individuals who would not otherwise have reached the ChemCo recruitment process in the normal way.

- This recruitment approach involves collaboration with external partners who understand the needs and special requirements of individual groups within society, and developing tailored recruitment process for identifying, recruiting and on-boarding such individuals.

- ChemCo does not compromise on the quality of candidates — the prime factor remains their match with professional requirements and personal abilities; however, in broadening the approach to recruitment and making changes to the recruitment process, and, in some cases, creating the potential for a greater pool of recruits through community involvement, ChemCo is able to resource its significant recruitment needs in a cost-effective way, while contributing to the fabric of the community by strengthening all sectors of the population.

*Malcolm Holmes, PeoplePower*

Sharon was impressed at this creative way of tracking down potential new candidates. She wondered if she ought to try to do something similar at Andromex. Perhaps it might reduce her recruitment costs. 'Oops,' she thought. 'Malcolm shouldn't have let me see this! If I start to work this way, we won't have the need for recruitment agencies like his.' She laughed to herself. Fortunately, her requirements didn't reach 1,000 new hires per year, as ChemCo do.

Sharon closed Malcolm's file. She asked herself what implications all these new insights in the area of sustainability recruitment held for her role as HR Manager of Andromex. Now that she knew this, what would she do differently? She made a few notes in her notebook:

## CSR and recruitment processes

- Ensure recruitment processes are ethical, truly non-discriminatory, broad enough to reach a wide pool of diverse candidates and requiring qualifications that do not automatically exclude large sections of the eligible working population

- Review how to ensure CSR is part of the employer brand of Andromex

- Train HR and functional managers in diversity and other CSR elements related to recruiting

- Actively seek out non-mainstream candidates through partnerships, go where the candidates are and revise recruitment processes to ensure this happens

- Leverage all contacts in the community, including via community involvement programmes, to get to where the candidates are, because not all of them will find you via the regular recruitment channels

An overwhelming wave of exhaustion swept over Sharon. She looked at Malcolm and saw that he was fast asleep. She gently placed the folder of jobs and notes in the seat-pocket in front of him, and put her own notebook in the one in front of her. Unpacking her eye-mask, she felt she had accomplished more than she ever could have imagined in this short trip to San Diego and back. And more quickly than it took to say Corporate Social Human Resources Manager, she fell asleep and started to dream of Richard Gere, in a new movie called 'Changing the World of Business'. Richard was the CEO of a large corporation and Sharon was the CSHR manager. No wonder she smiled all the way to London.

~

Arriving at Heathrow Airport was wonderful. No matter how long Sharon had been away, even if it was just for a day or two, she always loved that feeling of arriving home. She made her way efficiently through the corridors, escalators and baggage pick-up. She spotted Malcolm on the other side of the carousel and nodded a good-bye and mouthed another Thank You for his helpful sharing of information. They had exchanged business cards and she had no doubt she would be hearing from him again, as she assumed he would want to get a piece of Andromex recruitment action. Now, she turned her thoughts to her family, getting back home and the state of disorder it might be in, and enjoying a relaxing Sunday before getting back into HR, CSR, CSHR and whatever she decided would be the right way forward.

As soon as she stepped into the arrivals hall, Sharon noticed four smiling faces. Robert, Darren, Julia and little Michelle were all smiling in anticipation of her arrival. Normally she would have taken a taxi back home, but as it was Saturday, and she had been away for over a week, Robert had surprised her by bringing the children. 'Mummy!' she heard Michelle screech at the top of her voice and hastened her pace, though the trolley carrying her suitcase and another holdall full of conference papers and reports inhibited her step a little. Hugs all round, kisses and talking all at once lasted until Robert steered everyone to the car park, where they loaded the car and headed for home. Sharon still felt really tired, but satisfied, and glad to be home with her husband and children.

The rest of the day passed in family frenzy. Sharon called her parents and they announced they would be coming for lunch on Sunday. Robert told her of a new project at work — he was a marketing manager in a telecommunications company and was charged with leading a new innovative branding project. All the children needed Sharon for something: homework, sewing a button on a shirt, cleaning football boots, sorting out old socks and researching dinosaurs on the Internet. Even the family dog, Marbles, seemed to have lost his marbles and wouldn't let Sharon alone until she had found them, or at least, that's how she felt. Family Sunday was pleasant though intensive, and Sharon felt there was nothing like a warm, supportive family and she felt blessed.

Arriving on Monday morning in the office was good, too. As she walked into the office building, she was greeted by a steady flow of familiar and mostly friendly faces until she reached her office on the third floor, two doors down from her CEO. She dropped off her bag and went to see if her boss was in the office. It was 8.45.

Sharon's boss was a sharp, reasonably personable though not entirely charismatic leader called George Felton. He was aged 57. He had been headhunted from a leading high-tech company where he had been the CFO. This had been over nine years ago, after the company founders, two business partners who had their fingers in many pies, had tired of running the firm, and he had done a good job of keeping them both happy while quadrupling the company revenues, and doing so profitably. He had been somewhat of a risk, with Andromex being his first managing director position, but he had earned his spurs, so to speak, and appeared to have their full trust. He ran a tight ship, a lean organisation, and was very practical with a finger on the pulse of the software market. His analytical mind enabled him to assess the trends and new directions well, and his action-oriented approach enabled him to deliver multiple projects on time. He was not known for being a 'softie' but Sharon was pleased that he seemed to be a decent individual and always showed her and the HR function respect. In fact, as the company had grown more successful, he had begun to appreciate the good process and capability-building work Sharon and her team was doing, and around four years previously had elevated Sharon to corporate HR manager, and given her a place on the company executive team. They called this team ANDEX. ANDEX had seven members:

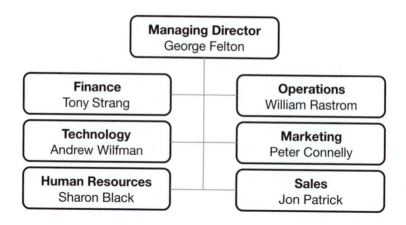

**George:** Well, good morning, Sharon, and welcome back. I hope you enjoyed your trip that cost us an arm and a leg.

**Sharon:** Look at it as an investment, George.

**George:** Fine. What's the ROI? Two weeks? A month?

**Sharon:** I will ask Tony to give us a view on that. Anyway, what have you been up to since I've been gone? Hired loads of unsuitable people? Fired half my team? Set up a new offshore operation that we will have to support?

**George:** No, nothing dramatic. Most of my week has been taken up with preparation for our IPO.[16] You know. It's a major change and I hope we are up to it. All the financials look good. The owners are very clear this is the way to go, so that we can expand significantly in Asia. I have to say I don't anticipate an easy ride.

**Sharon:** Why, George?

**George:** Well, once we float, our business becomes everyone's business. As a private company, we still have some sort of safety net in that our competitors don't quite know what we are doing, no one knows our pricing structure, no one takes too much of an interest in us. Going public will direct a spotlight at so many aspects of the way we work, and at the numbers we generate, that I feel it will put pressure on us to work differently. Right now, our owning partners are happy when we increase revenues and profits, and they don't breathe down my neck too much. In the future, we will be bound by many different priorities of different shareholders. You'd better get prepared, Sharon.

**Sharon:** What will I need to do differently, George? What does it mean for me?

---

16 An initial public offer (IPO) is the sale of shares to the public before the shares are traded on an exchange for the first time.

**George:** For a start, you need to be 195% sure that we are compliant on all labour laws. You need to be sure that we are managing our off-shores properly from an HR standpoint. And, of course, once we expand, there are going to be a lot more people to recruit and get into the business. Our projections show a move from 2,500 people today to over double that in two years. We need to expand or it is hardly worth going public. We have the potential orders right now, but our growth is limited because we don't have enough cash to invest in infrastructure. Anyway, we will be talking about all that at ANDEX this week. I have to get to a meeting with Tony and the lawyers now. Headlines of your trip?

**Sharon:** Trip was very worthwhile. Heard about interesting processes for training, employee engagement, employee performance development, talent management processes and some new ideas for internal communications. I also got a great grounding in CSR and what HR managers do.

**George:** CSR. Corporate social responsibility?

**Sharon:** Yes.

**George:** Oh no. I hope you aren't going to tell me we should contribute more to the community. We aren't making **that** much profit.

**Sharon:** IPO, George. People invest in companies that are good corporate citizens.

**George:** Uh oh. I have to go. I will check that your office still has Human Resources Manager on the door on my way out. You'd better check that it also has **your** name on it.

**Sharon** (laughing): Bye for now, George. I will send you my report within a few days.

Sharon returned to her office and made a point of calling all her ANDEX colleagues to check in with what was happening. No one else did that, and it made her feel good that she, as the HR manager, was setting a good example of teamwork and interest in the business and her colleagues. Then, she called each of the five HR managers that reported to her, got up to date on the HR headlines, and called in her secretary, Amanda, to run through the schedule for the week. Fortunately she had a clear couple of hours before her first meeting with Patricia, the Recruitment Manager.

At 11 a.m. exactly, Patricia came storming into Sharon's office. Even before Sharon could start to tell her about her experiences at ASTD, Patricia started to rant.

**Patricia:** Look, I am just fed up with this. Every time we get a good female candidate for the Senior Operations Role, reporting to William Rastrom, he just makes a whole load of excuses about why she is not suitable. We have the perfect candidate — take a look at this CV — she's just perfect. William is worried that she is not a strong enough team leader, although she has great experience as a group leader in two other companies. What really got my back up was that he also hinted to me that she would probably spend more time on maternity leave than she would in the technical centre. Sharon, this is just not right. I checked the numbers and of a total of 2,500 employees, less than 11% are women. You are the token women on ANDEX. Out of a total of 439 Managers, there are only 33 women – 33 out of 439. That's not even 8%. And frankly, they will all start to leave if we are such chauvinists in our recruiting policy. I have been waiting for you to get back to talk to you about this. It's not new, and you know it. Sharon, I want you to do something about this. We can't keep on ignoring the fact that we are discriminating against women in this company. The most women in the business are in HR, with some in Marketing and Finance. Most of the other parts of the business are just one big 'old boys club'. Whenever we find good female candidates, they are just not taken seriously. And as for William's remark about maternity leave, well, frankly, that's the last straw. Sharon, what are you going to do about it?

**Sharon:** Well, as the token woman . . .

**Patricia:** You know what I mean.

**Sharon:** Sure. Look, I can see that this has really frustrated you, Patricia. And I share your desire to turn Andromex into a gender-equal company. It's more than just because it's the right thing to do, it's our responsibility. It's part of being a good corporate citizen.

(Sharon chuckled to herself that she was using all the right jargon).

Let's say that I am with you on this. Let's say that I think we should be changing our recruitment practices and our hiring culture. With the best will in the world, such a change takes time – it's not something we can fix in two weeks. Let's say I would support a programme of change – have you got past your frustration and thought about what you might recommend?

**Patricia:** I knew you would ask that. Don't bring me problems, bring me solutions. I know the mantra. Well, Sharon, I want you to know that I spent the entire weekend on this. I am just not prepared to be part of a company where there is blunt discrimination. As an HR manager, I can't turn a blind eye and pretend there are no competent women in the entire UK that meet our requirements.

**Sharon:** Your recommendation, Patricia?

**Patricia:** Here it is. I also brought you this book.

Patricia handed Sharon a file and a copy of *Why Women Mean Business* by Avivah Wittenberg-Cox and Alison Maitland.[17]

---

17  Avivah Wittenberg-Cox and Alison Maitland, *Why Women Mean Business: Understanding the Emergence of Our Next Economic Revolution* (San Francisco, CA: Jossey Bass, 2008).

**Sharon:** This looks interesting. I hope I will have time to read it soon.

**Patricia:** Believe me, Sharon, this is the best and most authoritative book on why it is important for the business to tap into the talent of women that has ever been written. It has changed my thinking completely. If before I felt it was just morally wrong to discount women for all of these vague reasons, now I know it is a business disadvantage that prevents Andromex from achieving its true business potential. That's what gets me so annoyed with William Rastrom. He is making the wrong **business decisions** about people. You **have** to read this book.

Sharon smiled at Patricia, took the book and flipped to the contents page. 'Womenomics' stood out as the title of the first chapter. Another bit of jargon for me to use, Sharon thought, and then quickly chastised herself for being flippant, even if it was only a private thought.

Sharon promised she would do her best to read the book, and that she would give Patricia a view on her proposal within the coming week. In the meantime, Sharon suggested that they hold the recruitment of the Senior Operations Manager until she had had a chance to talk with William. After that, she and Patricia spent another hour working through the Andromex talent funnel and the plans for the coming three months. After Patricia had left, Sharon couldn't help but taking a peek at the proposal. Sharon thought it was quite fortuitous that she had returned from San Diego on a private mission to become a CSHR manager, and here was Patricia presenting her with her first opportunity. Or was it a threat? She opened the file.

---

To: Sharon Black
From: Patricia Rowland

### Recommendation to advance women at Andromex and ensure equality for women in recruitment practices

#### Background — the business reasons to advance women

Many studies demonstrate the value of ensuring gender equality in business. The general business motivations to ensure gender equality are as follows:

#### Improving performance
- Companies with more women in management make more profit
- Female employees are more motivated when they see women succeed
- Women represent half the potential workforce and exploiting the full range of available talent leads to improved business performance

#### Competitiveness
- Retaining and advancing women is cheaper than external recruitment
- Losing women employees means talent may go to the competition
- Women are an increasingly educated and skilled pool of employees

**Work culture that maximises variety of assets and creates new ones**
- Diverse groups are more innovative and creative
- Employees relate to female managers differently, often more positively
- Correlation has been shown between organisational excellence and women in management
- Female leadership offers a complementary balance of styles and approaches

**Women make most consumer purchasing decisions**
- Women can develop services and products more appealing to female consumers
- Employing women is an investment in the community and creates more consumers
- Diverse organisation reflects range of diverse stakeholders and facilitates understanding and dialogue

**Corporate sustainability and reputation**
- It is the moral obligation of a business to support equality and uphold human rights
- Capital markets and investors increasingly look for gender diversity
- A company which advances women enhances its reputation

The United Nations Global Compact states: 'There is consensus that empowering women to participate fully in economic life across all sectors and throughout all levels of economic activity is essential to build strong economies, more stable societies, and achieve internationally agreed goals for development and human rights.'[18]

A study by McKinsey & Co.[19] says: 'capital markets and investors are paying more and more attention to corporate performance in terms of gender diversity. For instance, investment funds such as CalPERS in the US or Amazone in Europe include this indicator among their investment criteria, while rating agencies (Core Rating, Innovest, Vigeo) are now developing tools to measure gender diversity.' . . .

'Correlation is not necessarily cause, but the correlation between organisational excellence and women's participation in management bodies is nonetheless striking. Such a correlation echoes a number of comments and remarks that we heard during our interviews with CEOs. 'When women sit on an executive committee, the nature of interactions changes'.

Ilene Lang, President and CEO of Catalyst, a non-profit organisation working globally with businesses to build inclusive workplaces and expand opportunities for women and business, says: 'It's not enough to recognize

18 'Advancing Women, Advancing Business and Supporting International Development Goals: Guiding Principles for the Corporate Sector', www.unglobalcompact. org/docs/news_events/Bulletin/Womens_Principles.pdf, accessed 5 June 2010.
19 McKinsey & Co., 'Women Matter: Gender Diversity, a Corporate Performance Driver', 2007, www.emberin.com/files/McKinsey%20Study%20-%20Women%20 Matter.pdf.

the need to advance women into leadership positions. It's time to execute on it . . . You cannot be a successful global business leader without women in your leadership. Catalyst research shows that companies with more women in leadership, on average, outperform those with fewer women, and those with three or more women board directors do even better. It's time businesses take action and leverage the talent that women bring to the workplace. It's good for women, good for men, and as our research demonstrates, good for business.'[20]

## Gender equality and diversity

Gender equality is just one aspect of an overall culture of diversity and inclusion. In principle, all businesses should be targeting to ensure that they recruit the best available talent from all sections of the population. Not only is it a competitive necessity, and seen to be demonstrating good corporate citizenship and strengthening the fabric of society, it also encourages openness, tolerance, respect, creativity and innovation, attributes that lead to improved business performance over time. As a first stage, gender equality seems the most obvious target. A business that succeeds in developing true equality between women and men will have a higher chance of developing greater equality and diversity in general, and therefore of delivering better overall business performance in the long term.

## Levels of women in business

In general, with the exception of some leading businesses, the numbers of women at board level in public companies, or at executive level, are still relatively low.

According to the 2009 Catalyst Census,[21] companies are still lagging in appointing women to board seats and very few women hold executive officer positions. Catalyst research shows:

- Women held 15.2% of board seats, a number that reflects little growth over the past five years
- Almost 90% of companies had at least one woman director, but less than 20% had three or more women serving together.
- Women's share of board chair positions remained flat at 2%
- Women made up 13.5% of executive officer positions and 6.3% of top earner positions
- Almost 30% of companies had no women executive officers

In a review of companies that published corporate social responsibility reports in 2009, there are several companies who employ over 50% of

20  Catalyst, '2009 Catalyst Census of the Fortune 500 Reveals Women Missing from Critical Business Leadership', (9 December 2009), www.catalyst.org/press-release/161/2009-catalyst-census-of-the-fortune-500-reveals-women-missing-from-critical-business-leadership, accessed 5 June 2010.
21  Ibid..

women in their total workforce, and the top companies reach 25–40% of women.[22]

An example of a company that has a good approach to developing diversity and gender equality is as follows:

## Vattenfall, a Swedish energy company

Total employees: 32,800, of which 7,774 are women: 24%
Board members: 11, of which 4 are women: 36%
Leadership team members: 10, of which 2 are women: 20%
(figures from Vattenfall 2008 CSR Report).

### Vattenfall's policy in gender equality

The target set for the Vattenfall Group is to increase the number of women managers in an effort to obtain an equal ratio between the number of women employees and women managers within the organisation. The minimal requirement for Vattenfall's work with diversity is that the company complies with equal opportunity laws in all countries where the company has operations.[23]

Gender equality activities:[24]

- Vattenfall's International Network for Women is used as a communication forum for managers and leaders at Vattenfall. About 130 women managers and young potentials are active in the network. In addition, Vattenfall is also a member of a network organised by CSR Europe, 'Women in Leadership Positions'

- In order to improve the recruitment process so that it evaluates and focuses on the applicant's competence and experience, it is becoming more common at Vattenfall to process applications anonymously. This is to ensure that only the applicant's skills are assessed and nothing else

- Diversity is highly integrated in the recruiting concept. Job profile descriptions are tailored to specific target groups, such as woman engineers. One way could be to highlight the message of 'work–life balance' at Vattenfall and advertise for a job with a picture of a woman

- Cooperation on promoting women with backgrounds in engineering and science. Mentoring programmes have also been developed to promote networking among women and create role models. To highlight the importance of work–life balance, 'keep-in-touch' and re-entry programmes are being developed for mothers and fathers following the early child-rearing years

- At the Ringhals nuclear power plant in Sweden, a local network for women managers was started in response to the large number of women managers leaving their positions after only a short period of

22 Based on a study published by Beyond Business Ltd, the author's consulting firm: www.b-yond.biz/en/sub_page.asp?sp=260&p=72.

23 report.vattenfall.com/csrreport2008/Menu/What+we+do/A+diverse+Vattenfall+pe rforms+better/A+diverse+Vattenfall+performs+better, accessed 5 June 2010.

24 report.vattenfall.com/csrreport2008/Menu/What+we+do/A+diverse+Vattenfall+pe rforms+better/but+action+is+being+taken, accessed 5 June 2010.

time. At monthly meetings, members are encouraged to speak out, and the result is that the number of women managers has increased. In the last year alone, Ringhals gained about ten new women managers, while the current managers are tending to stay in their position

## The position at Andromex

|  | Total | Men | Women | % Women |
|---|---|---|---|---|
| ANDEX | 7 | 6 | 1 | 14.3 |
| Senior managers | 48 | 43 | 5 | 11.6 |
| Other managers | 384 | 357 | 27 | 7 |
| Non-managers | 2,061 | 1,818 | 243 | 11.8 |
| Total | 2,500 | 2,224 | 276 | 11.04 |

In the last 12 months:

- Management promotions: zero women out of total 5 promotions
- External management recruitment: 1 women out of total 12 managers
- Women returning from maternity leave: 43%
- Managers leaving the company: 15 managers of which 9 were women

This demonstrates that women are not being recruited on an equal basis, are not advancing at Andromex, and are leaving the company in higher proportions than their male counterparts.

## Recommendations

- Appoint a Gender Equality Officer at Andromex (one of the male ANDEX members)
- Set targets to increase the level of women in all divisions in the business to at least 20% within two years
- Effective immediately, ensure all internal and external recruitment shortlists include women candidates, and create a new process whereby decisions on candidates are made by a Recruitment Committee, rather than the decision of one (male) manager. Decisions should be made based on a set of pre-agreed criteria and hiring should be by consensus
- Conduct a thorough review of salary and benefits levels between women and men, and assess discrepancies in similar jobs
- Hold round-table discussions with men and women managers together with members of ANDEX to discuss issues related to diversity, equality and inclusion. Use a gender equality specialist to help facilitate the discussions
- Conduct a company-wide survey on diversity, inclusion and equality
- Understand the differences in attitudes between men and women at different levels in the business

- Using the survey, identify the areas in which activities should be developed to address gender imbalance and create a work plan

**Note:** It is important to address gender issues as issues related to developing a culture of respect, dialogue, equality and inclusion, and not just a way of advancing women. In practice, it may be necessary in the first stages of the programme to boost the opportunities for women by setting targets and specific plans to advance women specifically. As the programme continues, this should be less relevant, and gender equality would become part of the culture and the processes of the business, without the need for specific focus.

Sharon was very pleased with this paper. Patricia had done all the work. She had done a good job bringing out the issues and Sharon felt her recommendations were sound. She thought she might have a chance at getting this through. She resolved to talk to all her ANDEX colleagues about this during the next week, and if she could get their support, she would take it to George. She was hopeful that most of this work-plan would be supported. She already knew who might have a problem with it, but she was determined not to let Mr William Rastrom interfere with her plans. HR might not be driving the business, but Sharon felt the time was right to start driving corporate responsibility and this was as good a test case as any.

Sharon heard a ping. It was Outlook telling her it was time for that marketing meeting on the marketing talent funnel. She picked up her phone and notepad and made her way to the fourth floor.

# 8

# Employee training and development

A week had gone by and Sharon hadn't had time to breathe. Having been away for over a week, she had suddenly come back to ground-zero with a ton of meetings to attend, emails to respond to, people to talk to, projects to progress, answers to provide, people to coach, metrics to review, problems to resolve, recommendations to write, recommendations to evaluate, Excels to study, PowerPoints to review and personal connections to renew. Not to mention the fact that her kids needed her attention, nor the fact that there was lots of stuff to do at home. Both her work and her family demanded her time, and she was on the go 18 hours a day in an intensive whirlwind of activity. She drove herself hard, trying to meet everyone's demands, deadlines and developments. In the midst of this, there had been a long ANDEX meeting taken up mainly with debates and upcoming communications processes around the IPO and product innovation issues. CSR was weaving in and out of her thoughts and she was experiencing a certain unrest as she felt she needed to start to do something with all these new insights. For now, she had no real alternative but to 'go with the flow' and catch up with all the tasks and projects she had left before her trip to San Diego. CSR was tucked away at a low level in her consciousness, gnawing away at the back of her mind, until she could break the critical mass of catch-up and have time to stop and think about how to organise herself to refocus her role and the company's culture.

It was almost 11 a.m. She was about to have a training review with her HR team. This was one area of her HR work she was proud of. As the company had grown, she had managed to secure increasing training budgets year-on-year, and a couple of years ago had overhauled the entire process to ensure improved identification of training needs, an annual training plan determined in advance, a multi-layered training system that offered a range of mandatory programmes for certain functions and employee groups, together with a menu range of options that could be selected to supplement the core programmes. In addition, she had instituted a training effectiveness system that tracked the way training was changing employee and management behaviour through time. These metrics were used in annual performance reviews and fed in to annual salary reviews and annual target setting processes. It was a comprehensive system that Sharon was very proud of and, she believed, that was supporting the delivery of business results. Her next meeting would be about assessing the first quarter metrics and fine-tuning the programme, or fine-tuning the ANDEX members about the need for training in their Divisions. She smiled to herself. Fine-tuning her colleagues on ANDEX. A couple of them needed reconstructive surgery, she thought, not just fine-tuning. But then, on the whole, she felt she was respected and supported by ANDEX. Sharon was about to pick up her notebook and walk to the third floor conference room when her phone rang. It was Arena.

**Sharon:** Hi, Arena. What a surprise! Good to hear from you. How have you settled in back home?

**Arena:** Great, thanks. How about you? What's happening?

**Sharon:** I am doing fine. Caught up in a whirlwind of things after over a week away. Wondering what I am going to do with all the CSR you drummed into me.

**Arena:** Small steps, you know. Small wins.

**Sharon:** Yes, though I need to think more deeply about where to start. Look, Arena, I am just going into a training review meeting, can I call you back later?

**Arena:** Sure. But you can start in your training review. If you were designing the training programme from the standpoint of a CSHR manager, rather than just an HR manager, what would you do differently?

**Sharon:** OK. Pass. What do you mean?

**Arena:** Well, who are the stakeholders of your training programme and what do they want? The business of course is the key stakeholder — it needs more skilled people. Then the employees — what do they want? Years ago, we might have said job security. People were hired for a lifetime of work and retired from companies they worked in for 30 years or more. Today, no company can guarantee lifetime employment, especially not after the global financial crisis. Today, people have different needs. They should be able to leave a company enriched with more skills and life-capabilities than they had when they joined. They should be able to leave a company knowing that they are more employable. The concept of employability is core to the concept of corporate responsibility. As employers, this is the way we can benefit our employees and society beyond just providing them with a pay-packet and subsidised meals. As you review your training programme, see what it's doing to make your employees more employable.

**Sharon:** But I'm training them because I want to retain them, Arena. Why would I want to help them become more attractive to other employers?

**Arena:** Sharon, it's a win–win. The more 'employable' they become, the more they add value to your business. The more they add value, the more they will find ways in which to contribute and feel motivated. You need to reward them accordingly, provide them with opportunities and they will stay. But businesses change. New skills are required. Old skills become less relevant. Businesses are bought and sold. Upsized and downsized. Resourcing needs differ. Sometimes the most valuable people today are less relevant in your business tomorrow, though they might be relevant elsewhere. Sometimes you have no choice but to let people go. And when you do, in the competitive market of today, with its changing landscapes, the concept of corporate responsibility invites us to add value to these employees so that they will be employable elsewhere. This helps them remain ambassadors for our business, which contributes to our reputation, and also help them continue to be economic value-adding members of society, which strengthens the basic environment in which we do business. Something to think about.

But the real reason I called was to invite you to meet Carl Barton, our Employee Volunteering Programme Manager who oversees IFC's global volunteering policy. He is based at IFC Head Office in London, like me. I have told him that you want an introduction to employee volunteering programmes, and he will be happy to meet. He loves talking, so I am sure you will have an interesting time.

**Sharon:** Thanks, Arena. That will be wonderful. I would love to hear about what you do at IFC.

**Arena:** I will SMS his telephone number to you. Fix with him directly. If I am in the office on that day, we can touch base, but if not, we will arrange some time to meet, just the two of us. Anyway, have to get moving now. Have a good meeting on employability.

**Sharon:** Training.

**Arena:** Ha, ha. You'll see.

Sharon looked at her watch. She was five minutes late for her meeting, so without stopping to ponder the concept of employability, she made her way to the conference room, and settled herself into the session. 'Arena has done it to me again,' she thought. All the way through the meeting, her mind was on what the training programme was doing to create employability, and not just what skills were needed on the job, or leadership capability or innovation techniques. She decided not to bring it up in the meeting but think about it afterwards, form an opinion and use it to develop her overall CSR strategy.

The training review came and went, as did another four meetings during the rest of the day. It was already five o'clock and Sharon hadn't had much time to think about anything, let alone employability. She decided to spend a couple of hours in the office to find out more about it. She had heard the term, of course, but hadn't really associated it with a company's responsibility. Settling herself in front of her screen with a cup of coffee and a banana, she prepared herself for some quality time in corporate responsibility research.

A search for employability brought up Wikipedia.[1] 'Employability is about being capable of getting and keeping fulfilling work.' 'Not mind-blowing,' thought Sharon. 'Get a job and keep it — what's the big deal?' As she continued to search, she realised that employability can often refer to the ability of a person who is not employed or never has been employed to enter the job market in the first place, such as graduates, or people from disadvantaged groups in the community. She recalled examples of government and corporate programmes that provided vocational training and up-skilling for people like this.

Her browser led her to an excellent report from an organisation called ENGAGE,[2] which encourages businesses to invest in 'sustainable community' programmes and is managed by Business in the Community[3] and the International Business Leaders Forum.[4] The report published in November 2008[5] was the result of a CSR Laboratory, demonstrating the effectiveness of employee community engagement in improving the skills essential for employment amongst disadvantaged and socially excluded groups of people within the EU.

Sharon delved into this report with great interest. She noted a list of essential skills for employability in this report, which included:

- **Basic skills,** e.g. literacy and numeracy

- **Thinking skills,** e.g. innovative thinking and learning skills

- **Job-ready skills,** e.g. CV writing and interview techniques

- **Self-reliance skills,** e.g. resourcefulness, drive, motivation, honesty, integrity, team skills, positive attitude to work, punctuality, dependability, self-confidence, positive self-image, accuracy, commitment and conscientiousness

- **People skills,** e.g. ability to coordinate projects and people, interpersonal skills, cooperative, assertive, good at listening and giving advice, leadership, able to motivate, energetic, customer orientation, friendly, caring and diplomatic manner

1   en.wikipedia.org/wiki/Employability, accessed 5 June 2010.
2   www.engageyouremployees.org.
3   www.bitc.org.uk.
4   www.iblf.org.
5   www.bitc.org.uk/global/skills_for.html, accessed 25 August 2010.

Sharon thought that it would be wonderful if all Andromex employees lived up to this description. However, this report was mainly about getting people into the job market for the first time. Some wonderful case studies were described, for example, a project called Employability Days, supported by businesses including Deutsche Bank, where volunteers run workshops for people of all ages from a part of London where the overriding majority of residents live in social housing and unemployment is around three times the national average. The workshops focus on interview skills, CV advice and the working environment. Another project highlighted in the report was the KPMG Mentoring Refugees programme, which prepares refugees with skills to work in the UK, specifically those who have qualifications in the financial sector in their own country, to prepare them for accountancy and finance work in the UK. KPMG volunteers act as mentors for the refugees. In 2007, 25% of the participants found work. Sharon found this Employability report fascinating because it related both to enhancing the employability of many different communities and groups, and also to employee volunteering as something which itself enhances the employability of those involved. She made a mental note to talk to Carl Barton of IFC, Arena's company, about this, when she went to meet him.

As she read on, Sharon recalled that Andrew Wilfman, Andromex's Technology Manager, was involved in some sort of academic working group to review vocational suitability of technology studies, to ensure that young technology graduates have skills that are relevant to industry. This was employability, she thought. She hadn't made that connection before. 'Hah!' she thought. 'Something to write in our first Corporate Responsibility Report!' She even recalled a conversation with Andrew where he had talked about corporate programmes to invest in vocational technology up-skilling — he had mentioned Intel and Cisco and others. Cisco, for example, established the Networking Academy[6] in 1997, a global education programme that teaches students to develop computer networks skills for increased access to career and economic opportunities. She took a quick look at Cisco website and noticed that this was Cisco's largest corporate social responsibility programme, aiming to improve socioeconomic conditions in communities around the world by increasing access to education and career opportunities, supporting the development of an educated ICT (information and communication technology) workforce, and promoting the growth of the ICT industry. Cisco also refers to helping to bridge the digital divide by extending learning opportunities to students in developing countries and those with disabilities and empowering women by 'encouraging gender equality within the ICT industry'.

Sharon was impressed with this as a community support programme, and with everything she had read about employability, but she felt sure that this wasn't what Arena had in mind when she talked about making in-house train-

6  www.cisco.com/web/learning/netacad/academy/index.html, accessed 5 June 2010.

ing programmes more aligned with this concept. She went back to the page on Wikipedia where she had started out and noticed an expanded definition: 'Employability is the capability to move self-sufficiently within the labour market to realise potential through sustainable employment'. 'This is different,' she thought. 'It's about moving *within* the labour market, moving from one job to another. Not getting into the market. That's more relevant to training and our internal needs.'

Sharon continued her Internet search and came across a small paragraph in the Corporate Responsibility Report for 2008 of Danske Bank.[7] The Bank reported that they used competency profiles in a systematic way to create a sort of competency inventory for all employees. They said that 'Targeted competency development increases the staff's employability and thus improves their ability and the Group's capacity to adapt to change.' The report gave an example from the Retail and Logistics Department, where increased digitalisation had the potential to eliminate jobs and, therefore, using the company development process, 'employees could gain a foundation for adapting to changes by proactively planning their careers'. Sharon also scanned what she thought was an excellent paper called the 'Industry Employability Index' produced by the ILO in 2004,[8] which looked at the concept of employability from an industry perspective and defined four drivers of employability: technological developments, organisational developments, economic developments (mainly related to competition) and demographic developments. The paper referred to three elements that make up developing employability as being mobility, training and functional flexibility. Then Sharon jumped to a Working Paper developed at Cardiff University called *Employability in a Knowledge-Driven Economy*.[9] She read the following paragraph three times:

> Employability is also seen to reflect the shift away from the bureaucratic career structures of the past that offered stable career progression to significant numbers of white-collar workers (Collin and Young, 2000). The large corporations have become leaner, flatter and prone to rapid restructuring making them incompatible with the expectation of a bureaucratic career. This led companies to highlight the need for employees to not only remain employable within their current jobs but in the external labour market, if they should find themselves in the category of 'surplus' employees (Sennett, 1998). A feature of work reorganisation in the last twenty years has been the democratisation of insecurity. Redundancy is no longer restricted to semi-skilled and unskilled workers. Technicians, engineers, manag-

7 Danske Bank Corporate Responsibility, www.danskebank.com/en-uk/CSR/ Documents/CR_report_2008.pdf : 20.

8 www.roa.unimaas.nl/cv/degrip/industry.pdf, accessed 5 June 2010.

9 Phillip Brown, Anthony Hesketh and Sara Williams, *Employability in a Knowledge-Driven Economy* (Working Paper 26; Cardiff, UK: Cardiff University, 2002, www.cf.ac.uk/socsi/resources/wrkgpaper26.pdf, accessed 5 June 2010).

ers and professionals, have all discovered that the long tenure career bargain is dead (Cappelli, 1999; Peiperl, et al. 2000). For some business gurus such as Drucker (1993), employability also represents a powershift in the nature of global capitalism. There is less need for those with initiative, energy or entrepreneurial flair to commit themselves to the same organisation for decades in order to make a decent career. If organisations depend on the knowledge and skills of the workforce then power rests with those that have the knowledge, skills and insights that companies want (Micheals, et al., 2001). The shift away from long-term company careers has given the educated classes greater economic freedom. This has enabled young knowledge workers to short-circuit organisational hierarchies to arrive in senior managerial positions often in their thirties.

The democratisation of insecurity. Sharon was fascinated by this concept. The shift of power in global capitalism from the business to the workers. Extraordinary, she thought. She hadn't truly thought about these concepts before. She was familiar with outplacement programmes, to help people find alternative occupation and support them when they are fired from their jobs. She had even used outplacement services for a number of vulnerable employees whom she had had to lay off in one of the data aggregation departments, because of the changing nature of technical skills, and because, at over 50, they didn't stand a very good chance of finding other jobs. She had intuitively felt that it was the right thing to do to assist these employees. She hadn't thought of calling it anything to do with enhancing their employability, or even as a responsibility of the company. She had thought it was just the decent thing. Now, she was wondering if she might have been able to assist them in enhancing their employability earlier on in their employment with the company and what a difference this might have made to them and to Andromex.

Sharon started to gather her thoughts and, as she was in the habit of doing, prepared a short paper on employability, creating her own definitions and rationale out of everything she had read in the last hour and a half, placing emphasis on the internal business benefits of addressing the concept of employability and the HR function.

# Employability and the responsibility of the HR function

## Definition

Employability is the result of a shared investment in the contribution to the personal and professional skills of employees such that they are equipped to maintain their attractiveness to potential employers in a competitive and changing job market.

## Employability is necessary because:

- **Business.** Professional skill requirements change as markets and economies evolve. This is essential to maintain competitiveness
- **Social.** Communities need to develop towards greater economic stability with higher levels of employment and economic prosperity, and inclusion of underprivileged groups in the labour market
- **Individual.** Individuals have greater chances of being employed and are able to achieve personal growth and self-esteem and contribute to society

## Benefits of investing in employability

**Business benefits:**

- **Increased ability to retain employees** as job needs change reduces costs associated with turnover of employees
- **Increased flexibility and mobility of workforce** reduces recruitment costs and maintains business continuity
- **Increased motivation of total workforce,** which appreciates employer's efforts to develop people in the business and commitment to employees even if requirements change
- **Increased pool of available potential employees.** The business depends on local communities for recruitment of a qualified and adaptable workforce
- **Corporate responsibility.** Community contribution, workforce development and equality of opportunity are enhancers of business reputation

**Employee benefits:**

- Employees ensure their professional skills and competences remain relevant to current and changing job demands, providing them with greater opportunities to stay in work
- Employees increase their opportunity to stay with a company as job requirements change, providing stability and continuity in an employee's life
- If dismissed, employees can expect shorter time needed for job search when between jobs
- Employees gain the potential to increase earning power through acquisition of new skills that are more in demand

## Employability depends on:

**Business:**

- A strategic, clear commitment to programmes that enhance the employability of its employees
- A budget to support relevant programmes

**Employees:**

- The employee's basic skills and competencies
- The employee's attitude to change and ability to learn and adapt
- The employee's physical mobility to move to where the jobs are

## Achieving employability

The employability of an employee is the combination of efforts by both the employee and the company. There is a shared responsibility and creation of mutual benefit. The ways in which employability is delivered through a combination of several factors:

**HR strategy**

- Analysis of changing job markets, business strategy and company skill requirements
- Strategic planning of resourcing needs over a medium- to long-term period

**Core HR people development processes**

- Performance development processes
- Competency assessment
- Identification of skill gaps and training/development needs
- Performance review
- Establishment of performance development targets for all
- Talent management process

**Training and development**

- Delivery of training and measurement of its effectiveness
- Career counselling
- Mentoring
- Job move — promotion or sideways moves, or cross-functional moves

**Transition management**

- Preparation for leaving the company through dismissal or retirement
- Coaching for success in finding a new job
- Assisting with contacting potential new employers and/or giving recommendations

**Employee mind-set alignment**

- Helping employees understand the risks and opportunities related to their current employment and future potential

- Ensuring employees take shared responsibility for their own employability

**Corporate responsibility programmes**
- Employee volunteering programmes to assist disadvantaged groups and minorities in becoming more employable
- Development opportunities for employees with an NGO for a period of time to provide mentoring
- Leadership opportunities for employees for internal CSR programmes
- University and college partnerships to define future employability skill development and academic programme content
- Partnerships with NGOs to develop skills of minority and disadvantaged groups

Sharon felt pleased with herself. She had got to the bottom of this employability thing, at least in a basic way. She felt sure there was more to it, but at least now she understood that there was a clear overlap between traditional HR processes, such as talent management, and HR deliverables, such as training, with business benefits related to supporting business strategy and corporate responsibility. She would have to work out the cost implications for programmes that required more than just tweaking current training content, but she felt that this was one area at least that was entirely within the jurisdiction of the HR director and could be developed without too much debate and involvement of ANDEX.

Sharon looked at her watch. It was half past seven. She hadn't intended to stay so late in the office. Work–life balance. There is no such thing, she thought. She quickly packed up all her papers, flipped her laptop shut, hunted out her car keys, and dashed out, happy that no one else was around to delay her. As she drove home, she thought about food. 'Maybe I will go vegetarian this evening,' she thought. 'I wonder if I have a recipe for nut cutlets.'

# 9

# Employee communications

Sharon never ceased to be amazed at the fact that once you become aware of something it pops up everywhere. As someone once said about green pigs, or purple elephants, or something like that, the minute someone talks about them, they suddenly seem to be everywhere. So it was with corporate social responsibility. No sooner had Arena turned Sharon's antennae to this new way of thinking about her role, and about business in general, it seemed that CSR was just everywhere.

Sharon was having lunch. For a change, she had decided to grab a sandwich in the office, rather than go to the dining room and have lunch with colleagues or other employees, so that she could work through some of the email backlog that she hadn't managed to catch up with. Only 343 emails in the inbox; 140 unread. Not bad. As she unwrapped her sandwich, she noticed that the latest edition of *HRM Practitioner,*[1] her favourite monthly HR professional journal, was in her in-tray. Her physical in-tray, not her electronic inbox. She liked to read the journal — there was always something new to learn, or something else to think about. Not that she needed anything to think about. A trip to San Diego and hours of Arena, Ilana and many other interesting people had given her more than enough to think about. Not being able to resist the temptation, she picked up the journal, took a bite of her sandwich and a sip of water and scanned the contents list. And then, the inevitable happened. Something she could absolutely not pass up reading, there and then. Of course, it had CSR in the title. Another mouthful of sandwich, and she began to read.

---

1 *HRM Practitioner* is a fictional journal. The article was written by Nirit Cohen and Revital Bitan especially for this book.

# Where HR and CSR meet

## Intel Israel works to create the optimal employee experience

Nirit Cohen, Intel Israel HR Director and Revital Bitan, Intel Israel CSR Manager

At Intel, Corporate Responsibility is driven to create bold advancements in technology that enhance people's lives. Explore how Intel is cultivating the spirit of innovation and promoting the concept of sustainability in our operations and in communities worldwide. With 6,500 employees, Intel Israel is the largest private employer in Israel. In 2009, Intel Israel celebrated its 35th anniversary.

## Intel values

The statement 'Conduct business with uncompromising integrity and professionalism' is part of the formal Intel values and expresses our commitment to upholding the highest standards of corporate governance and business ethics in our day-to-day activities at Intel and in our engagement with external stakeholders. We continuously work to develop a strong culture of trust through open and direct communication, and are committed to accountability and transparency in our work on public policy issues.

As Intel Israel HR Manager, my aim is that every employee at Intel Israel can honestly say: 'I believe in the company, I belong to the Intel team, and I matter to the company and its success.' I know that to attract and retain the talented workforce we need to maintain our leadership in innovation, and we must continue to effectively empower, motivate, and reward our employees for their achievements. We encourage them to pursue challenges and take well-informed risks, and we provide resources to help them manage their lives — both on and off the job. We also set clear, consistent expectations for our managers and leaders: we want them to be responsible both for the business goals and for employees'

growth, including adequate recognition of their contribution.

## Diversity: a way of life

Making corporate responsibility an integral part of Intel's strategy means seeing diversity as a way of life. We believe that our ability to innovate depends on ideas, and great ideas come from great people. The wide range of perspectives that we gain by hiring and developing talent from a diverse labour pool gives us a better understanding of the needs of our customers, suppliers and communities and helps us advance our leadership position in both technology and corporate responsibility. In my experience, employees working in a diverse environment tend to feel more fulfilled, creative and productive on the job, resulting in increased productivity, efficiency and innovation. Intel promotes equal employment opportunity for all applicants and employees, regardless of non-job-related factors, including but not limited to race, colour, religion, gender, national origin, ancestry, age, marital status, sexual orientation, gender identity, veteran status and disability. Our policies apply to all aspects and stages of employment — from recruiting through retirement — and prohibit harassment of any individual or group. We offer all employees extensive intercultural training and mentoring programmes. We have also tailored several initiatives to meet the needs of targeted employee populations, for example, women in senior levels and technical jobs, with comprehensive programmes designed to improve work–life balance and flexibility, career options and cultural awareness.

Intel Israel is the high-tech company in Israel with the largest number of employees from the Arab sector. Therefore, Intel is well positioned to lead a change in perception in the hope this will expand further to include the entire business sector. In an enterprise like Intel, where the profit line plays a significant factor, employing Arab people is a unique opportunity to demonstrate boldness, creativity and global business. The assimilation of Arab engineers in Israeli high-tech companies is a breakthrough initiative for Intel Israel and makes good business sense for all the parties involved. As part of this, Intel is active in Kav Mashve,[2] a non-profit organisation that promotes Arabs with academic qualifications in the high-tech sector. Intel was the first company in a coalition of Israeli companies supporting Arab employment.

## Best place to work

In 2009, for the second year 'The Marker' and 'BDI Coface' both voted Intel Israel as the best place to work for (in two categories: all Israeli companies and all high-tech companies).

Having worked at Intel for the past 19 years, I feel that employee satisfaction in the high-tech industry has changed over the past decade. In addition to good pay, employees primarily seek to work in a stable company which is also a technological leader and innovator. Other preferences include the ability to learn and grow on the job and the feeling that they make a significant contribution. Just as importantly, employees would like to work in a pleasant environment, be rewarded based on their performance and receive competitive benefits. To top it all, they appreciate an opportunity to contribute to their community.

Central to our goal of making Intel a great place to start and advance a career is our belief that career development is a partnership between our employees, their managers and the company. Our employees grow by continuously learning — on the job, in the classroom and by connecting with others. We encourage employees to work with their managers to align their job assignments with their strengths and interests, as well as with the needs of the organisation. When employees are ready to try new challenges, they can 'test-drive' short-term assignments by providing coverage for employees on sabbatical leave or by taking advantage of one of our rotation programmes.

I see part of our HR role as ensuring that our managers are effective: they should care about people, know how to delineate the road ahead, provide the tools and processes, develop their people and have technological as well as business understanding. We give them the opportunities to acquire these critical skills and knowledge by attending internal and external courses, connecting with other managers, and taking on new challenges.

2  For further information on Kav Mashve, see their website: www.kavmashve.org.il/hebsite/content/t12.asp?sid=101&Pid=324, accessed 6 June 2010. Employment of Arab university graduates in the Israeli high-tech sector is low compared to the potential. Intel's reference to the Arab population in Israel is against the background of a significant issue that needs to be corrected in a just and open society. In taking a leadership position on this, Intel Israel is influencing the entire high-tech sector.

## Open communications

One of the things that gives me great pride is Intel's open-door approach, which gives employees access to all levels of management to address concerns. Employee surveys indicate that our open-door philosophy contributes to organisational health, improves productivity and decreases turnover. In planning our corporate communications, we work to demonstrate this philosophy of openness and two-way give and take.

A development strategy for employees and managers is part of our corporate responsibility strategy that has contributed to our reputation as a valued corporate partner, protected our ability to operate in local communities and enabled us to attract and retain a talented workforce.

Intel's success depends on all employees understanding how their work contributes to the company's overall business strategy. As such, we have a wide mix of electronic and interpersonal channels to keep employees informed. Through news articles, open forums, webcasts, cyberchats, quarterly Business Update Meetings, and informal brown-bag lunches, employees receive information, ask questions and get candid answers from executives. 'e-CENTER, our intranet employee portal, provides corporate and local Intel news along with information about workplace services and benefits. Employees increasingly participate in Intel's social media channels, such as blogs, vlogs (video blogs) and online forums. Senior leaders and other employees publish provocative personal essays to open up dialogue about business issues, challenges, and opportunities. Regular employee surveys ensure that Intel's managers and leaders obtain feedback and track the health of organisations so that adjustments can be made as needed. Employee surveys include, for example, the Manager and Leader Feedback Survey. Through this survey, administered twice a year, employees evaluate how well their manager is communicating, motivating and developing his or her team. Managers are strongly encouraged to discuss the survey results — both strengths and areas for improvement — with their teams and develop action plans. Roughly every two years, we conduct our worldwide Organizational Health Survey (OHS) to learn what employees think about our workplace. The OHS helps identify strengths and areas for improvement in our business groups in Israel, and provides data for planning and improvement.

All these communication channels create an impactful dialogue between management and employees that strengthens employees' sense of involvement. In addition it connects employees to Intel's direction, their role in the company's success and the rewards of working at Intel.

## Rewarding employees

Intel's approach to employee compensation also contributes to overall business success and employee satisfaction. We call it the Total Compensation plan, or 'T-Comp', approach, which aligns company, employee and stockholder interests, and provides employees with incentives to focus on meeting or exceeding business objectives.

T-Comp is based on five guiding principles that support our philosophy of rewarding both individual performance and corporate success: meritocracy, market competitiveness, alignment with business performance, promotion of health and welfare, and balance between employee and stockholder needs. Base pay for each job is determined in accordance with local market rates for comparable jobs, our business targets and the employee's relevant education, skills, experience and job performance compared to his or her Intel peers.

Managers meet employees periodically to review quarterly goals and to define ongoing priorities. These meetings provide opportunities for recognition and discussion of performance issues, and contribute to overall improvement in team performance, execution, and business results. A formal performance review is held annually and in order to gain an objective, 360° view of employees' performance and effectiveness. The 360° approach is applied to prevent personal bias by managers, as each employee is evaluated by a selection of managers, customers, peers, and subordinates.

I believe that our variable pay policy reflects the company's success and employees' contribution to that success. In addition to receiving base pay as described above, all employees participate in bonus or results-related incentive programmes that include Intel's financial and operational performance metrics. By linking a portion of each employee's total cash compensation to Intel's performance, these variable-pay programmes recognise that each employee contributes to the company's overall success.

Aligned with our corporate responsibility approach to provide employees with incentives to focus on meeting or exceeding business objectives, some years ago, Intel expanded the bonus payout to all employees (previously it applied only to the executive management team). A further development of the programme was applied in 2008 when we added criteria related to environmental sustainability metrics.

Another CSR aspect which supports the compensation programme is Intel's employee rewards and recognition programme. We believe that employee recognition should be structured and planned to achieve the right impact. It should start with everyday 'thank-yous' and continue with banquets. Diverse forms of recognition are used to reward employees for their accomplishments. We encourage managers to celebrate the accomplishments of their business organisations, teams and individuals through our company-wide recognition programmes, which include global corporate-wide programmes that apply to less than 0.5% of the total employee population, as well as local programmes created by individual business groups to address specific goals or recognition that may be given at any time to show appreciation to a peer, subordinate or manager. The rewards may include cash, a gift card or other reward. As corporate responsibility has a direct link to our recognition strategy, Intel also recognises employees for their years of service, for volunteering efforts, contributions as instructors for 'Intel University', and for environmental achievements, including efforts to conserve energy and prevent pollution.

Intel also believes that employees who contribute to our success should benefit from it, as stockholders do. We grant equity to more than 90% of our employees annually through stock option/restricted stock plans. Through our broad-based stock programme, employees obtain the right to receive an equity interest in the company, acquire a stake in Intel's long-term growth, and potentially benefit from capital appreciation. In 2006, we expanded our programme to include restricted stock units (RSUs), delivering more predictable value to employees while meeting our commitments to stockholders. Although all employees who receive stock grants receive RSUs, our more senior level employees have a larger percentage of their stock grant in the form of stock options. Regular full-time and part-time employees are eligible to receive stock option grants from the day they are hired and may be recommended for additional stock option grants during annual or mid-year performance reviews. In addition, by enrolling in the employee stock purchase plan, eligible employees can purchase shares of Intel stock at a discounted rate through payroll deductions. All regular full-time and part-time employees and interns are eligible to participate.

## Work-life management, health and wellness

Managing a career and personal life can be challenging. Intel is committed to making it easier. We want to help our employees make the most of both worlds. One of my major responsibilities as HR Manager is to deliver on our commitment to provide a portfolio of health benefits and wellness programmes that help our employees evaluate, maintain, and improve their health and the health of their families. Our Health for Life 3-Step Wellness Check is based on the concept that the more employees know about their health risks, the better they can manage them. The programme provides a gateway for employees to access resources that focus on positive health and wellness lifestyle choices. The programme features a baseline health evaluation, an online health risk assessment, and confidential meetings with an on-site personal health coach to develop an individual health action plan. Quarterly surveys show that more than 96% of the respondents were very satisfied or satisfied with the Health for Life wellness programme and plan to make changes to improve their health.

Intel Israel is a leader in offering consumer-driven health plans. We strive to optimise health plan designs and suppliers, and to provide employees with flexibility and options so they can choose the plan that best meets their needs. Intel Israel's health programme is one of the best among Israeli companies. It covers employees' families and children up to the age of 24.

We maintain a range of options for employees to take time off from work without fear of losing their job. This includes special leave programmes and various opportunities such as a sabbatical programme. Intel Israel employees receive a double annual vacation on completion of each seven years of service. Female employees on maternity leave can benefit from a phased back-to-work part time scheme up to 12 months from childbirth.

Our comprehensive, global approach to work–life effectiveness includes providing tools and creating an environment that supports the needs of different employees, both women and men. Programme options may vary by business unit and job type and are tailored for each employee based on his or her needs. Managers accommodate reasonable requests for flexibility whenever possible. There is no 'one size fits all' solution to flexibility. Work–life options are most successful when they begin with open and honest discussions between managers and employees and address specific issues or needs.

Flexibility is about making Intel's workforce more productive, both on and off the job. Flexibility solutions do not reduce performance expectations nor do they shift the focus away from our customers. Our flexibility options are intended to help our employees navigate, not eliminate, work–life conflicts.

Intel Israel was one of the few companies that introduced telecommuting as early as the year 2000. As a global company, we communicate regularly with various groups in different time zones around the world. While in the past employees were expected to stay in the office until late to communicate with their overseas peers, today they can interact with their peers from home

We host employee's families with many events throughout the year such as special summer on-site back-up childcare, and holiday care, special kids and family celebrations. During the past several years, Intel Israel has sponsored near-site childcare centres in Jerusalem, Kiryat Gat and Haifa. We provide a comprehensive intranet site with resources for employees and their families. We also provide on-site cafeterias, fitness centres, cash-dispensing machines, dry-cleaning services and private rooms for nursing mothers.

## Community involvement and environmental protection

Last but not least, Intel Israel employees participate in multiple activities for the community, either as part of or after work hours. In this way, they can fulfil a sense of giving, whether in education, technology, environmental responsibility, safety or community engagement. Intel Israel has emerged as a leader in this field.

Intel Israel has been operating since 1974, when the first Intel development centre outside the United States was opened. In 1985, Fab 8, the first non-US production plant, opened in Jerusalem. The CSR operations of Intel Israel are therefore not limited to international initiatives but include additional locally driven ventures. The 'localised' CSR policies are reflected in Intel Israel's CSR report. When Intel started in Kiryat Gat, expectations were high. At that time, we were beginning to formulate our community involvement model. For example, before getting started, we set up teams that included representatives from the local community. Together, we reviewed how to cooperate for mutual benefit. We felt it was important to promote and develop the city, to communicate with our stakeholders and to be transparent in our operations.

Throughout 35 years in Israel, Intel Israel has intensified its involvement in innovative educational programmes in addition to our ongoing support of universities, colleges and research institutions to help develop human capital for the high-tech industry. Our commitment to environmental performance generates long-lasting benefits. We ensure all our new buildings are built with 'green' construction methods. We have also launched the Membrane Bio Reactor (MBR) to treat waste-water from our Fab 28 plant in Kiryat Gat. The MBR is the first waste-water treatment facility in the world established by Intel and the largest of its type in Israel. Since Intel first opened its R&D and production centres outside the USA, Intel Israel has been responsible for some of the breakthrough technologies and products that transformed the nature of computing. We are proud that the energy-efficient developments that lead Intel's new computers were conceived in Israel. We regard our advanced technological developments as an opportunity to nurture the communities in which we operate. In addition, Intel Israel successfully harnessed its personnel and economic resources. Intel purchased from Israeli suppliers equipment, products and materials. Intel further expanded its operations within the framework of the new Israeli Industry Development (ISID) programme to include encouragement of foreign investment in the Israeli market and development of local suppliers instead of importing materials wherever possible.

## In summary

Three main reasons motivated Intel Israel to take the lead on driving CSR as part of the company's management strategy:

1. 'Being an asset to our communities' is one of Intel's values. It is rooted in the basic perception that businesses must give back to the community in which they do business

2. Our employees are a most valuable asset and bring a unique and valued

perspective to Intel. Their creativity, productivity and experience make it possible for us to remain innovative and competitive

3. Intel's continued success as a company depends on our ability to meet the needs of our global, diverse workforce. We are dedicated to making the Intel environment a place where our employees thrive creatively and intellectually

Overall, HR and CSR meet in all of these places. Values, diversity, great workplace, work-life effectiveness, health, wellness, compensation, community involvement, environmental protection and more, all of these processes live at the interface between human resources management and a corporate responsibility strategy. As an HR manager, I see the alignment of CSR and HR as not only beneficial, but also critical to total performance. Having experienced this for several years at Intel on a personal level, I also know that it is possible. ∾

**Nirit Cohen** serves as Human Resources Director at Intel Israel. She joined Intel in 1991 as a Finance Analyst with the Israel Design Center and later moved to Human Resources to start the Compensation and Benefits team. Nirit held various positions in HR, including HR Information Systems Manager for Israel, HR Manager for Mergers and Acquisitions in Israel and HR Manager for a business group in Israel. In 2001 Nirit relocated to Intel corporate HR in Santa Clara, CA, as Worldwide Compensation & Benefits Manager for the Technology and Manufacturing Group at Intel and then moved on to manage the design and implementation of a global performance management system. In 2004 Nirit returned to Israel to manage Intel Israel HR. In 2007, she managed a global project, the HR implementation of an Intel Divestiture and during 2008 she acted as Intel Corporate Compensation & Benefits Director. Nirit sits on the managing board of the Israel Human Resources Management Organization (non-profit) and is a frequent guest speaker at academic institutions and conferences. Nirit holds a BA in Economics and Business Administration from the Hebrew University in Jerusalem and an MA in Technology Policy & Innovation Management from the Maastricht Economic Research Institute of Technology at the University of Limburg, Netherlands.

**Revital Bitan** serves as CSR Manager at Intel Israel, She has worked at Intel in various capacities since 1987, including marketing, communication and community relations. Throughout her career at Intel, Revital has driven numerous local community projects and national educational programmes to help bridge the digital divide. In 2004, she was part of the eight-member pioneer global team that worked towards driving Intel's CSR strategy and achieving global leadership in socially responsible investments. In 2008, she was part of global team that was responsible for Intel's 40th anniversary 1 million-hours volunteer programme, including the design and implementation of the Intel Involved Matching Grant Programme. Revital believes that women are catalysts for creating positive social change. She participated in Harvard University's programme 'Women and Power: Leadership in the New World'. Revital holds an MBA from the Haifa University, Israel.

Sharon hadn't finished her sandwich. She put the magazine down and stared out of the window as she took another bite. She was inspired. To see an HR manager writing about HR- and CSR-driven practices was quite an uplifting experience. Nirit Cohen was obviously a CSHR manager. She obviously knew how to leverage both elements of her role. Sharon was impressed with what she felt were fantastic examples of so many different aspects of CSHR — the manager-appraisal programme, near-site childcare centres, sabbaticals, variable pay based on environmental performance — so many interesting approaches to motivate employees so that they deliver more. She looked at her screen: 357 emails; 154 unread.

Sharon passed the magazine to her secretary, Carol, and asked her to photocopy the article and circulate it to all the HR team. 'Can you print on both sides of the paper?' she asked. 'Oh yes,' Carol said with a knowing smile. 'Haven't you noticed? I've been doing that for some time. All the secretaries do. We have to be conscious of the environment, you know.' Sharon was surprised and pleased but felt a little foolish. All this CSR brainwashing had been such a revelation to her, and here was her very own secretary preaching to her about the environment. Perhaps her company was more environmentally friendly than she thought. Perhaps she should not be so quick to judge, but should keep an open mind and ask what actually goes on.

One thing that had struck Sharon in the article she had read was the point about communications. It seemed to her that communications processes were critical to developing a CSR culture, and as HR Manager, she had responsibility for internal communications, though she knew that many HR colleagues did not. One of the things that had been big at ASTD in San Diego was the subject of internal communications, and she recalled having attended a couple of sessions and picking up some new insights, particularly about the use of social media in HR communications. It was interesting to hear the Intel HR Manager talk about Intel's social media channels, such as blogs, video blogs and online forums. These were tools that Andromex had not yet developed; in fact, the company didn't have a social media policy at all. The cornerstone of CSR, it seemed to her, was good internal communications, and the use of social media platforms seemed to her to be the way forward, not replacing personal contact or even traditional internal communications channels, but as a complement to that. She had been hearing a lot about this. She wondered how many of her HR team was already using social media, because she certainly couldn't pretend to be an expert herself. She also wondered about the connection between social media and CSR and thought there must be a connection that was more than random.

Sharon picked up her office phone and dialled Arena's number.

**Arena:** Hey, Sharon, great to hear from you. What news?

**Sharon:** News? Apart from the earthquake in Haiti?[3]

3  In January 2010, Haiti was affected by a massive earthquake near the capital Port-

**Arena:** Yes, apart from that. But since you mention that, did Andromex do anything to support the Relief Fund? At IFC, we sent around 15 containers' worth of food products and held an employee donation drive which the company matched. In total, our cash donations were over $1 million.

**Sharon:** Ah, no, we didn't do anything specific, actually. But I am thinking about our community involvement. I have been learning more about it and am looking forward to meeting with Carl Barton.

Sharon felt a little embarrassed. Perhaps she should have thought of initiating a discussion at ANDEX about how they might contribute to the Haiti Relief effort. She had to admit that, while she had sympathised with the situation, and felt extremely sorry for all those who were affected, those thoughts hadn't extended to organising a specific response by Andromex. This didn't seem to upset Arena.

**Arena:** Ah OK. Yes, Carl told me you had arranged to meet. He is looking forward to it too. He loves talking.

**Sharon:** Yes, you mentioned that. Anyway, I was calling to ask you about something else. I was wondering about the use of social media and CSR. I know communications is a core element of CSR in many ways, but I was wondering specifically what this means for the use of social media. It seems that social media can offer many new opportunities. I was sure you would know how to advise me on that.

**Arena:** Of course, social media is an essential tool for advancing the business in many ways, not just for CSR. Social media is used in marketing, customer service, even crowdsourcing new brand development and more.

**Sharon:** Crowdsourcing? What's that?

**Arena:** It's where a company opens up its technology or other aspect of its business and requests the general public to play a part in the development. It might be a technology, or a brand or even a cause marketing programme. Cause marketing, you know, where the company develops a marketing campaign that promotes the brand and contributes to the community simultaneously. Didn't you hear all the buzz about the Pepsi Refresh programme earlier this year? Pepsi took the bold decision not to spend huge amounts of advertising money, around $20 million, I think, at the Super Bowl, and instead used the cash to crowdsource a social campaign about ideas which make the world a better place in a range of categories such as health, education, arts and culture, food and shelter and others.

---

au-Prince. The earthquake devastated the city, leaving over 200,000 people dead, and over a million people homeless. During the following days and weeks after the earthquake, and its aftershocks, there was massive corporate support from businesses all over the world, donating money and resources, supporting medical treatment and more. Corporate donations reached over $140 million — a non-exhaustive list of examples were recorded by the Business Civic Leadership Center on their website www.uschamber.com/BCLC/Haiti_CorporateDonations, accessed 6 June 2010.

Each month, Pepsi awards grants up to $1.3 million to the winning ideas, which the public votes for. Take a look at the website — refresheverything dot com. They leveraged this through social media including a page on Facebook. I recall an article by Bonin Bough,[4] the Global Director of Digital and Social Media at Pepsi, in which he said that they received over 1,000 ideas in the first 72 hours. I am not sure how much the HR function had to do with developing this campaign, but just think of the ways HR could tap into this project and energise its own workforce, and not just the external world.

**Sharon:** Yes, I had seen something about that. Amazing initiative. How can I learn more about social media quickly, Arena? I want to complete my understanding of all aspects of CSR and how it interrelates with the HR role, and then pull a strategy together which I can recommend to my executive team. Communications is an important chunk of that, but I haven't got time to spend weeks studying this.

**Arena:** My recommendation would be to get a consultant in to talk to you. Someone who understands the world of social media and also the world of CSR. My recommendation would be to bring in Rona Parkville.[5] She is quite an expert. She works with Liam, whom you met in San Diego, at Ecoveg Café, remember?

**Sharon:** Oh, yes.

**Arena:** If I were you, I would invite Rona to come and give you and your HR team a presentation about the use of social media in business and in subjects related to CSR. You can reach her by email. I will forward it to you.

**Sharon:** Good, I will ask her to come in. The problem is that my team doesn't really know too much about CSR, so it might be a little over their heads.

**Arena:** Don't worry. Rona will be able to help you with that.

**Sharon:** OK, thanks. I will email her. Hope to see you in the office when I come to meet Carl.

**Arena:** Ah, I don't think I will be there. I have a regional meeting in Milan. But, after that, let's talk and arrange to meet, just the two of us. I'll be interested to hear how you are thinking about becoming a CSHR manager, and how I can help.

**Sharon:** Thanks, Arena. Sounds great! Have a good trip!

Sharon replaced the telephone receiver and immediately tuned to her laptop and punched out an email.

---

4  beth.typepad.com/beths_blog/2010/02/pepsi-refresh-project-an-insiders-view-guest-post-by-bonin-bough.html, accessed 6 June 2010.

5  Rona Parkville is a completely fictional character, invented by the author.

> From: Sharon Black <Sharon.Black@andromex.com>
> Subject: Social Media and CSR
> Date: 21/10/2010 14:32
> To: Rona Parkville <rona@parkville.com>
>
> Dear Rona,
>
> Arena Dardelle of IFC recommended I talk to you. I am the HR Manager at Andromex, a private software company employing 2,500 people. I have been thinking recently about CSR and would like to develop our approach to social media and its use in business and specifically in CSR communications. Arena thought that you might be able to give our HR team a lecture on this subject, so that we can first of all understand what the world of social media is all about, and how it applies to us as a business, and how it can be used to develop CSR awareness.
>
> I would like to do this fairly quickly. Can you be available some time during this month to do this? I was thinking of a lecture of about 2 hours, including time for questions. We are based in Bristol, a couple of hours west of London.
>
> Many thanks,
>
> Sharon Black
> HR Manager
> Andromex Ltd
> www.andromex.com

Send.

Good, Sharon thought, another step forward. Almost immediately, a reply pinged back onto her screen:

> From: Rona Parkville <rona@parkville.com>
> Subject: RE: Social Media and CSR
> Date: 21/10/2010 14:4
> To: Sharon Black <Sharon.Black@andromex.com>
>
> Hi Sharon,
>
> Thanks for getting in touch. I would be happy to come and lecture. Let's touch base by phone and agree expectations and fix a date. Please let me have a number I can call you on.
> Warm regards.
>
> Many thanks,
>
> Rona Parkville
> Sustainability Consulting Ltd
> rona@parkville.com

Sharon wrote back and later that day she and Rona had a telephone conversation about what Sharon wanted. They fixed a date for the session, two weeks hence. And, for the time being, Sharon put social media, CSR communications and all things related to those topics out of her mind, and concentrated on preparing an HR status report for her upcoming ANDEX meeting.

Days came and went, always busy, always interesting, always provoking Sharon into deep thought about her role and contribution. However, these days she was thinking about her contribution in a different way. Pre-Arena, as she called the period before she had boarded that flight, she had thought about her contribution in primarily two dimensions: how she led the HR function to contribute to the business, and how she led HR to contribute to the people. She had always through in terms of HR's role as building business capability and building individual capability. And even that seemed like a complex set of priorities to juggle with. Now, Sharon was continually asking herself about the wider contribution — the contribution beyond the business and the people to society, community and environment. She was continually checking with herself just where that boundary lay. She was thinking about the extent to which the HR role changes when it functions within a business that is CSR-minded, like Arena's company IFC, versus a business that is less CSR-oriented. She wondered which was harder, or more challenging, or more rewarding. One thing, Sharon felt, was that sooner or later it ceased being a question of choice and became a compelling imperative that was just the right way to do things, and not a conscious selection from a range of options. It was as though she had seen the light, though she was very wary of becoming too 'evangelistic' and preaching to everyone she came across. She found herself holding back from being too enthusiastic about suggesting CSR perspectives, and contented herself with asking the occasional question, making the occasional observation, circulating the occasional article. Until Sharon had clarified in her own mind just what her own role was, and what was right for the business, she didn't want to burn any of her boats.

Part of this internal search for answers prompted Sharon to do her own private survey.[6] In an burst of impulsive energy one evening, Sharon had constructed a brief survey and sent it to a range of HR colleagues, some of whom she knew well and some she had met just briefly. The survey was completed anonymously so she had no way of knowing who had responded to what. Sharon received 16 responses. Nine of the sixteen respondents claimed over ten years' HR experience — which Sharon thought brought some depth of perspec-

---

6  This was an actual survey conducted using SurveyMonkey.com, issued by the author in early 2010 via the Internet. There were 16 actual respondents and the responses indicated are the real responses by these respondents. In some cases, the author has slightly changed the wording to make it more legible, and had omitted a small number of irrelevant comments. However, all the data is correct. Participants came from Israel, the USA and Australia.

tive to their responses. Six of the sixteen worked for large public companies, and three for private companies. She recorded the results.

## HR Professionals Survey — Corporate Social Responsibility

**Question 1: As a human resources manager, what does the concept of corporate responsibility mean to you?**

**Responses to Question 1:**

- It means that as an organisation, you have the possibility to contribute to others

- That we should look at our environment and community, understand their needs and see where we can help and contribute

- The business organisation should act fairly. Today, community involvement is a key ingredient in HR services. It's part of the organisation culture to take ownership and leadership in projects related to our social community

- It means, in an HR sense, to consciously treat employees as valued assets, to be successful in making the workplace happy, efficient, law compliant and profitable. HR now also has a leadership role, especially in communications, to foster CSR awareness and provide opportunities to all to make a positive social and environmental impact within the company's sphere of influence

- It means that my organisation treats its employees fairly, contributes to the community in which it operates and also contributes to the empowerment of different populations

- Being accountable and highly responsive to all levels of the organisation and shareholders. It means all facets of business conducted are done in a responsible way. It also means that the company has the job of making sure it is above board in all transactions and that it undertakes initiatives that give back to employees, shareholders and the community at large.

- Dealing with the issues of quality of work life and environment, improving company results by enhancing human and employee rights

- For me, being a responsible company is one of the most important aspects of being a sustainable company which will appeal to employees.

- All employees are trained annually and told that unethical behaviour in the organisation will not be tolerated. Also, the customer service initiative makes interaction with clients very transparent

- Corporations are responsible for their employees, their shareholders and their customers to provide them the proper service or product that was promised

- Sustainability

- I am a CSR and Sustainability consultant as well, so besides a way of living it means a constant effort to assist companies in making a 'switch' in their form of thinking and bring new ideas and best practices to companies
- As a leading company that works in an advanced technology environment, we choose to focus on technology and education, in order to give a better chance to children and youth in our neighbourhood
- To support programmes that put education, job readiness and workplace training within the reach of everyone. We would like to give people a rod and not just a fish
- Involvement beyond the traditional boundaries of business, encompassing engagement with a range of both internal and external stakeholders

### Question 2: Does the role of HR Manager require an understanding of corporate social responsibility?

### Responses to Question 2:

16 (100%) responded yes.

### Question 3: In your HR role, do you have specific responsibilities to progress elements of the company's corporate responsibility programme?

| Responses to Question 3 | Number of responses | Percentage of respondents |
| --- | --- | --- |
| Yes, it is part of my ongoing role | 8 | 53% |
| Yes, relating to specific projects or initiatives | 5 | 33% |
| Yes, but only relating to internal communication of CR | 1 | 7% |
| No, it is not part of my role | 1 | 7% |
| Total | 15 | 100% |

### Question 4: Beyond HR core policies and practices, what elements of corporate responsibility practices of the business are you involved in as part of your role as human resources manager? (Please check all that apply)

| Responses to Question 4 | Number of responses | Percentage of respondents |
| --- | --- | --- |
| Ethics | 12 | 75% |
| Community involvement | 12 | 75% |
| Customer service | 8 | 50% |
| Environmental protection | 6 | 37.5% |

| Responses to Question 4 | Number of responses | Percentage of respondents |
|---|---|---|
| Corporate governance | 8 | 31.3% |
| External communications | 5 | 31.3% |
| Cause marketing | 3 | 18.8% |
| Product development and innovation | 2 | 12.5% |
| CSR reporting | 1 | 6.3% |
| External stakeholder engagement | 0 | 0 |
| Supply chain practices | 0 | 0 |

**Question 5: Do you believe that HR Managers need special or new skills to support the CSR strategy and practices of the business? If yes, please provide your insights below.**

**Responses to Question 5:**

- They should have CSR skills
- Yes, if they want to do it in a professional way
- They do not necessarily need new skills since much of CSR can be learned on the job. However, I think the executives who hire HR managers should look for individuals who are aware of CSR and have the personality and propensity to be open minded to integrating CSR into HR or building on what is already there. Ideally, you would want to hire someone who has solid HR skills and CSR job experience (a tall order though!)
- Basic training needed for HR staff:
- Basic instruction on sustainability/CSR and where HR Managers should be involved
- Conscious leadership training
- Going beyond law compliance and benefits of HR innovation
- Corporate philanthropy and volunteerism (many company's do not have a separate dept for this and rely on HR to execute)
- Internal CSR functions, programmes, goals
- Some may and some may not. It would depend on the individual's needs
- No, what they need are negotiation skills to deal with objections to implementing CSR in the organisation
- They need to deeply believe in the company values
- Yes, HR managers need to understand how corporate social responsibility is part of their and everyone's job. This could be in the form of business training, marketing and public relations
- Yes, business understanding
- No

- Yes, I think they need skills and tools that will help them in viewing the company through a prism that is wider than HR, i.e. understand the brand, the marketing strategy, the focus on triple bottom line, etc.
- More exposure to the regulations
- Web
- Yes. Strategic networking competencies; capacity to work cross-functionally

**Question 6: Is any part of your performance evaluation linked to your activities relating to the Corporate Responsibility programme of the business?**

| Responses to Question 6: | Number of responses | Percentage of respondents |
|---|---|---|
| Yes, I have specific CSR targets | 5 | 31.3% |
| Yes, my CSR activities are reviewed in my annual performance review | 1 | 6.3% |
| Partially: it is discussed but not specifically measured or recorded in my performance evaluation | 4 | 25% |
| No, I am only evaluated on my HR performance | 4 | 37.4% |
| Total | 14 | 100% |

Sharon looked at these results and tried to see if there were any insights she could gain. The most interesting result, she felt, was that 100% of the respondents said that HR managers needed to have an understanding of CSR. Clearly, the respondents, other HR managers like herself, believed that CSR was here to stay, and that it was important enough to require them to understand its implications for the business. The second thing she noticed was that most of the CSR activity of HR managers was related to ethics or community involvement. This indicated to her, based on what she had already learnt, that CSR was still very embryonic as part of the HR role. Ethics and community involvement were the two basic areas of CSR that most companies embrace as a first stage. She noted that 13 HR managers had said that they have some form of CSR responsibility but that only five of these had specific targets relating to CSR. Finally, the other point she noticed was that there was a wide variety of responses relating to what HR managers needed to know in order to be effective CSR partners.

Sharon thought this was interesting, especially the fact that all HR managers said they should understand CSR but only some of them had CSR-related responsibilities and targets. She realised that if she wanted to develop a CSR programme for Andromex, she would have to ensure that all the HR team had adequate CSR knowledge and skills to play their role.

$\sim$

It was Wednesday at 9.30 a.m. Rona had arrived and set up her presentation and most of the HR team had arrived. Sharon opened up the day by referring to the need for the HR team to think long term, think about the future of work and the key drivers of change and the implications for HR strategy. She referred briefly to CSR, defining it as the way the company does business to deliver both business gain as well as positive social and environmental impact. She knew her team wasn't very well versed in this concept, but she had been routing all sorts of information and articles on this subject to them over the past couple of weeks, and had had separate conversations with many of the team. Sharon felt they were beginning to understand. Sharon welcomed Rona, explained that she would introduce herself, and Rona took the floor.

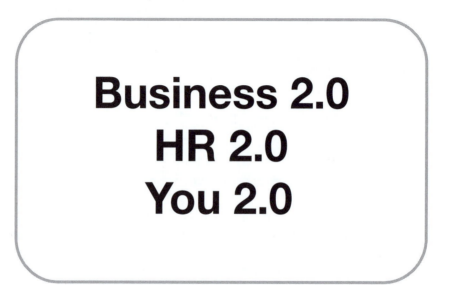

Good morning, everybody! Thank you to Sharon for inviting me to talk about my favourite subjects. We have a long session today, at Sharon's request, in which I want to present some thoughts about the way business is evolving, and the way Web 2.0 is changing the landscape of business, and the implications of all of this for HR and for the individuals in the organisation. In doing so, we will look at the concept of CSR and how that fits into the mix. I am not going to go into a lot of detail about the broad business use of Web 2.0; that's something you can get from your Marketing people, and from general independent research on the Internet. The Internet really is a place you can learn anything. Web 2.0 as it is commonly called, is the opening up of the Internet to allow interaction and participation in many forms and channels. It's the personalisation of the Internet, where anyone can create content and share it with the world. Bloggers have become almost as important as journalists; some might say more important. Peer-created brand development has made traditional brand agencies partially redundant. Customer service is now more instant and more personal.

We should have plenty of time for discussion, so don't hesitate to ask questions throughout my talk. I have structured this session to give you a broad range of insights regarding the way business communications are changing, and what that means for HR. I won't use too many examples, in the interests of time, so that we can cover the main points in the course of the next couple of hours. After this introduction to the subject, you and Sharon can decide what further training needs you might have. Anyway, first, let me introduce myself, and then I would like you to introduce yourselves.

I have had over 20 years of business experience, most of which has been with multinationals. I have worked in Marketing, Corporate Affairs and Strategic Business Development. I formed my CSR consulting practice about five years ago, and I specialise in CSR communications, especially via social media. I am married with two cute but noisy children, have a passion for social justice and ice cream.

Rona paused as the HR team all introduced themselves and their roles at Andromex. One asked why Rona hadn't brought some ice cream if she was so passionate about it. Rona promised to do so next time, thanked them, and then continued.

# Business 2.0

## The infinite possibilities of fast, global, accessible connectivity

The bottom line is that businesses need to sell their services in order to survive. Ideally, they should make a profit. But first, they need to reach their customers. The opening up of the World Wide Web has done two things: first, it has enabled businesses to reach customers directly, immediately, all over the world, and second, it has enabled the possibility of interaction with customers — direct dialogue. I attended a talk by Biz Stone, the founder of Twitter, some months ago, and he said that one of the first uses of Twitter was by a small bakery who tweeted immediately a new batch of loaves was being taken out of the oven. This led to people flocking to his bakery store in droves as soon as the bread was ready. That bakery's business increased massively due to this simple, direct way of reaching customers using social media. By the way, Web 2.0 is the name that is used to refer to the second generation of the Internet, which is interactive and collaborative, far more than the first generation, which was mainly about pushing information out. People are even starting to talk now about Web 3.0, which is more about opening up programming interfaces and allowing people to create new tools and be much more personalised with applications that meet your very specific personal needs. As our discussion is about social media and interaction and connectivity, we will stay with the concept of Web 2.0.

There is nothing — well, almost nothing — that you can't do online these days. Over ten years ago, I used to play bridge on Yahoo! It never ceased to amaze me that I could log into the Games area and join a table with live people, each playing in the comfort of their own homes in different corners of the globe, engaging in conversation, forming friendships and maintaining a virtual interaction over a game of bridge. Later, I went on holiday to the USA and met several of the players I had met virtually online. It was as though they were old friends that I had known all my life. The power of the digital era to connect all sorts of people who would have never otherwise met is incredible. That's what is happening in business. The power of businesses to reach so many customers through so many different applications of digital media is simply mind-blowing. Businesses all over the globe, large and small, are harnessing this power creatively, innovatively, and with great success.

How many businesses do you know now that only trade online? How many businesses use online commerce as an addition to their physical retail outlets? Think of almost any retail store. I do my grocery shopping online, for instance, and it all gets delivered to my home within a few hours. I just wish they would empty all the packages and stock it in the refrigerator and cupboards as well! How many businesses don't have a website, today? If you don't have a website, you are invisible. More businesses are writing corporate blogs and using social networks such as Facebook and microblogs such as Twitter to leverage their communications. Many use these fast, instant communication channels to interact with customers directly and provide immediate solutions to customer service problems. Many have been alerted to customer service problems via online complaints and have had the opportunity to address them. Businesses use online PR to get their message out further. Traditional newspaper circulation has been in decline for the last few years. Think about what that has done to the job market and the change of skills required. It is not the purpose of my presentation here to go into detail about how this is happening. Our focus will be the implications of this digital revolution for business culture and human resources management, and the individuals in your business. But in these tip-of-the-iceberg examples, there is already a wealth of change that I think you can appreciate.

What does all this mean for HR and HR communications?

# HR 2.0
# The digitisation of HR!

- Need for more digitally skilled employees
- New virtual working formats
- Transactional HR – greater digitisation and personal ownership of HR data
- Online recruitment – now commonplace
- Employees are linked to *all* stakeholder groups via multiple digital platforms
- More information about employers *and* employees available on the Internet
- New possibilities for web-based internal and external communication platforms
- New ethical issues

**The new digital perspective of HR**

**–**

**Optimise digital employee engagement**

The future of work is changing, not only because of Web 2.0 but also largely as a result of the new accessibility and connectivity that Web 2.0 has made possible. No HR team can ignore the implications of this for their business. Even small businesses stand to gain significantly by welcoming the digital age and leveraging it in their business, perhaps even more than large ones. All of this has far-reaching impacts on the HR function and the way it does its job. If traditionally the HR function has been about building the capability of the organisation and of individuals, and supporting the development of an appropriate organisational culture, now this is equally about building the digital capability of the organisation and the appropriate culture within a digital framework. Don't get me wrong. Andromex is a software business. This is close to your core competences. But I am talking about all businesses. This is relevant to every single business, even if their core skill is remote from digital processes. No company, small or large, can let Web 2.0 and its implications for the way people work, communicate, collaborate, learn, develop and act pass by without making the relevant adjustments to structure, staff, systems and culture. That is, if they want to stay on the radar and even make some money.

As an HR team, you have to judge the scale of this intervention for your regular HR processes. As a very minimum, you yourselves have to enhance your awareness of the way the nature of business is changing and the implications for Andromex. This will govern your creation of a new partially digital HR strategy which will support the new business strategy. You might call it HR 2.0.

But Web 2.0, Business 2.0 and HR 2.0 are not the only things that have been happening in the past few years. Before I move to focus on the communication implications, risks and opportunities, I wanted to look at the concept of CSR and how that is also having an impact on the nature of conversations and relationships that business are building on Web 2.0 and Business 2.0 platforms.

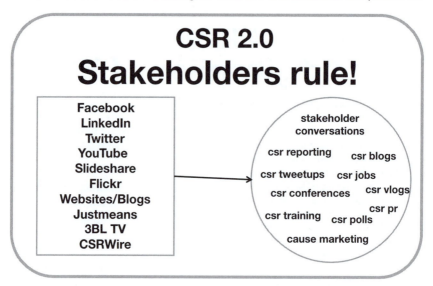

The concept of CSR relates to a company's responsibility, accountability and transparency. This requires platforms for dialogues with all stakeholders. The opening up of the web has progressively made this dialogue possible and enabled processes and practices specifically related to CSR that were not possible before. Companies are communicating their CSR, using cause marketing to deliver business results with social and environmental benefits, participating in virtual CSR conferences, webcasts and podcasts and webinars, or in CSR training events. Cisco technology such as Webex conferencing services makes it possible for anyone in the world to attend a conference, see a set of slides, ask questions and join in the conversation. Companies are even writing CSR blogs. Look at CSR@Intel[7] or FedEx citizenship blog,[8] for example. As companies drive CSR and sustainability programmes, they are opening themselves up much more to dialogue via social media and Web 2.0.

In a way, social media has become a catalyst for communications in general and for CSR communications specifically. Given that CSR is, or should be, a core element of business strategy, we are progressively seeing general business communications becoming flavoured with CSR messages, or alternatively, more and more CSR-related messages being pushed out there and generating reactions. The Zipcar Company has a CSR room on their website which is dedicated to news about their impacts and CSR activities.[9] We are seeing much more user-generated content by company employees in the CSR space than ever before. Many more internal resources are required to support the collective external communications impact, fielding many different kinds of communications on a number of fronts simultaneously. More employees are necessary not just to get the message *across*, as has been the case in traditional media platforms, but also to get the message *through*. How do you know the message has got through? Social media gives you very quick measurable feedback — people respond, people follow, people ask, people react. ANY reaction you generate via social media means that you are getting through to your stakeholders. More and more employees are engaging in those conversations. As this happens, we are seeing the convergence of *internal* and *external* communications. More messages are more transparent to more stakeholders, and more people are more involved in creating more content. No longer can HR content itself with an internal newsletter, or an intranet platform which is disconnected from the outside world.

CSR reports are a measure of how difficult it is to achieve this balance. The CSR or sustainability report is designed to provide a review of the entire spectrum of company performance in terms of sustainability for any stakeholder that has an interest. This may include stakeholders who have historically been interested only in one aspect of the company's business — the financial results, the employment practices, or the customer offering and so on. More and more, we are seeing multi-stakeholder interest — an employee might be a shareholder, and a local community member, and an environmental activist, and a disabled war veteran. His or her interest may go well beyond that of a single-dimensional employer–employee relationship. CSR reports have not managed to achieve this balance very well, on the whole, as despite the objective, finding the right pitch, style, tone and balance of content which will appeal to such a broad range of stakeholders is not an easy task. Let's put this all together in terms of HR communications.

Before our very eyes, we are seeing the convergence of the corporate communications architecture.

7  blogs.intel.com/csr, accessed 6 June 2010.
8  citizenshipblog.fedex.designcdt.com, accessed 6 June 2010.
9  zipcar.csrroom.com.

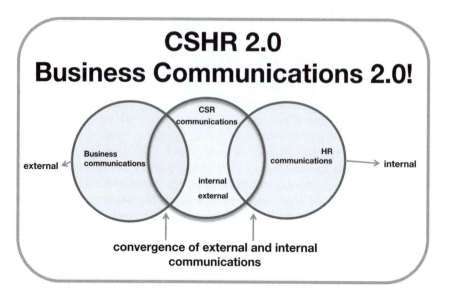

This is complex, I know, so let's take it a little more slowly. I am going to run through that flow again.

- In order to compete, in today's connected world, an organisation must play well in the digital space

- Transparency, which was once demanded by only regulatory or owner-ship bodies (governments and shareholders), is now demanded by a wider range of stakeholders

- In addition, companies can no longer control the reach of information that circulates about them or their actions, as information reaches large audiences anyway through the Internet

- Corporate communications strategy must take this into account. Typi-cally, corporate communications are now including much more CSR-type content

- As this happens, corporations must mobilise a much larger proportion of their workforce to engage in communications which may include direct stakeholder contact

- In order for this to be effective, total consistency between internal and external communications must be achieved

- HR communications, which typically were focused on an internal popula-tion, now risk being totally transparent to all stakeholders. So again, such communications must be consistent with those messages that external stakeholders are hearing from the business communicators

- This is what we mean by convergence. There is no difference any more between internal and external communications

- And finally, as more employees are needing to engage in this process, the organisation culture of ethics, responsibility, transparency and accountability must be completely assimilated at all levels of the organisation. This requires HR strategy to ensure employees have the tools, skills, knowledge and capabilities of becoming the organisation's digital ambassadors

- This spans the entire business communications cycle and its relation to CSR. In order to develop successful digital ambassadors, CSR needs to be effectively embedded. In order to embed CSR, digital tools are key. This is all part of the same story

I want to pause here to see if that's clear, before we look at some of the specific strategy elements and tools that can be used within the Social Media range of options. Are there any questions at this point?

Several HR team members indicated that they wanted to ask a question. Rona took the questions one by one.

**HR team member:** Rona, I understand what you are saying. We always try to ensure our external communications items are available to employees, but they are very different types of communication. Isn't the first rule of communication to tailor your communication to your audience? If the company is putting out new product information, it needs to formulate this with the customer in mind, not the employer. How can convergence be achieved if people need different messages?

**Rona:** Great point. In the past, we played by the rules of the past. I maintain that these rules are changing now, and customers do not exist in isolation from all other stakeholder groups. It is possible that a customer may be a relative of an employee, or a neighbour, or a former employer. People talk. People pass on information. There needs to be consistency in all internal and external messages. The essence of the company values and principles need to be reflected in all communications. One voice should apply internally and externally. That's not to say that some audiences might require different levels of detail, which can be offered separately from core communications messages. But if you think about it, you have an engaged, motivated, interested workforce, particularly one that is digitised, hooked in to various social media channels; there is absolutely no risk in ensuring everyone has the same message. Indeed, the more your employees are treated like your customers, the better ambassadors they will be, digitally or otherwise.

**HR team member:** But Rona, maybe you are talking about companies who market retail brands to mass consumers and therefore need to have a visible presence in the marketplace. We are a small software firm. We have a limited number of business customers. We don't sell to private individuals. Surely this is going a little too far.

**Rona:** Yes, that's usually a question I get about CSR in general. Small companies, or private companies, or business-to-business companies tend to think it doesn't apply to them. But nothing could be further from the truth. Remember who your stakeholders are. You have no idea of knowing what other connections your customers have to other stakeholders. You are also operating in a local community, recruiting from local communities, impacting on the local environment. All of these factors mean that you are probably more transparent than you think, and more vulnerable to stakeholder influence than you think. The more you leverage the power of your workforce in supporting your company's mission internally **and** externally, the more effective your company will be. There is another advantage too – and that is that your workforce becomes empowered, employees become more motivated. Instead of just doing their job, they are part of the corporate information flow and feel a shared responsibility. Of course, this assumes that the company is treating them with respect and decency. A good values-driven ethic is essential for any of this to happen.

**HR team member:** Suppose we accept what you are saying, that internal and external communications must be aligned, what does this mean for HR? Should we stop dealing with communications and leave it to the PR professionals?

**Rona:** Another great question. Not every company positions internal communications with HR. There are many companies who have communications professionals running one department where internal and external communications are managed in sync. There is no single answer. However, where there are two functions driving the communications strategy and practice, Corporate Affairs or Marketing and HR, then these must work in close synchronicity to ensure 100% alignment. There are always specific and separate internal and external communications that need to be generated. Your employee handbook, for example. That's not something you automatically publish to your shareholders (though personally, I can't see why such a document could not be in the public domain). Basically, an internal communicator needs to think with an external hat on and self-check at every step of the way regarding what would happen if internal communications were made public? And an external communicator must think with an internal hat on and self-check the other way, asking what would happen if an external communication was distributed internally. In designing an employee handbook for internal purposes you must consider the external stakeholder who might see it by accident. We often do this intuitively, but the 2.0 world requires us to think deeper about this. In addition, both internal and external communicators should think about gaining maximum leverage from all stakeholders with every communication.

In a global high-tech business I consult to, internal 'green' communications are outstanding – green is all over their intranet, there are posters on the walls, letters from VPs, internal messages when the latest ISO 14000 audit is successful and more. Technical development processes include comprehensive procedures for including environmental considerations in new product design. It's really impressive. But when I looked at their external website targeted primarily at customers and investors, I could find almost no reference to their 'green' positioning. So what about all the potential environmentally conscious employees that would like to join this company? What about local communities that are worried about carbon emissions from their distribution systems? What about the local community that now has an expectation of environmentally responsible behaviour of businesses? Wouldn't it be advantageous to have all these stakeholders see the 'green' activity of the company on the corporate website? Similarly, customers appreciate purchasing from environmentally responsible suppliers because it makes their own responsibility shine a little more. Investors give extra points for environmental responsibility because such a business is seen to be more sustainable. Clearly their HR team is passionate about 'green', and is doing a great job of buzzing that up internally. But the corporate communicators are ignoring that as far as external stakeholders are concerned. What a wasted opportunity. The same internal 'green' newsletter that goes to employees should be available to all stakeholders. Maybe, just maybe, a potential customer might see that an internal team led by his brother-in-law is doing great things for the environment. Stranger things have happened. Business is personal. People want to know who is behind a business, not just what the business is offering. Making business more personal by making communications more aligned and more available to everyone creates more personal connections that weave in and out of the traditional boundaries of the business. That's a great opportunity.

**HR team member:** Yes, Rona, but it's also a great risk. Why should we publish our employee handbook, so that our competitors can copy it or criticise it? Why should we give details of our employees so that headhunters can approach them? Why should we bother employees with formal announcements to shareholders when we want them to focus on their work without having to understand the complexities of stock markets? Surely, too much transparency is risky?

**Rona:** Good. I love being challenged. Your thinking is spot on. As far as it goes. Think about it further. What are the risks? Someone might criticise your employee handbook? What if they are right? They did you a service. Someone might copy it? What if they do? It's not the handbook that determines your business success, it's the way you develop your culture and processes and relate to your people. The fact that someone takes a handbook, or a code of ethics, or any other internal document and copy-pastes with their own logo will not help them. First, they are missing out on the process that is essential to generating internal commitment and second, they do not necessarily have the tools to ensure implementation in alignment with something they have just copied. What about headhunting?

I looked at Alcoa's website recently. They have a page on the site[10] dedicated to employee insights and quotations about sustainability. Around a hundred of them, I think, with their pictures, job titles and quotations. An open invitation to headhunters. Didn't they think of that before they posted that page? Maybe they did, maybe they didn't. But let's face it. Any employee worth headhunting almost certainly knows his or her way around the World Wide Web, and almost certainly has about 20 different profiles on networking sites, and almost certainly is ripe for the picking whether or not he or she appears in a company communication. So what retains employees? Not hiding them. My view is that exposing them is a stronger motivation for them to stay with a company. Giving them their own corporate webpage shows them how well respected they are, and empowers them to be better company ambassadors. There are always exceptions to this rule, of course, but by and large, the risk is there anyway.

And finally, you suggest that ensuring employees understand the messages to shareholders and external stakeholders could risk diverting them from the focus on their work. In my experience, the most common failing of businesses is precisely that they don't ensure their employees are informed about what's going on in the external reality of the business. By talking to them about business results, shareholder reactions, anything that can affect how the company is being viewed externally is in my view about treating your employees as partners, giving them respect and ensuring they are aware of what is driving decisions in the business. Done well, internal communications of this nature can be a major empowering and motivating force in the culture of the business.

**HR team member:** Is it all that easy — just put everything out there and see what happens?

**Rona:** Ah no, transparency has to be managed and this does require effort and investment. There is potential for significant harm to the business if communications are not formulated with due care and attention. First, all communications must be carefully thought through and executed. Second, the company must be consistent. You can't cherry-pick the good bits of news and leave out the tougher messages, and you can't communicate one week and skip the next. Third, the company needs to be prepared for all eventualities including unfounded attacks on the company's integrity or radical suggestions from extreme thinkers that even though they may be totally off-the-wall, must be responded to. Like the time that the animal protection NGO, PETA (People for Ethical Treatment of Animals)[11] suggested that Ben & Jerry's use breast milk in their ice cream instead of cow's milk. They were serious but no one could take that suggestion seriously, of course. However, it needed a response. Fourth, there needs to be a lot of internal work to generate alignment and understanding across

10  www.alcoa.com/sustainability/en/employees.asp, accessed 6 June 2010.
11  www.peta.org.uk.

the company. Yes, of course there are risks, and I would recommend increasing levels of transparency gradually rather than the short, sharp shock approach. On balance, though, through the long term, it is my firm belief that managed transparency pays, and those companies that behave transparently seem to succeed over time.

**Sharon:** I think we ought to move on, now. There will be more time for questions at the end.

**Rona:** Fine. This has been a great discussion. I see your HR team is right on the ball, Sharon.

**Sharon:** You are doing well that they are all still awake.

Rona flipped to the next slide and continued her presentation.

# CSHR 2.0 communications[12]

"... the best practices that define success in social media and in CR are one and the same: The key driver is transparent, authentic, and engaging communication with all constituents. While the barrier to entry is low, the price of not participating is quite the opposite."

See this quotation? I am not the only one who thinks like me. Just in case you still have any doubts. See this chart as well.

12  Paul Argenti, 'Corporate Responsibility and Social Media', *Ethisphere* (24 February 2010), ethisphere.com/corporate-responsibility-and-social-media, accessed 9 June 2010.

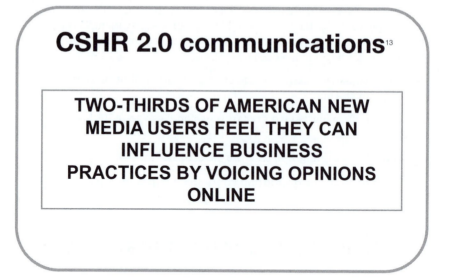

Given that the world of work is changing, and that HR needs to align itself with the new work reality, and encourage a culture where digitalisation is the norm, what do HR Managers need to think about? Let's look at what is being communicated in and by the organisation.

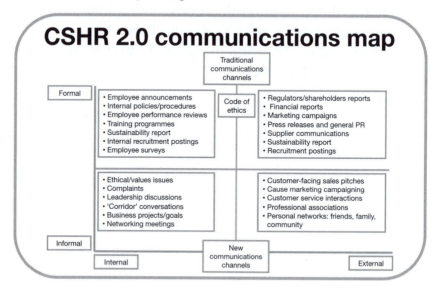

What does this chart tell us? On the vertical axis we are looking at the split between formal and informal communications. On the horizontal axis, we have what is traditionally split between internal and external communications.

Formal/external are the traditional communications that have an external focus and that are not generally communicated internally. Formal/internal are those employee types of communication that are not usually communicated externally. The formal communications are usually spread via traditional channels — printed press, TV, brochures and booklets, posters, notice boards, and I include email and electronic documentation in the 'traditional' category because it has been around long enough to be part of the standard repertoire in any business. The company has a good degree of control over these forms of communication.

Informal/external are those conversations which all employees have with the outside world through sales, customer service, involvement in professional associations, conferences and networks, word-of-mouth promotion of company marketing activities and so on. Some might be consumer-facing interactions, some might be personal interactions with an employee's diverse networks. It's what employees are saying about the company to anyone outside the company, even if they are doing this as part of their job as customer service representatives, etc.

Informal/internal is what employees are saying to each other about the company. This is the informal water-cooler chats, meetings outside work, planned or unplanned, complaints about things or people in the company, discussions about the process of business projects or company performance. Typically, the company has little control over these forms of communication and can only hope that employees are sufficiently engaged, aware of the company principles and business objectives and positive towards the company so as to make each of these informal interactions one which advances the company. Each of these interactions is an opportunity for the company. It's HR's job to deliver processes which enable and promote this. The vital importance of values is what brings HR into the arena of CSR. This is where the role of HR becomes so complex. Influencing something you have no control over. Enabling a culture in which most of these informal interactions will be positive and developmental for the company and reflect the company's core values at all times.

The formal/internal communications are easy and this is what HR departments usually excel at. Printed brochures, announcements, glossy booklets — these are all usually developed to perfection, though the degree to which HR departments ascertain to what extent they are assimilated or used is generally low.

You will note that the corporate code of ethics is usually one of the formal company communications that is communicated internally and externally. There are very few others.

---

com/news/request.php?id=2614, accessed 9 June 2010.

**HR team member:** What about the annual financial report?

**Rona:** In general, most companies do not make efforts to communicate this internally. It is externally available and employees can view it if they wish, but most companies do not make sure employees see it. At best, there is an annual performance review meeting to which managers are invited at which the CEO presents the headline results. That's my experience, anyway.

To continue, what you should note about this chart is that most of the formal communications take place in traditional media. This is slowly changing but, in general, this is still the case. Most of the informal communications take place in the new media channels. I will describe those in a few minutes.

What is the challenge here? You note that I said the company has high control over formal communications, but low control over informal communications. The challenge for HR is to create an environment where more informal communication is within the organisation's control. By that, I don't mean telling people what to say. But I do mean bringing these conversations into an open space, which is more visible to more people within the company, so that issues can be addressed as they arise. I mean that informal communications should become more transparent. Suppose a manager is complaining about a certain company policy. If he does this to a friend, or to a colleague, the manager may not get a balanced response and the complaint may stay in his mind, possibly shaking his motivation for a while at least. If this same complaint is made in a communication channel which is open and safe, the company can (a) know what's bothering this manager, and (b) address the issue in a constructive way. The new media channels give HR the tools to move informal communication into an open, collaborative, constructive space. Similarly, if these new media channels are used for both internal and external communications, we have for the first time a possibility to fully align our communications as a company, and understand what is being said to and by all stakeholders, face the issues that arise boldly, and gain greater reach for the positive messages. Does that make sense to you?

The HR team was concentrating hard on this. It was rather new to them. They needed some time to see if they agreed. There were a few nods around the room, and Rona chose to keep going.

Let's look at these new media communications options and we'll come back to the concept in a second.

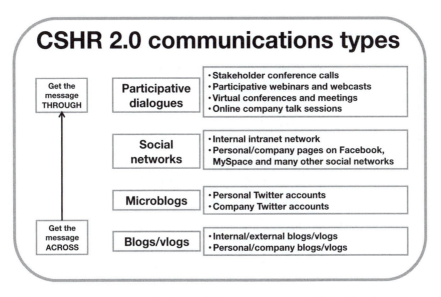

There are many categorisations of the way new social media channels are used, and this is my own version. You will probably find many other representations. What you can see here is the way the use of social media develops from a kind of *push* action — writing a blog post, pushing information out into the blogosphere, to a kind of *pull* action — generating sufficient interest such that both internal and external stakeholders will want to participate in interactive and participative dialogues. The more of this that is out in the open in transparent frameworks that the company representatives and digital ambassadors are a part of, the more the company stands to gain from these interactions. In general, as you go from push to pull, you increase the development of relationships between people — often between company employees and external stakeholders. This gives the company a personal face and creates an emotional bond which, if managed correctly, works in the company's interest in the long term. So as you pull, and as you develop stakeholder relationships, you also influence stakeholder thinking, ensuring your message gets through, rather than just getting across.

**HR team member:** What's a vlog?

**Rona:** A vlog is a blog on video. More companies are using short video films to provide their news to stakeholders. More companies post to YouTube today than ever before. More employees are making videos and posting them to YouTube and Vimeo and other platforms. People want to see people.

Let me give you a few brief examples and then I think we should stop and discuss a little what all this means for HR.

As you can see from the above headings, everyone is doing something: 22% of Fortune 500 Companies had blogs in 2009 and 45% of the Inc. 500, which are the fastest growing private companies in the USA; 19% of the 2009 Fortune 500 are podcasting and 31% are using video on their blog sites; 35% of companies in the Fortune 500 had an active Twitter account in 2009. This data is from research published in 2010, conducted by Dr Nora Ganim Barnes of the University of Massachusetts Dartmouth and Eric Mattson, CEO of Financial Insite.[14] They used a small group of companies. If we broadened out the research to include medium-sized and smaller companies, I believe the figures would be much higher. We don't have time to go into all these examples one by one, but you can look them all up on the Internet and form your own opinions. Perhaps I will just highlight one of the best CSR blogs: Intel.[15] The CSR blog is actually only one of a set of themed blogs on the Blogs@Intel website. It is frequently updated by employees who talk freely about their experiences and insights related to new Intel products or initiatives, market trends, report on attendance at conferences or events, or, something that is most popular, their experiences in Intel corporate volunteering programmes. This is an impressive way of leveraging employees in the business to spread the Intel message. The employees that write for the blog reinforce their own engagement in doing so. In the case of Timberland, the company CEO is personally very active as a blogger and a Tweeter. Pepsi used the Internet to solicit submissions for their

14 Nora Ganim Barnes and Eric Mattson, 'The Fortune 500 and Social Media: A Longitudinal Study of Blogging and Twitter Usage by America's Largest Companies' (2010), www.umassd.edu/cmr/studiesresearch/2009F500.pdf, accessed 6 June 2010.

15 blogs.intel.com/csr, accessed 6 June 2010.

charitable-giving programme. I could go on forever about this. The point is that communications are changing from one-directional delivery of information to multi-participant conversations and dialogues. The culture of a business needs to change to support this, and the values of CSR need to be clearly embedded for it to be effective and reduce risk. Change management processes are what HR is all about. How many of you have a private Facebook account?

Around half the hands in the room went up.

How many of you have a LinkedIn account?

Around a quarter of the hands in the room went up.

How many have a Twitter account?

Around a third of the hands in the room went up.

Of those of you who have Twitter and Facebook and LinkedIn accounts, how many of you have used these accounts to promote something related to Andromex?

Very few of the total account holders' hands went up.

How many more Andromex employees are doing this? What would it take for you to engage more of your employees in social media to build awareness for Andromex and contribute to Andromex's positive reputation?

I'm going to stop here for now. I want to leave you with this thought. The business environment is changing. It's becoming more digitised. The HR function needs to change to ensure it delivers the right business and individual capabilities to keep pace with digitisation. As CSR becomes more embedded, so HR has a role to play in supporting the way the company communicates with employees and the way employees communicate with all stakeholders. And you too, the HR team at Andromex, need to start changing in order to be able to lead the way.

Thanks to you all for listening and for your questions. I think we have a few more minutes if you would like to discuss anything. I am going to leave you with some guidance about how to develop a social media strategy and a social media HR policy.

Everyone clapped. Sharon stood up.

**Sharon:** Thank you Rona so much for that fascinating overview. I certainly learnt a lot from your presentation and I am sure the HR team did too. I admit to not having made the plunge into social media myself, and to having had little knowledge of the way it can be leveraged in the business. Also, I hadn't realised what HR benefits there are in encouraging use of social media among employees. I am sure that your recommendations make a lot of sense. We will be working over the next few weeks to develop a proposal for a CSR strategy and that should include social media. I hope my colleagues on our executive team will be receptive. In the meantime, thank you very much.

Everyone clapped again. One of the HR team wanted to ask a question and put up her hand. Rona nodded.

**Questioner:** Rona, it really does sound fascinating, thank you. The thing that is bothering me though is the time all of this takes. I use Facebook and Twitter. I do it in the evenings when I have time, not at work. Just keeping up with friends takes forever. I follow the HR streams on Twitter, and just keeping up with the things that are posted means you have to be online every day. I tried to write a personal blog about my hobby, photography, but I gave up after a burst of about six posts because I just couldn't make the time to keep it up. How can we expect our employees to do the same? This is a major drain on people's time, and everyone is always so busy as it is.

**Rona:** Yes, that's another great point. The beauty of blogging and tweeting in a corporate context is that the burden is shared. One corporate tweet account can be managed by several users. One corporate blog can have several contributors. However, there does need to be a single digital communications coordinator or manager who is responsible for driving the implementation in a consistent and continuous way. Most companies have someone doing that as a full-time job or at least part time. Some companies use an external communications company or freelance consultant to help them. Certainly there is an issue with individuals in the workplace and their use of social networks and this needs to be encouraged but appropriately managed.

Sharon was delighted. Her team seemed to have understood the message and she felt positive energy in the room. It had been a while since she had brought them a new, innovative topic to discuss, and she felt a little excitement as they walked out of the conference room, talking about tweeting and profile pictures on Facebook and other things related to the lecture they had just heard. Rona declined to stay for lunch as she had another appointment and thanked Sharon for the opportunity to come and present to her team. Sharon felt that she had closed another gap in her CSR knowledge, and she was looking forward to her trip to IFC so that she could develop her understanding of employee volunteer programmes.

# 10
# Employee involvement in the community[1]

Sharon was excited. Today was the day for her visit to International Food Company Ltd, Arena's company. She was to meet Carl Barton, the Employee Volunteering Programme Manager who oversaw IFC's global volunteering programme at a policy level and was very much involved, so Arena said, in local volunteer work in the UK. After a pleasant train journey to London, a rather less pleasant, stressful ride on the Underground and a short walk, Sharon arrived at IFC Head Office. Her name was displayed on a large plasma screen in the entrance: 'Welcome to Sharon Black of Andromex'. That made her feel quite at home.

Carl Barton collected Sharon from the lobby and took her to the corner meeting room on the second floor. On the walls of the long corridor leading to the meeting room, and in the room itself, Sharon noticed many posters — framed, enlarged photographs of people engaged in different activities: having fun at a party, cleaning parks, working in what looked like a children's playground, poses of adults and children together with big smiles.

---

1  This chapter was written in collaboration with Chris Jarvis and Angela Parker of Realized Worth, a leading employee volunteering and CSR consulting firm based in Canada: realizedworth.blogspot.com. Chris and Angela provide training and hands-on involvement in the design and implementation of outstanding and sustainable employee volunteer programmes for businesses interested in leveraging their CSR programmes and differentiating their corporate culture. Their frameworks, concepts and insights, in particular the Seven Steps of Employee Volunteering were invaluable in developing this chapter. They are regular tweeters at www.twitter.com/RealizedWorth.

**Sharon:** What are all these pictures, Carl?

**Carl:** Ah, glad you noticed. All these pictures were taken by employees during volunteer activity. We hold an annual photo competition for our volunteers; the best ones are awarded a prize and the photos enlarged and framed and hung all over the company. There are hundreds! Each year, we replace them and the photographers get to keep their own framed photos. We like to make sure we have as much evidence and documentation of our volunteer activities as possible, so the photo competition keeps volunteers alert and they just snap away at every opportunity. People like photos! We have a large archive of photos, covering all our activities. It's invaluable as a record of what we've been doing. I think next year the Corporate Sustainability Report will feature many of our employee photographs as the main design theme.

**Sharon:** Oh, great. What an exciting idea.

**Carl:** OK, how about a coffee before we get started?

Carl and Sharon poured coffee from the thermos in the meeting room, and then settled back into the roomy black swivel seats. Carl reopened the conversation:

**Carl:** So, Sharon, tell me something about yourself and what you want to get out of this meeting. Arena briefed me a little. She said you met on a flight?

**Sharon:** Yes, a few weeks ago, now. We were both travelling to a conference in the States, and by chance, though perhaps it wasn't by chance, we sat next to each other on an 11-hour flight. As we got talking, we realised we were both going to the same conference. Each time I think back to that, I find it incredible, actually. The fact that we sat together. Arena changed my professional thinking on that flight. I have been in HR since the start of my career, and I love my work with Andromex. Andromex is a privately owned software solutions company. We do quite well, and I like the company. I have been there now for nearly six years. We have around 2,500 people. Not as big as IFC, but quite a large operation all the same. Anyway, Arena introduced me to corporate social human resources and the way that HR managers can contribute to building a sustainable culture. One key element of that is corporate social responsibility strategy and how it relates to employees and everything HR managers do to create CSR awareness and competences in the HR profession. Arena took me through all the basic concepts and gave me some fabulous ideas as to how to proceed. The area of employee volunteering is something I haven't been able to develop in my company, partly because the CEO doesn't believe that it's necessary. After hearing Arena, I am more determined than ever to make something happen at Andromex. Arena suggested I come and see you, so I could learn how you do it. I don't mind hard work, but I don't want to reinvent the wheel.

**Carl:** Good, thanks for that. I hope we can help. I used to be a full-time

HR manager myself. I was part of IFC's HR management team, but then they outsourced all transactional HR functions, and I didn't have a job any more. Arena, who is still my boss, offered me this role. I didn't quite understand at first what it would mean, but, you know, it was better than standing in line at the Job Centre. That's what I thought, at first. Any job is better than no job, especially at IFC where the people are so great! But then, once I got into the action, I realised that this is probably one of the best roles I have ever had, and in many ways more personally rewarding than my former HR roles. Anyway, I hope I can help you. Let's get down to business. Using Arena's brief, I prepared a short agenda for your visit. Take a look.

He handed her a printed page of A5.

**Carl:** How does that look?

**Sharon:** Fantastic. I am sure that will cover everything. You are very thorough, Carl. Thank you for all your efforts. By the way, I note you printed this on A5-size paper. Do you print everything on A5? Is that in order to save paper?

**Carl:** Yes, of course. We use only recycled printing paper and half size to ensure we use less. We print on both sides. Since we started this policy, our paper consumption has reduced by over 40%. Just by reducing the size of the paper we print on.

**Sharon:** That's a great idea. It's something I believe I could implement immediately at Andromex. I am sure the buyers would be interested, as it would yield savings, irrespective of the environmental benefit.

---

Sharon Black, Andromex:
Visit to IFC

Purpose: Learn about IFC Employee
Volunteering Programmes (EVPs)

Visit leader: Carl Barton, EVP Manager

Participants:
Jenny Garford, UK EVP Champion and
Marketing HR Partner
Brian Redman, Global Strategy Director

11:00: Introductions and plan for the day
11:30: Different types of EVP
12:00: Elements of an outstanding EVP
12:30: HR objectives in EVPs
13:00: Lunch
14:30: Seven steps to designing an EVP
16:30: Close

---

**Carl:** Yes, you will find that about employee volunteering, too. It delivers real business benefits, and HR benefits in particular, irrespective of the community contribution. That's true about most aspects of CSR. Anyway, as we have now officially started our programme for the day, perhaps you would tell me your thoughts on employee volunteering? What have you managed to pick up so far?

**Sharon:** I think it's great for companies to be involved with charitable work. I believe in helping people, and I think we have a responsibility to give back to the community in which we work. More than ever now, I understand that we cannot operate in a vacuum. A business is part of society, and it is important for us to strengthen that society as we do business. This also makes it easier for us to do business as our stakeholders value businesses that get involved. Stakeholders — that's a term I wasn't using so freely before Arena brainwashed me.

**Carl** (laughing): Great. Have you ever done any volunteering work yourself? Either as part of a business programme or privately?

**Sharon:** You know, I'm ashamed to admit, hardly anything. When I was at secondary school in Bristol, I ran a History Club for the younger kids. I would pick events in history, and we would turn it into a short playlet, and the younger kids would act it out and perform for the rest of the class. They learnt a lot, because a condition of joining the club was to read the briefing papers I prepared for them on each subject. I did this voluntarily and, actually, I reinforced my own learning as well. All the History Club members did well in their end-of-year exams. All the teachers loved me, you can bet on that.

**Carl:** Nice.

**Sharon:** Also, during my school holidays, I helped out at a local home for disabled kids. It was an experience — my first real exposure to people very, very different from myself. At university, I volunteered and was elected to the Student Council. But then, I started my career and, well, I am afraid, really, that I haven't give it much thought since then. Just managing myself, my family — I've got three children — and the dog, and holding down a full-time job, I haven't even thought about volunteering. Over the past few years, I have been more and more aware of companies developing volunteer programmes and felt it was something we ought to be doing too. I have tried to get my CEO's approval for me to get something going, but I haven't been successful yet.

**Carl:** Yes, I know how life takes over and we tend to become very focused on our own lives and everything we have to pack into our days. I will say upfront though, that setting a personal example is a big advantage. One of the reasons Arena picked me for this EVP job is that I have been an active volunteer here in London for quite some time. I help out with the British Red Cross[2] in helping refugees get accustomed to life in Britain, and I also work with a local food charity called FareShare.[3] It's a food community network that acts to relieve food poverty and ensure food is not wasted. Actually, working for a food company, I was able to leverage some of my

---

2 www.redcross.org.uk.

3 www.fareshare.org.uk. Author's note: FareShare is an actual non-profit organisation in the UK, selected at random by the author. However, the author has no personal experience of FareShare and has not volunteered with that organisation.

internal contacts here at IFC to provide food items and some funding for the organisation. But my connection with them was my own initiative, and I go out once a week in the evening to deliver food to homeless people and I go in at weekends, sometimes, to help sort food. Believe me, I meet all sorts of people that I would never meet in the normal course of my daily life, I have learnt new ways of talking to people, and if ever I am frustrated with anything, just feeling that I have made a difference in someone's life gets me through that frustration. The point is, Sharon, that setting a personal example is important. It not only demonstrates to people that you are serious, but it also gives you a position of authority from which to advance your case. Your CEO will be more inclined to listen to you if you practise what you preach and can give him examples from your personal experience, rather than if you just tell him that it's a good thing to do.

**Sharon:** Carl, you are right. You are absolutely right. How can I hope to develop a volunteering spirit in the company, or convince my boss to do so, if I can't speak from experience? I hadn't thought about it that way. Frankly, I am feeling rather stupid now.

**Carl:** Hey, come on, I didn't tell you that to make you feel bad. The fact that you are here now is a great thing. And every day brings new opportunities. But, I guess, I just wanted to say, before we go to the book approach on developing an EVP, that if I were you, the first thing I would do is examine your own motivations, and your own willingness to make a difference in the community on a private level. If you are not willing to make time yourself, then you will understand the challenge you have ahead with your 2,500 employees. If you want, I know that FareShare have a branch in Bristol, and I can put you in touch. But I am sure there are many other opportunities.

**Sharon:** Thank you Carl. I agree with you. I will take up your challenge, and I will be happy to go and talk to FareShare.

**Carl:** Good. Let's move on to the first point on our programme. Different forms of EV programmes. Let me take you through the EVP continuum. There's a broad continuum when it comes to corporate engagement — that's reflected in the many different names for similar programmes: employer-sponsored volunteering, volunteer service, global stewardship, workplace volunteering, community involvement programmes, corporate volunteer programmes, corporate volunteering, employer-supported volunteerism, employee engagement programmes. We call it EVP, Employee Volunteering Programme. Fairly straightforward, right?

**Sharon:** Right.

**Carl:** Take a look at this continuum:

## Employee volunteering continuum

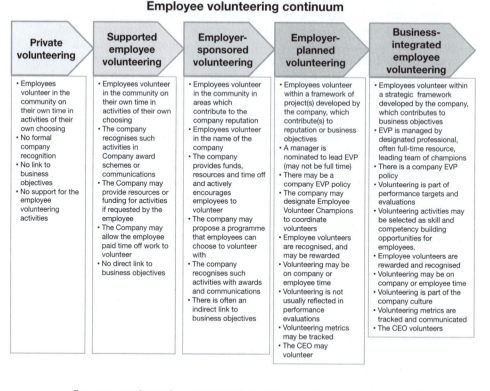

| Private volunteering | Supported employee volunteering | Employer-sponsored volunteering | Employer-planned volunteering | Business-integrated employee volunteering |
|---|---|---|---|---|
| • Employees volunteer in the community on their own time in activities of their own choosing<br>• No formal company recognition<br>• No link to business objectives<br>• No support for the employee volunteering activities | • Employees volunteer in the community on their own time in activities of their own choosing<br>• The company recognises such activities in Company award schemes or communications<br>• The Company may provide resources or funding for activities if requested by the employee<br>• The Company may allow the employee paid time off work to volunteer<br>• No direct link to business objectives | • Employees volunteer in the community in areas which contribute to the company reputation<br>• Employees volunteer in the name of the company<br>• The company provides funds, resources and time off and actively encourages employees to volunteer<br>• The company may propose a programme that employees can choose to volunteer with<br>• The company recognises such activities with awards and communications<br>• There is often an indirect link to business objectives | • Employees volunteer within a framework of project(s) developed by the company, which contribute(s) to reputation or business objectives<br>• A manager is nominated to lead EVP (may not be full time)<br>• There may be a company EVP policy<br>• The company may designate Employee Volunteer Champions to coordinate volunteers<br>• Employee volunteers are recognised, and may be rewarded<br>• Volunteering may be on company or employee time<br>• Volunteering is not usually reflected in performance evaluations<br>• Volunteering metrics may be tracked<br>• The CEO may volunteer | • Employees volunteer within a strategic framework developed by the company, which contributes to business objectives<br>• EVP is managed by designated professional, often full-time resource, leading team of champions<br>• There is a company EVP policy<br>• Volunteering is part of performance targets and evaluations<br>• Volunteering activities may be selected as skill and competency building opportunities for employees.<br>• Employee volunteers are rewarded and recognised<br>• Volunteering may be on company or employee time<br>• Volunteering is part of the company culture<br>• Volunteering metrics are tracked and communicated<br>• The CEO volunteers |

Can you see how the concept of employee volunteering progresses in a graduated way until, ultimately, it becomes part of the fabric of the business, adding value to the community, the business and the employees?

**Sharon:** Yes, this is very interesting.

**Carl:** I must point out though, that is what I call a descriptive continuum, not a prescriptive one.

**Sharon:** By which you mean . . . ?

**Carl:** This is not necessarily the way we would prescribe planning and developing a programme. An organisation doesn't have to work through each of these phases one by one. However, as most companies don't sit down and plan upfront, it does tend to be descriptive of how EVPs progress in organisations. OK? I am not recommending that you start at phase one, but it is important for you to recognise phase one because it might already exist in your organisation.

**Sharon:** I understand.

**Carl:** Let me take you through each of the stages:
The first phase is **private employee volunteering**. This is what I started out doing. I was just a regular guy, wanting to contribute to the community.

I went out and found causes that I wanted to contribute to, some with my own time, some with my hard-earned cash, and I just went and did it. I didn't look to the company for any support and didn't ask for any company resources, always volunteered in my own time, in the evenings or at weekends, and occasionally I took some of my vacation days, for example, at Christmas and Easter when there is always more work to do. In fact, the company didn't even know. Some of my colleagues knew, including Arena, because I often talked of my experiences, and a couple even joined me at the Red Cross, but in general, it was something private between me and my community and the company wasn't involved. When I went as a volunteer, I went as Carl, not as IFC HR manager. I suspect that there are many people in many companies who are like this.

**Sharon:** Yes, I am tempted to do a survey to see how many people at Andromex are actually volunteering in the community. I might be surprised.

**Carl:** And yes, this is important. Know why?

**Sharon:** It seems to me, that if all these people are investing their time in things that are important to them, they could also be investing their time in things that are important to them **and** the business. This would create a win–win–win: employee, community, business.

**Carl:** Right. In addition, their volunteering activity provides you with insights to them as people and as leaders. Through their volunteering activity, you might find that they have skills you didn't know about, which might be of value in the business context.

**Sharon:** I hadn't thought about that.

**Carl:** OK, next phase:
We call this **supported employee volunteering**. This is where the focus is still a private one, the employee is doing his or her own thing, but the company recognises there is value in this and actively finds ways to support the employee. This support may come in the form of paid time off to volunteer, or a time-off matching scheme, you know, where the employee donates one hour of paid company time for every two hours of personal time the employee volunteers, or something like that. Alternatively, the company will have a fund for employee volunteering, from which the employee can request funding for certain activities. Suppose the employee volunteers at FareShare, for example, like I do. I might be aware of the fact that FareShare need a new rack of shelving in the warehouse, or a new truck for deliveries, or a new trolley. I go to the company and tell them that this is an organisation that I am volunteering with, they need this or that, and request the funds as a charitable donation. Rather than give to just any charity, the company prefers to give to me, as it might motivate me more as an employee if the company supports something I believe in enough to donate my time to. In addition, the company quite likes the idea that its employees are contributing to the community, so it makes a fuss of

them in employee communications, maybe features them on the company intranet, or an article in the company in-house magazine. But in this phase, the company is still not reaping any focused business benefit, other than, perhaps, an increase in motivation of a small number of employees. This is still not linked to the business in any significant way, but it certainly goes further than the previous stage and demonstrates some form of company support for the community.

**Sharon:** Yes. I understand. I have to admit that at Andromex, we haven't even considered this stage. Would you recommend starting with this stage or should a company jump straight to one of the later stages?

**Carl:** That's a great question. I admit that I tend to believe in evolutionary processes. My organisational development training tells me that organisations have to be mature enough to absorb new processes, and the best chances of long-lasting success come when there is evolution not revolution. Generating a culture of volunteering, starting to change the mind-set in small ways, as a precursor to a more formal and strategic approach is a good idea, in my view, but it is not absolutely necessary. We didn't really apply this stage at IFC. When I took over the EVP role, IFC was already at the third stage, where the company was actively putting its name to volunteering programmes. But if I were starting from scratch, in a company where no efforts whatsoever had been put into employee volunteering, I would go though the stages. First, I would find out what people are doing anyway. Then, I would encourage and assist them. Then, I would provide frameworks for more people to do things that motivate them, in terms of volunteering. I am talking about larger businesses that employ more than a few hundred employees. In a smaller company, it might be possible to skip these steps, as the connections between people are tighter, gaining consensus is easier and quicker, and communications are more direct. But in large companies, I believe this approach would offer an advantage.

**Sharon:** I understand. It makes sense.

**Carl:** Good. So the third phase is what we call **employer-sponsored volunteering**. Up until now, the employee has been the driver. He or she has selected an activity and if the company has been involved in any way, it was at the employee initiative or request. With the third phase, we turn the corner of having the company take a more proactive role in driving employee volunteering and actively establishing frameworks in which the employee can volunteer. See the difference?

**Sharon:** Yes. The first two phases are driven by personal motivations of the employees. The third phase starts to mesh employee motivation with the business interest.

**Carl:** Correct! In a very basic sort of way. For example, take IFC. This is what was happening when I took over as EVP Manager. Here is one example. A group of local employees at our plant in the south of England, many of whom live in the same area, were interested in supporting the local community centre. The community centre is actually a registered charity, and a few employees were involved anyway. They identified a list of activities that could be beneficial to the centre, such as helping kids with homework, providing meals for the needy, renovating the sports ground, conducting family finances workshops to help families manage on a tight budget, holding cookery and woodwork classes, setting up a computer room and more. A few of these employees approached the HR Manager based at the plant and suggested that, instead of them volunteering on a private basis, the company 'adopt' the community centre as a CSR activity, so that more employees could volunteer. They wanted the programme to be a company programme, with cash support and use of company resources.

The HR Manager was supportive and, to cut a long story short, managed to obtain a modest budget and established a new policy of giving employees who wanted to volunteer an allocation of two paid hours per month provided they contributed a matching two hours of their own time. She formed a Factory EVP Team to agree on the focus of the employee volunteering activities. They made a plan and each took on roles to move things forward. A core of about eight employees who were already volunteering on a regular basis grew to 80 employees (out of a total of 450 employed in the plant) within six months. Today, there are more than 200 employees volunteering on a regular basis, at different community centres. During that first phase, though, the company contributed £25,000 to help renovate the sports centre, and the community centre kitchen, so that there would be a better facility for providing meals. The company also contributed food products and ran a cookery course with the company chefs and others, who volunteered their time, and a nutrition course with the company nutrition team. The employees who volunteered went as company representatives, not just private people. This was a real win–win–win: the company gained many benefits, the employees were delighted, both the original initiators of the programme and the new volunteers, and the community centre popularity within the local community increased massively and made an important contribution to strengthening the local community fabric. The HR Manager was able to leverage this to advance other activities in the business. She also ensured that volunteering employees gained recognition and after the first year, she had the Plant Manager award an Employee Volunteer prize to the most deserving volunteer.

There were other, similar, examples of employee volunteer initiatives that the company accepted sponsorship of, some developing as a result of this first example, like additional community centres in other areas, and some in completely different fields. When I took over my job about three years ago, I was faced with a mish-mash of unrelated projects which had been developed at grass roots, all highly successful by all accounts, though metrics didn't feature in the vocabulary at that time. All of them had some proximity to our core business activity – food – though there wasn't a clear tie-in to business strategy. But lots of energy, lots of activity, good volunteer levels and, all in all, fairly positive stuff.

**Sharon:** How wonderful! When you took over your job, there was already a start-up volunteer culture in the business.

**Carl:** Yes, indeed, but it still wasn't recognised as anything really important. It was seen more as a way to motivate employees, sort of giving them a benefit that would motivate them. It was very sporadic. Some sites had two or three programmes running, other sites did nothing. Wherever the grass roots were strong, the company responded with sponsorship. Where there was no grassroots pressure, the company did nothing.

**Sharon:** I recall reading about eBay[4] in the USA, and the way their EVP developed entirely through grassroots activity. The Director of the eBay Green Team, Amy Skoczlas Cole,[5] said that the 'CSR efforts of the company grew out of employees' own work',[6] and that the entire eBay activities to develop community involvement and support activities to improve the quality of the environment were the result of employee suggestions rather than a top-down initiative. Today, they have an eBay Foundation that includes matching employee gifts and employee volunteer time.[7] It sounds like a phase two activity that has become a corporate programme and leveraged for the good of the business, more phase three.

**Carl:** Yes, I have seen the eBay programme. It's quite impressive. I see you are getting the hang of this. Let's move on, as we don't have a lot of time if we want to complete our schedule for today.

**Sharon:** OK. Fourth phase.

**Carl:** Yes, the fourth phase is one we call **employer-planned volunteering**. This is where the employer effectively takes responsibility and drives the employee volunteering programmes as a business initiative, rather than waiting for the employees to come up with a request. The company takes the initiative, determines what level of resources it wants to assign to community involvement and employee volunteering, appoints someone to lead the efforts and generates frameworks which have some element of mutual advantage — community and business in most cases. In a few cases, the company may develop frameworks which are not related to core business, but more often than not, if a company gets to stage four, it's because they have realised that there is a certain business value they can gain, albeit they haven't reached the ultimate stage of fundamental integration of employee volunteering as a business strategy. So employer-planned volunteering is the same as sponsored volunteering, except that the drive comes top-down and not bottom-up; though often even

4  pages.ebay.co.uk/aboutebay.html.
5  www.communitelligence.com/pwps/pwpsite.cfm?sys=2373, accessed 6 June 2010.
6  Quotation noted by the author during attendance on Day 2 at the virtual conference *New Models of Social Responsibility,* hosted by Communitelligence and Cisco, 5 and 9 November 2009: www.communitelligence.com/content/ahpg. cfm?spgid=377&full=1#day2, accessed 6 June 2010.
7  pages.ebay.co.uk/aboutebay/employeeinvolvement.html, accessed 6 June 2010.

top-down activities are developed with a certain degree of consensus. In a typical employer-planned initiative, you have an annual work-plan with objectives and maybe some quantified targets, a leader who may or may not be full time, a corporate employee volunteering network, recognition programmes, resources, perhaps even a written policy, and, if they are really serious, a CEO who personally and outspokenly backs the programme and may even volunteer him or herself. It is possible that some of the metrics may be tracked — like how many employee volunteer hours, or how many one-time or regular volunteers or whatever. IFC transitioned into this phase from phase three. It wasn't an easy transition and required quite a change in mind-set both at management level and at employee level. But we did it and saw a lot of benefit. Now we are trying to develop into phase five.

**Sharon** (smiling): Yes, I suspected you would tell me you are at phase five.

**Carl** (smiling back): We are getting there. Phase five — the ultimate level in EVPs. **Business-integrated employee volunteering**. This is where EVP is seamlessly integrated into the fabric of the business, part of the way of life of the company, used as a tool to leverage the business as well as provide employees with personal and professional benefits, and ultimately, serves the community and or the environment in a way which produces positive outcomes. This kind of EVP has all the characteristics of any other business process. It's part of the management agenda, it's planned as part of the strategy and annual planning process, its benefits are known and quantified, and it has targets, objectives, goals, metrics, everything you might expect. It fits in with performance evaluations, remuneration and bonus allocation. It's clearly present in any internal and external communications strategy, and there is a clear leader, who, depending on the size of the company, may well be a full-time management resource. There is a written policy, procedure and methodology. The company forms community partnerships which are long term rather than one-off initiatives. Anyone who comes into contact with the company sees what's going on, feels the spirit and hears employees talking about their experience. I must say that very few companies ever reach this Utopian stage of phase five. It takes complete embedding of a sustainability culture and thorough understanding of the total scope of the strategic value of employee volunteering to achieve this. Not many companies have achieved this level of sophistication, and IFC is certainly not there yet in a comprehensive way. Phase six is not on this chart. I am working on how to move to phase six as another future challenge.

**Sharon:** What is phase six?

**Carl:** See this:

> ## Business-advancing employee volunteering

- **Strategic employee volunteering** characterised by strategy, policy, goals, objectives, targets, metrics, senior management visible commitment, reward and recognition for volunteering programmes and strong communications platforms. Provides opportunities for all employees who wish to volunteer in a way that is aligned with core business advancement, community and environmental needs, and the personal and professional development of employees

- **Involvement of external partners** (customers, suppliers, outsourcing units, consumers etc.) in employee volunteering programmes to generate greater leverage and positive outcome thought the entire value chain

- **Tracking and measurement of outcomes** — the focus on metrics relating to social impact — not just social input or actions; the measurement of the outcomes of the volunteering and community involvement activities over time, quantified in terms of community beneficial outcomes achieved and where possible, employee and business outcomes

**Sharon: Business-advancing employee volunteering**. Hmm. I see the difference. What you are saying, Carl, is that the ultimate is to take employee volunteering programmes even further — so that they become another route to interaction with upstream and downstream partners, and that the actual effects or outcomes are evaluated, and not just the amount of time people volunteered or the number of initiatives which were completed.

**Carl:** Yes. Phase six carries some additional risks, as well as opportunities, so I am being rather cautious in my approach. There are no well-developed methodologies for measuring longer-term outcomes, so we are treading in uncharted territory.

**Sharon:** Carl, this is all very impressive, very clear, very logical. I don't think I could have learnt all this in a better way anywhere else. But what, I am wondering is, how long does all this take? In a company like ours with 2,500 people, half of them work on the same site, others are in different locations. We have no volunteering mind-set at all, unless its phase one, which I am not aware of. How long do you think it should take to get to phase four and then to phase five?

**Carl:** Of course you know that I can't be specific, but broadly speaking, I would say that you can get through phases one to three within a matter of months. Phase four requires some management commitment and, by definition, alignment and perhaps even a little internal politics as you agree on who pays the budget, who releases the employees, where best to invest energies and so on. I would expect something like Year 1, phases one to three. Years 2 and 3, phase four. Years 4 and 5, phase five. And if your experience is good at phase five after three years or more, you could start to develop towards phase six, on a carefully selected pilot basis, as I am thinking of doing at IFC. We are talking about a minimum five-year commitment to get to a successful contributing programme, and more than five years to deliver true business value throughout the value chain.

**Sharon:** Yes, I imagined that would be the case. I think you are even a little optimistic. But basically, if I get my skates on, we can be at phase four in another 12–18 months. I think I probably will have enough ammunition to fight a successful battle with my boss and my management colleagues to get us to phase three, employer-sponsored volunteering. I think my CEO might go for that. I can probably generate enough data to support that it's a good approach.

**Carl:** Yes. Look, I need to take a natural break. How about we take a short pit-stop, you can grab yourself more coffee if you like, and then we can move to the next item on the agenda, which is how to build an EVP and the key things you need to do to make it work.

**Sharon:** Fine. Thanks so much so far.

**Carl:** No problem.

Carl left Sharon in the office, pondering over the EVP phases handouts he had given her. So organised, so professional, she thought to herself. Not what she had imagined at all. She had tended to think of employee volunteering as something that sort of managed itself — employees want to volunteer, you set up a framework and people volunteer. 'Everything that Carl has told me so far indicates that this is quite a professional activity, one that demands the same degree of professional attention as other processes,' she thought. She was delighted and excited and overwhelmed and scared all at the same time. She felt this was exactly what she needed to do, but that it wasn't going to be as straightforward as she thought. Elephants, she thought to herself. How to eat an elephant slice by slice. She recalled a book she had read about total quality management with this title.[8] She remembered that the opening page contained a quote from an elephant who said 'TQM is an activity almost as frustrating as herding cats!', and secretly hoped to herself that developing an EVP wouldn't be quite in the same category.

Carl returned, bringing with him a young woman who smiled at Sharon.

8  John Gilbert, *How To Eat an Elephant: A Slice-by-Slice Guide to Total Quality Management* (Liverpool Academic Press, 3rd edn, 2004).

**Carl:** I thought you might be a little sick of the sound of my voice, so I brought Jenny in to help us out. Jenny is our EVP Champion in the UK. There is a team of EVP Champions, with people at each site, but as we have three sites in the UK, Jenny oversees it all. When she is not doing EVP, she does a little HR.

**Jenny:** Funny, Carl. I knew I could trust you to introduce me properly. Hello, Sharon, I have heard about you from Arena, and I am pleased to meet you. I hope Carl hasn't scared you off with EVP theory. But don't worry, I will help you make sense of it all, and how it works in practice.

**Sharon:** Hello Jenny, I am pleased to meet you too. Thank you for making the time. Carl has been great, but I will be happy to learn about the practical side, too. I admit to starting to feel a little overwhelmed!

**Jenny:** Fine. Carl asked me to take you through the key elements of a successful EVP. Let's assume we are at phase four. You know the phases by now, right?

**Sharon:** Engraved on my heart.

**Jenny** (laughing): Great. Phase four: employer-planned volunteering. This starts with the need to establish a framework that the company drives. It's more than just planning an event and inviting people to come and volunteer. At first, someone suggested we organise one big volunteer marathon in the UK, and others in the other countries we operate in. After checking this out, we realised it's more complex than that. We began to understand the implications of accounting for volunteer time. Timberland, for example, offers employees 40 paid hours per year for volunteering, to engage in the company's CSR agenda. You can download their 2009 report on their Global Stewards Program.[9] They have done an amazing job. I read in the Optus CSR report[10] for 2009 that their policy is to allow every employee one volunteering day a year, and they have around 15% of total employees who volunteer. Optus is a large Australian telecommunications company. They have over 10,000 employees so 15% is quite a lot of people. Eli Lilly, the pharmaceutical company, has an annual 'Global Day of Giving'[11] where employees contribute their time to big, highly visible and high-impact events to clean up neighbourhoods and contribute to the quality of life with a big sense of team spirit. There are so many examples. We had high expectations and we were searching for the best way to establish an infrastructure that would carry EVP forward and meet all these expectations, at minimum cost and resource expenditure for the company.

---

9  Timberland, 'Engaging Employees', tbl.imageg.net/include/csr_reports/ Timberlands_Global_Stewards_Program_2009_report.pdf, accessed 10 June 2010.

10  Optus Corporate Responsibility Report 2009, www.optus.com.au/portal/site/ aboutoptus/menuitem.ee0ee21ac9cce722d0b61a108c8ac7a0/?vgnextoid=0c7f3dd4 813b1010VgnVCM100000c8a87c0aRCRD. Page 75 describes employee volunteering programmes.

11  thelillybrand.com/dos.

**Sharon:** What kind of expectations do you mean, Jenny?

**Jenny:** Well, you know, I laugh about it now, but we thought that the minute we established this great framework, then everyone would jump to volunteer. We thought just by creating the opportunity, people would rush to take part. We thought they would involve their friends, both at work and outside, and perhaps even their families. The reality is that the average participation rate among businesses our size is about 20%. And out of that 20%, the average number of hours volunteered is just three. Per year![12] Another thing is that we thought that the minute we approached some non-profit organisation or community partner, they would fall at our feet and just beg that we would engage with them. In practice, most of them reacted as though we were Martians, and that the concept of employees volunteering was too ridiculous to be true. Some even saw it as an affront.

> **Eli Lilly values**
>
> - Integrity
> - Excellence
> - Respect for people
>
> www.lilly.com/about/
> compliance

**Sharon:** No! That's exactly the opposite of what I would have thought. Surely they would welcome companies offering to help them out. All you hear about these days is how hard it is for non-profits. Why would they refuse help?

**Jenny:** Yes, that's exactly where we were. As soon as we mentioned donating money, their eyes lit up and they were ready to accept any amount. But when we talked about volunteering, they refused to listen. Said it wouldn't work. Said they had nothing we could do. What they needed was money to fund their projects. They just didn't want to hear about volunteers. Like you, I was astounded. Anyway, Carl, you've seen him in action this morning, he wouldn't take no for an answer, and insisted on meeting with non-profit organisations in various sectors, and talking with their leadership. We heard the same story five times over, from different organisations, in different words, different tones and different shades, but the message was always the same. Companies who volunteer are not reliable and can do more harm than good. They want to provide their employees with a jolly, a way of getting out of the office for a while, a lollipop to make them more motivated, and they don't really know what the non-profits want or what they need. Short-term interventions, or promises that aren't kept, can shake the delicate nature of relationships in the non-profits and create a lose–lose situation for everyone.

**Carl:** That's right, they felt we were unreliable for the long term. Managers come and go, employees come and go, while creating relationships, especially in the non-profit sector, with real people who have real needs,

---

12 Bea Boccalandro, *Mapping Success in Employee Volunteering: The Drivers of Effectiveness for Employee Volunteering and Giving Programs and Fortune 500 Performance* (Chestnut Hill, MA: Boston College Center for Corporate Citizenship): 30.

is a year-after-year thing, not just a one-off. They even went as far as to say that we were insulting them by coming in and offering to help them out, without considering their professional needs, as though we felt they were not professional, just nice people trying to make a difference, without any real skill. You know, they were probably right. We felt they were just nice people. Good values, Generous. Humanity-minded and all that. Not professionals who we could regard as equal and develop a partnership with on equal footing. Right, Jenny?

**Jenny:** Yes, you're right. That's pretty much how we felt. They threw that back in our faces in no uncertain terms. If they could have thrown us out of the window, they probably would have done. They made it quite clear we were wasting their time. The bottom line was: If you want to help us, make a donation. Don't bring your employees, who will probably do more harm than good.

**Sharon:** But what about a big event, the sort you talked about? A one-off event which could generate a lot of publicity and awareness, even if it doesn't establish an ongoing relationship; surely that could offer benefits?

**Jenny:** Not really. The amount of effort and planning and discussion and organisation that needs to go into a big annual event, which includes non-profit people as our employees, like renovating a playground, or old peoples' homes or cleaning a river bank, frankly, far outweighs the benefit of any publicity that it generates. We thought like you at that time, but now I see just how naïve that was, and how insulting we must have seemed. Anyway, in designing our EVP we thought about the levels of volunteering we could reasonably expect, the way we needed to approach community partners and what sort of community partners would be appropriate. Partners who we would work with as equals, with shared objectives. Another thing was selecting a programme that would add value. Really meet true needs and deliver a social return and a business return. This means understanding very clearly what the business stood to gain, both in terms of advancing our reputation and our brands, and creating opportunities for employee motivation and skill building, and also understanding clearly what needs existed in the community that were aligned with our business objectives. Once we figured that out, we had to know how to measure it so that we could see that there was a return in all directions.

**Sharon:** Can I stop you here for a minute? Carl referred to this earlier, and now you, Jenny. I mean, I am all for an employee volunteering programme delivering benefits, but you both seem to be referring to it as just another business project which has a rate of return and goals and targets and a money bottom line. What about values? What about the desire to benefit the community? The desire to give back? Doing the right thing? Altruism? Is it all just about money, resources, planning? Isn't this a sort of mercenary approach to EVP? If that's all it is, it's sort of disappointing. I would rather stay at phase one or two.

**Carl:** Hah! I wondered when you would come to that, Sharon. You are going through everything we had to agonise over ourselves in the early days. Jenny can tell you how many hours and hours of debate we had about that point.

**Jenny:** Carl's right. We did agonise over it. At one level, volunteering in the community is about values. At another level, we are a business. Businesses have to consider the return on every activity and every investment. The more important thing is that, without considering these factors, the return on investment factors, we would never know if we were making the sort of difference in the community that we wanted with the resources we had committed to allocate. We would never know if what we were doing was optimum or just average, or if we were actually delivering beneficial outcomes, or just doing things to make ourselves feel good. Even if our motivation was solely values-based, this information is critical to know if we are making an impact. We found the answer somewhere in the balance of all these factors. Identify, evaluate and make decisions based on where we think we can meet the most relevant needs in the most comprehensive way with the resources we are able to allocate. In delivering the programme, ensure that we are doing so because we believe in the value of the personal involvement and dialogue and interaction in the community. Otherwise, it would have been much easier to ask the CEO to sign a cheque and send it off to the non-profit without ever meeting the people. That's what some companies do, and they even call it 'strategic philanthropy'. I call it strategic cheque-writing. Don't get me wrong, donating money is good, and it always helps. But it's philanthropy, not community involvement. It's not what we were about at all. We wanted to understand the issues we were addressing and be a part of the solution, not just pay for it.

**Sharon:** I understand. You wanted to engage the community on the right topics in the right way with the right resources.

**Jenny:** Yes, and once we had reached that conclusion, we had to achieve alignment within the business even before we selected the community partners that were willing to give us a chance. We had to create a framework that would serve the business, be exciting and fulfilling to employees, be viable within a reasonable budget, be manageable in a consistent way over time, and deliver measurable outcomes for the community in the way we all wanted. Internal alignment was also a tough thing. Employees' requests to volunteer ranged from helping old people, children, stray animals, disabled people, hungry people, foreign immigrants, community groups, environmental groups, women's empowerment groups — anything that's out there, someone wanted to do it. We had to figure out a way to combine all these options and find something that everyone would feel comfortable volunteering with, and have some leverage for the business. We had to look for unifying factors between the interests and values of our company, our community and our employees. Finally, we had to be clear how we would manage it all. Putting

Carl in place was the outcome of all these discussions that we had been generating. The fact that Arena listened, understood, and was willing to allocate one of her HR resources to EVP on a full time basis is a credit to her. I know she gained the approval of the CEO and the Exec team, but only by promising not to increase the number of people in the HR team, though the Exec team did allocate a budget for the EV programme itself. All of us in the HR team had to commit to taking on Carl's HR workload without increasing manpower. But the good thing about Arena is that she made the decision together with us, so we were all committed to making it work.

**Carl:** Our assumption was that we would be able to create a network of champions who would help us move the programme forward throughout the company. This has been the experience of other companies that we had heard of. Champions like the extra leadership status, and if you pick them well, they will drive the EVP with energy and commitment, meaning that all the leg-work doesn't fall to the HR team. That is how it should be of course, because HR is the facilitator, not the owner of this programme. HR can create the framework, but it is the line who implement, as with most HR processes. Champions also learn leadership skills that are useful in their work and other interactions on teams.

**Sharon:** This is so useful. You guys should write a book about your experience with EVP. I am sure your experience could help many HR managers like me who have no idea that this is an activity requiring this level of thought and planning.

**Jenny:** Would you two excuse me now? I have a meeting starting in a few minutes. Sharon, I hope I have been some help.

**Sharon:** Thank you so much, Jenny. Your insights have been invaluable. I can see why you are a champion.

**Carl:** OK, OK, let her go before she starts blushing. Thanks, Jenny. Appreciate your help.

Jenny left. Carl picked up the programme for Sharon's day and read out loud: **HR objectives in employee volunteering programmes**.

**Carl:** Good, we are doing nicely, Sharon. The last thing I wanted to cover quickly before lunch is the way HR defines its objectives in the framework of EVPs. We have already referred to this, perhaps in a roundabout way, when talking about some of our dilemmas, but let's just run through the key points before we go to lunch.

**Sharon:** Fine.

**Carl:** Take a look at this chart and I will walk you through it briefly. We have touched on some of the points already.

## Ways in which employee volunteering contributes to HR objectives

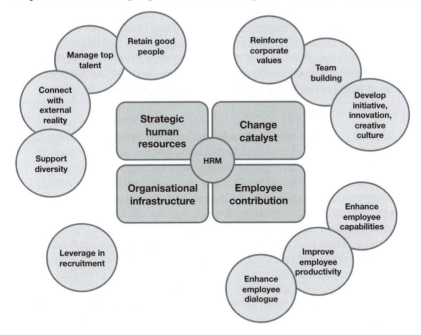

**Carl:** It's fairly self-explanatory. I think you get it, right?

**Sharon:** Right.

**Carl:** I have to admit that when I first took up the role of EVP Manager, I thought it would be a nice morale booster, but not much else. It was only after I started to research and listen to others, much in the same way you are doing now, that I realised there is a world of positive potential beyond making people feel good, or increasing motivation. I found several surveys that indicated that employees like to work in a company that contributes to the community, but I couldn't find anything that actually correlated this with recruitment metrics or retention numbers. I mean, do employees really stay with a business because of the volunteering aspects? I doubted it then and, even now, it's a little far-fetched, though certainly a volunteering programme enhances the value of a company in employees' eyes. I have a friend who was the HR director of one of the local Unilever subsidiaries,[13] and she told me that employees in a manufacturing plant which was downsized, and where several employees lost their jobs and others were taking pay cuts, were still happy to participate in the company's community efforts and volunteer. When the company chairman

---

13  The author served as Unilever VP for Human Resources in Israel between 1997 and 2005, and initiated a series of employee volunteering programmes. This is a true story from that period.

came to visit, after offloading about their own hardships and issues related to job security, they thanked him warmly for the opportunity to do something positive in their local neighbourhood. Clearly, this is a benefit, and as part of an overall approach to positive and responsible workplace management, it makes a contribution. Anyway, as you can see from the chart, there are many aspects of EVP that support HR objectives. We use the model developed by Dave Ulrich — do you know that? He introduced it in his book Human Resources Champions several years ago.[14]

**Sharon:** Yes, I am familiar with the model.

**Carl:** Good. If you consider the core HR roles in the centre, here, you can see that EVP has something to contribute to all the roles which make a big difference in the business. In a good, well-managed EVP, where employees are directed to activities they can personally engage with, where they can experience new skills and learn new things, where they can meet new colleagues, develop new ways of dialogue and interaction, see what's going on in the external world which might impact on their own business, the direct and indirect effects on the business are real. All this contributes to what HR is trying to create in terms of strategic support for business objectives, transformational change in culture and practices and enhancement of individual employee contribution.

How do we calculate this? What's our return on investment? The benefits are often indirect, and so the metrics need to be correlated with other metrics to make sense, but there are some things that we can measure:

- **Employee job satisfaction**. When employees are given time within their working day to volunteer, their overall motivation increases. This can be measured in performance evaluation conversations and in employee surveys

- **Recruitment**. More employees want to apply to work at a responsible company. When this is used as part of the employer brand, and applicants or new hires are surveyed, we can see the relevance of this

- **Employee skill building**. This can be tracked through the employee performance evaluation process

We include questions about volunteer activities in the annual employee performance evaluation process . For example, we're interested in leadership and skill development. Our employees can be evaluated in the community as well as inside the workplace. We use a 360-degree evaluation process, and employees can choose colleagues from their volunteer work to fill out the evaluation. We also ask new hires to tell

14 Dave Ulrich, *Human Resources Champions* (Watertown, MA: Harvard University Press, 1996), one of the leading transformational books about human resources management which has influenced many of the developments we see in transformational human resources today.

us if our CSR and EVP strategies had influenced why they joined us. We compare that information to the programmes that they participate in over the first year. If they indicated that community involvement was really important, but they didn't volunteer anywhere in the first year with the company, we ask why. That can lead to some insightful conversations that help us make better management decisions. And here's an interesting thing. Over the past two years we've been comparing the performance reviews of those employees who volunteer with those who don't. Employees who volunteer seem to be 6–7% more productive than those who don't.[15] This is a piece of data we are monitoring closely to make sure we have got it right, but if it is substantiated over a longer period with a broader base of employees, it will be very significant. It will mean that our EVP pays for itself several times over in the space of a year.

Another thing we tried out last year with a close community partner we have been working with for some time, was to engage in volunteering activity which would specifically help us meet a key HR objective of developing a team culture. We agreed to try this with one activity and then move forward. We selected the cleaning up of a river bank with a group of disabled youngsters. This was work with required good coordination and communication between team members both to do the work and also to do it jointly with a team of disabled kids. This worked very well. Many employees who were not ordinarily in team leadership roles took on responsibilities for part of the work, and even surprised themselves with their abilities to get the work done, through their teams. People who didn't ordinarily work together met each other for the first time, creating new team bonds within the company. And, this is important, some groups worked in their organic teams, and their feedback was incredible. One guy who works in a brand group, when we debriefed them in small groups said: 'Carl, now I know what team-working is all about. This has been a more effective lesson than most of the training programmes I have been on. It was even more worthwhile because we contributed something to the community.' Many others gave similar feedback. Believe me, I was mind-blown. I couldn't wait to start thinking how we capture more of that, reapply it in a more consistent way across the business. HR today is living in a new world. We need new tools. We need to think out of the box.

**Sharon:** It does sound quite incredible, Carl.

**Carl:** What I think would be more incredible right now is the sound of lunch. I'm starving, how about you?

**Sharon:** Yes, me too. You certainly deserve to be fed. I can't thank you enough for your help so far.

Carl and Sharon made their way to the company dining room. Sharon was impressed by the variety available, including low-calorie, organic and vegetar-

15  Based on recent research by Kathleen Day and Rose Anne Devlin at the University of Carleton; data and source provided by Chris Jarvis of Realized Worth, Canada.

ian options. She noticed that each dish had a label showing the nutritional value, calorie value and other relevant information such as whether it was organic, contained nuts, gluten or additives. There were posters on the walls of the dining room with advice about healthy eating under the IFC Healthy Eating Programme, and also about physical exercise, the ICF Be Fit Programme.

**Sharon:** Carl, 'Healthy Eating Programme', 'Be Fit Programme'. IFC does a lot to encourage employee well-being, I see.

**Carl:** You don't miss anything, Sharon. Yes, we promote the healthy option wherever we can. Many of our roles are sedentary, or in factories which require little physical exertion. As a food company, we are more than aware of the fact that we are what we eat. Part of our responsibility to employees is to help them understand how to manage their personal health and fitness, and give them tools to do so.

**Sharon:** I am going to go for organic risotto. See, you have influenced me already. It also looks delicious.

During lunch, Sharon and Carl were joined by other colleagues from different departments. Naturally the subject of EVP came up, and Sharon was impressed that everything Carl had told her was reinforced by the things she heard around the table. It was very clear to her that Carl had been talking to her about a programme that was actually working, not something that looked good on paper, and then when you asked questions Pandora's box opened. Sharon was beginning to understand what it takes to develop a complete assimilation of a CSR mind-set. She also took the opportunity to interrogate the other lunch-partners on different aspects of CSR at IFC, and she was impressed by how engaged they were by different aspects of the company's programme. CSR did seem to be buzzing at IFC.

After lunch, Carl and Sharon went for a brief but pleasant walk in the area outside the London office. Carl explained that he couldn't spend a whole day in the office without getting some fresh air and stretching his legs. Sharon thought how many days she spent in the office from nine in the morning to sometimes after seven in the evening without ever seeing the light of day, and resolved to make a walk around her office building a compulsory part of her day, too. They returned to the small meeting room, past the amazing volunteer photo exhibition again, and reinstalled themselves in the ergonomically designed seats, ready for the next part of their programme. Carl was already on the phone to Brian Redman, the IFC Global Strategy Director, telling him they were ready for him to call in.

**Carl:** EVP is something that has to fit with company strategy. So before we go into the design of the EVP, I wanted you to hear a little from Brian Redman, who looks after strategic development at IFC.

**Sharon:** Great!

The door opened and Brian entered.

**Carl:** Hello Brian, glad you could join us! Meet Sharon.

Sharon and Brian introduced themselves and Carl took the lead again.

**Carl:** I wanted you to talk about your approach to strategy and where EVP fits in.

**Brian:** Take a look at this model. It's the way I think about strategy development. You won't find it in any textbook and it's probably not perfect. I keep wondering if I should have a box to include 'risks', for example. I might update it, but in the meantime, these are the factors I try to ensure are on my radar when I look at how we should be developing our business strategically.

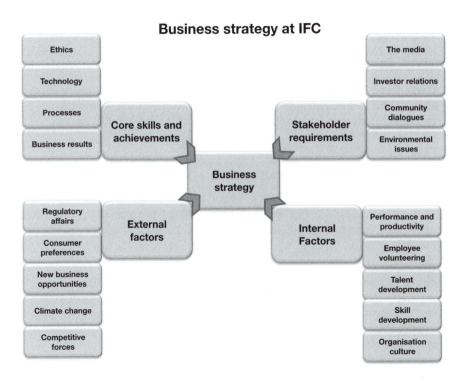

As you can see, there are a number of elements that relate both directly and indirectly to CSR. In fact, I look at CSR as the **way** we do business, whereas strategy is more about **what** we will do. Everyone knows, however, that sometimes these two are interrelated and, in certain cases, how you decide to do things might influence what your business decides to work on. Take General Electric's Ecomagination,[16] for example. That's both a 'way' and a 'what' strategy. Think about the entire new Clean Tech, or Low-Carbon economy — that's both 'way' and 'what' strategies coming into play. Sometimes the border between the 'what' and the 'way' is a little fuzzy. This makes my job much tougher these days, I can tell you that. In the past, the questions of climate change or regulatory risk or even stakeholder opinion were not significant determining factors in the approach to strategy. Take any strategy textbook written just ten years ago and you won't find mention of CSR or stakeholder dialogue on CSR issues.

**Sharon:** I understand.

**Brian:** As you can see from my chart, there are many CSR-type factors that swing our business. Even something such as consumer preferences is loaded with CSR content, as consumers are going for different types of food brands, healthy options or organic content and move to vegetarian options with less red meat and so on. The financial crisis has meant less eating out and more home-cooking. Kind of a back-to-basics approach to food. Our ability to respond to changing consumer preference is in part connected to our stand on CSR.

**Carl:** Brian, I don't think we will have time to go through this entire chart, though I know how much you love to talk about it. Sharon, Brian is so proud of his strategy chart that I think he is going to submit it for the Guinness World Records as the most talked-about strategy chart in the history of business.

**Brian:** Don't give me ideas, Carl.

**Carl:** Ha ha! I was just wondering, Brian, if you could focus on the EVP part. Sharon is only here for a short time, and her purpose today is to learn about EVP. Sorry to cut you off in your prime, but that would be really helpful.

**Brian** (smiling): Sure, Carl. Completely understand. Your loss! Sharon, as you can see, I now include employee volunteering as an element on my radar for the development of business strategy. I don't think you will find many companies who think in this way, but what I have learned to appreciate is that the opportunities that can be developed through employee volunteering programmes can actually leverage the things we want to do in the business, and not just the development of internal capabilities and competences and culture. I mean the way we can leverage our employee network in the volunteering space to assist in the achievement of business results.

**Sharon:** And in English?

**Brian** (laughing): Take an idea for a new food product. Through volunteering in the community, we can talk to people about their food likes and dislikes, in a way which marketing surveys don't always capture. This might just give us a thought that could lead to a new product. An example. We held a sports day recently with one of our community partners. I volunteered to lead the basketball competition between two groups of schoolkids. In chatting to them, I understood that they leave home with breakfast cereal in bags to snack on. They are not buying snack bars, or granola bars or things like that. They just grab a bunch of breakfast cereals. Their mothers think it's healthier than fried snacks such as potato chips or chocolate snacks, of course, but the kids want the feeling of dipping into a bag and eating a snack one by one, not taking bites of a bar. This way, they can also share with their friends. I went to talk to our marketing people about that and now they have initiated a piece of research about kids' cereals-snacking behaviour, because that's an area of healthy eating we would like to explore. The point is, I could have had that thought anywhere, even by just talking with my own kids. But the fact is, I didn't. I gained this particular insight, and began to think about it, in my volunteering activity. There is something about the volunteering context that makes you more open and more attuned to what's going on around you. You listen more.

**Sharon:** OK. I get it. But it's quite a random effect, is it not?

**Brian:** Yes. But the more we have employees volunteering, the more insights we will gain. I take what's happening in EVP as a way of potentially leveraging, or contributing to business strategy development and execution. It's only one input, of course, and certainly not the most significant. But it's there and I take it into account as far as I can assess and evaluate it. The more the effects of EVP can be measured, the more the true cyclical impact can be understood. We volunteer, get an insight, use it in the business, business succeeds, we volunteer more. Get it?

**Sharon:** Got it.

**Brian:** Look, I have to get to a meeting now. I will be happy for you to be in touch with me if there is anything more you need to know. I am sure Carl has already given you my details.

**Sharon:** Thank you so much, Brian. That was fascinating.

Brian stood up to leave and Carl opened the conference room door for him, patting him on the shoulder as a gesture of thanks. Carl took the helm once again.

**Carl:** Good. That was helpful, I hope. Now you understand the fit with business strategy, and of course, by implication, human resources strategy, which is a derivative of the business strategy, let's talk about the **seven steps of designing a successful EVP**:

1. Identify the contribution of the employee volunteering programme

2. List the outcomes

3. Consider the cost-to-benefit ratio

4. Determine how the corporate volunteering programme fits within each business unit's own strategies

5. Select the cause(s) or non-profit with which to partner

6. Identify the pressing socio-economic-environmental issues in the local community

7. Find out what employees are passionate about

Step 1 looks like this:

| **Identify the contribution of the employee volunteering programme** | |
|---|---|
| Decide on the structure, purpose and parameters of the employee volunteer programme. Examples may include: | |
| For the business: | • Nature of community partnerships<br>• Paid time to volunteer<br>• Budget considerations |
| For the employees: | • Work outside their professional skill areas |
| For the community: | • A focused organisation-wide cause<br>• Individual volunteer work supported by the company via training, technology or financial assistance |

This is arguably the hardest step. It requires you to think through all the possible ways the overall EVP will contribute to its various stakeholders. To do this, you need to assemble a range of different stakeholders, internal and external, and map the entire potential for multifaceted contributions that we would like the EVP to deliver. This chart lists just a couple of examples, but at this stage, you really must think about the framework, and the non-negotiables, that your EVP will have to fit into. If the company management insists that all volunteering is on employee time, and not paid time, this may dictate another kind of volunteering programme. One that cannot be carried out during working hours, for example.

Let's move on to Step 2. This step is listing the outcomes. Dr Stephen Covey in The Seven Habits of Highly Effective People[17] coined the phrase 'Begin with the end in mind', the second habit. That means knowing what you want to achieve before you set out trying to achieve it. It's no different with EVPs except that we want to go further than what we want to achieve, we want to design for what will happen as a result of what we achieve.

**Sharon:** We want to design for what will happen as a result of what we achieve. I need to think about that.

**Carl:** We want to achieve a vibrant EVP where almost everyone will be volunteering, and they'll bring their friends, non-profit partners will love

---

17  Stephen R. Covey, *The Seven Habits of Highly Effective People* (New York: Simon & Schuster, 1989).

us, and we will conduct lots of successful activities which everyone will feel good about. At different stages in the programme, there will be things we can count — number of food baskets distributed, number of people trained, number of volunteer hours, number of kids tutored in their school homework. Many things that give a measure of the time and energy we have invested. But, you know, so what? If I don't know the outcome of all that activity, it's hard for me to know exactly what impact all this time and energy had. What we really want to achieve is the number of kids who pass their exams as a result of tutoring, or the level of increase in school attendance rates, or decrease in absences, or the skills that our employees learn in the hours they spend volunteering, or the number of people that increase their nutrition levels as a result of the food baskets we distribute. Some data is hard to get to, but there are specific outcomes we can target. This requires some discipline of thought. The following chart shows some examples.

### List the outcomes

List the desired outcomes of the programme. Quantify as far as possible. This may include:

| | |
|---|---|
| For the business: | • Improved reputation<br>• Improved brand recognition<br>• Positive media coverage<br>• Improved employee motivation and commitment |
| For the employees: | • Skill development<br>• Team support |
| For the community: | • Improved performance in schools<br>• Improved quality of life in the community |

To assist us in this, we use a technique called **'horizons'**. Let me explain. We look at three horizons, sometimes more, when trying to determine desired outcomes.

**Horizon of the originators.** The originators are the people who have a vested interest in developing an employee volunteer programme. Often, the originators, if they maintain their motivation, can be a singular driving force in the success of an EVP, so it is important to take their views into account. In our case, it was the HR team. In other cases, as we have mentioned, it may be grassroots employees. It might even be the CEO of a company who says he wants an EVP. It might be a non-profit partner who approaches the company with a community investment request. But the point is that these originators often have some specific ideas about why they want an EVP in the company, and maybe they also think they know what the parameters should be. They may also have a list of factors, which should determine how the programme would be run, or how it should not be run.

**Horizon of the participants.** This refers to anyone who would be actually involved in volunteering projects. For an EVP to matter to anyone, it must take into account the numerous and personal reasons for getting involved in the first place. If the participants do not feel personally connected, they will not stay interested. Oh, and by participants I don't just mean employees. We also include here the external participants in the community.

**Horizon of the work.** Each volunteer project has its own rules and possible outcomes. For example, if the originators wanted to see team-building as one of the main outcomes of the EVP, an after-school tutoring programme would be a poor choice. Not because it's a bad idea for volunteering, but because tutoring is primarily a solo volunteer role. The genre of the volunteer work always comes with specific parameters that allow for certain outcomes. The horizon of work will only allow for certain objectives to be achieved.

Ultimately, all the horizons need to fit together harmoniously. It's like this. When my interests are aligned with the interests of others, everyone benefits. But when my interests compete with those of others, I may feel forced to choose what is good for me at the expense of others. Companies need to offer EV programmes where employees can discover their own personal motivations for volunteering. When that happens, volunteering becomes important. It's no longer just a good thing to do, it's personal. People who previously had little or no time for community activities find themselves spending significant time for the benefit of the organisation they volunteer for. Why? Because it all becomes very personal. The motivators move from an external construct of 'It's the right thing to do' to an internal and personal place of 'For me to be right, I have to do it'.

**Sharon:** Let me get that again. 'For me to be right, I have to do it.' That's a powerful sentence.

**Carl:** Yes. I regret that I didn't invent it. I heard it from a great guy called Chris Jarvis. He is an expert EVP consultant based in Canada, and I heard him talk at a conference here in London a few months ago. That's his sentence. I also found it very powerful. The Horizons approach is his too. And the Seven Steps. You can see where the Horizons model helps you define the outcomes from the different perspectives of all the different stakeholders, and ensure that they are aligned before you decide what it is you are going to do. Chris Jarvis calls it convergence of horizons. He says that this is where many EVPs really begin to suffer. The only outcomes that matter are those of the originators. Everything else is seen as good, but not essential. By forcing an EVP team to look at the programme from each perspective and see the horizon as each group would see it, we change our priorities.

Step 3 is next. This is the one the finance people like to get their teeth into. It's about determining how much bang you get for your buck. In other words, your cost-effectiveness, and the critical allocation of resources to ensure that the maximum return, or outcome, is delivered for the amount of resources the company and all the volunteers plan to expend.

### Consider the cost-to-benefit ratio

Based on the linkages with other strategic goals in the company, and the community benefits, determine the financial and time expenditure value of the programme

Evaluate the substantive quality of the metrics that have been chosen. Do the metrics support the cost?

Decide on which best practice benchmarks or ranking systems to utilise to support the cost-to-benefit ratios you have chosen

This is very important, though many companies do not really address it. If we can demonstrate a real return on the work we are doing inside the business as well as in our community, then the programme is more able to achieve everything it was designed for. Our objective is not philanthropy. We want this to be a key asset that differentiates our corporate brand and our culture. To do this we need to engage other departments to collect data for measurement (PR, Marketing, HR, R&D, etc.) and use the partnership with non-profit organisations to discover how they calculate the social benefits they deliver as a result of our intervention. We also try to benchmark metrics against any international and industry-wide standards. There are some more sophisticated calculations which people call social return on investment, or SROI,[18] but I won't go into that now, it's a little complex. Suffice it to say that, for our needs, we must select some measurable benchmarks of effectiveness and rank the various community investment and EVP options against these, to determine which programme is optimal. This is, of course, a fairly straightforward approach used in many other business decisions. The difference is that, as we have said, getting a real measure for outcomes is not easy over the short term.

Let's move on to Step 4. This next stage requires drilling this down a little further. We have said that the programme should be aligned to the overall corporate direction and strategy. Even so, it will only work if the specific department heads support it. Therefore, this stage looks at what benefits such a programme would deliver in each and every department of the company. There is always something. Sometimes, there are very specific things that show up as benefits in a particular department, whereas in others it might be more generic. For example, I have found that working at FareShare, as I mentioned, helps me understand issues related to food safety and food handling and storage. This could be very beneficial to marketing and sales employees who would not normally have this experience in their jobs.

---

18  For a more detailed view on the concept of SROI, see SROI Europe, www.sroi-europe.org. Most businesses are not at the level of an SROI calculation for their community activities. At best, they calculate basic outcomes, but do not work with a full SROI methodology.

**Determine how the corporate volunteering programme fits within each business unit's own strategies. Two examples are shown below:**

| Public relations and reputation building | Human resources strategy |
|---|---|
| Improve customer perceptions by connecting brand to community interests | Enhance recruitment success |
| Gain brand loyalty by including customers and vendors in EVP activities | Contribute to improved retention rates |
| Enhance existing CSR efforts to strengthen brand trust among customers | Improve employee satisfaction |
| Utilise social media to promote activities and tell stories of employee activities in the community | Improve employee motivation and commitment |
| Improve or alter corporate image and reputation | Improve or develop organisation culture and team working improvement |
| Demonstrate clear commitments and company priorities towards the health of communities to leaders and government officials | Provide platform for skill and competency development |

In a publication by Junior Achievement Worldwide on the benefits of employee volunteering,[19] they say that 'there is ample evidence that volunteering can strengthen work teams and build employee skills as well as contribute to professional development. However, beyond personnel development, there is additional evidence that company-supported EVPs can also contribute to the bottom line.' Here is a summary of some of the excellent data quoted in this report:

**Selected data from Junior Achievement, *The Benefits of Employee Volunteer Programs* (2009)[20]**

- 81.7% of corporations focus their employee volunteer programmes on core business functions
- 52% of companies stress a commitment to community service in their corporate mission statement to help build a cooperative corporate culture

Companies are tying their workplace volunteering programmes to:

- Address public relations goals (83%)
- Meet marketing and communications objectives (64%)

19  www.ja.org.

20  Junior Achievement, *The Benefits of Employee Volunteer Programs*, www.ja.org/files/ BenefitsofEmployeeVolunteerPrograms.pdf: 4,5, accessed 1 June 2010.

- Develop employee skills (60%)
- Recruit and retain employees (58%)
- The 100 companies rated as 'the best to work for' received 1.9 times more applications per post than average, offering a wider choice of candidates for each role
- Employers whose employees volunteer gain a more highly skilled workforce, with competency gains showing up at 14–17% as a direct result of volunteering

Step 5 moves us on a little. So far, we have spent a lot of time and energy looking at the framework of the programme, the structure, the rationale and the overall fit of whatever it is we design as our EVP. It's now time to consider how to distil the right cause, or causes, and the right partner, or partners, from the thousands of options available. Sooner or later we have to make a decision, right?

**Select the cause(s) or non-profit with which to partner**

Evaluate brand alignment between the company and the non-profit organisation or cause

List the obvious areas where the company's work in the community would be visible to employees as well as customers and the wider community

Hold exploratory meetings with potential non-profits to discover if there is a good fit between the values of the company and the mission and values of the non-profit organisation

Survey company's stakeholders  (internal and external) to determine the driving perspectives of the non-profit organisation, community issues and potential alignment with various causes

Step 6 is about relevance. To paraphrase Stephen Covey again, you have to be sure that the ladder is standing against the right wall. As we mentioned earlier today, we must ensure that we identify a need that is relevant to the community, not just something we feel we want to do, for our own diverse reasons. There are many sources of assistance we can call on to do this, and it is critical to ensure the development of a balanced view here. If the EVP ends up being something the CEO is passionate about, but it does not really serve what is perceived to be a pressing community need, it won't work. The wider the consultation process, the greater the chances of success.

### Identify the pressing socio-economic-environmental issues in the local community

Perform a community audit to determine the pressing socio-economic-environmental issues. Identify and utilise individuals who are active community builders, activists and academics to guide in these assessments to ensure they are balanced

Review resources within the company that may be employed in addressing these issues

Involve stakeholders by determining their awareness of the company's present community and employee volunteering initiatives, if any, and of competitive company programmes

Survey stakeholders in order to assess the influence these present initiatives have, and the influence any new/expanded initiatives may have

Interview a representative sample of employees in order to identify present areas of involvement within the community

Finally, Step 7. Even if employees are not currently volunteering, they have latent passions in areas in which they would volunteer, given the right platform. Again, the more closely we can hook into these existing passions, the more successful our programme will be. Mark my words, Sharon. Everyone has something they are passionate about., I promise you. Not everyone will want to bring his or her passion to an employee volunteering programme, but everyone has potential. It might take more than a survey to find that out, but even a simple employee survey of potential volunteering interests could give some indication.

### Find out what employees are passionate about

Survey or talk to employees to know what currently captures their attention and passion

Review to what extent the connections are between the company's core business and the passions of employees

And that concludes all the seven steps of designing an EVP. All we need after that is execution. Piece of cake!

**Sharon:** Absolutely. This is so clear, Carl. How did you develop this?

**Carl:** As I mentioned, I adopted the plan that I heard Chris Jarvis present. These are his Seven Steps. But there is something else Chris Jarvis said that I haven't mentioned. It is very important that you understand that there is a difference between transactional volunteering and transformational volunteering.

**Sharon:** OK. Definition, please.

**Carl: Transactional volunteering** involves an exchange of goods or services. We show up with a group of volunteers and give our time and some resources to a cause or non-profit and in return, we get publicity, or the benefit of team building, or a fun day out of the office. That's transactional volunteering. As you have probably guessed, this is not our prime objective. Even if it means a bit of a morale boost around the company.

What we're after is **transformational volunteering**. Our goal is to see people changed in meaningful ways by getting involved in areas of life they may not have considered before. Let me give you an example of what I mean. A friend of mine, quite the affluent type from Kingston, began volunteering with us at FareShare, as a food sorter. At first she stuck out like a sore thumb. There she was, dressed in smart suits, Armani earrings and painted nails, standing next to some of the most modest, not-so-affluent folk from the area. The kind of people who could make the value of a pair of Armani earrings last for a year of Sunday lunches, with custard. Some who had themselves been recipients of FareShare food baskets. You know, it is often the people who have been on the receiving end of charity that are the first to volunteer. This friend was a fish out of water. I don't think she had exchanged more than two words with people like those she met at FareShare until that point, unless they were tradesmen or check-out staff. She was obviously out of place. She had only started volunteering because she was bored and doing nothing much that she deemed of value. Slowly, she started to tone down both what she wore and the way she talked. She didn't become a totally different person, but after a few months, she was really looking like one of the team, ready to do her bit and blend in. She made an effort to understand some of the hardships that those around her had gone through, and they respected her for that. She listened and listened and listened. You know what, her manner is now much more open and tolerant. Even her husband and children say they see the difference in her whole outlook on life. She is listening differently and appreciating her own ability to make a difference in a new way. She admitted to me that she feels she is getting more out of volunteering than she believes she is contributing. As extraordinary as it sounds, what she experienced was transformation. She had stumbled on her highest level of contribution. The volunteering we do isn't about how much work we perform, even though that's important. It's about seeing the world differently. It's about seeing ourselves differently. This is transformational volunteering. The more we can gain this type of benefit for employees in our volunteering context, the more they will personally benefit and the more they will bring these new qualities into play to advance the business. That's what we feel EVP should be about. Our highest level of contribution is not limited to our skills or stature in society. We have something valuable to contribute that comes out of who we are, out of our own intrinsic value. And the more we believe this about ourselves, the more we have to offer everyone around us. That's the greatest benefit to having this programme here at work. It builds self-esteem in a way that almost nothing else can.

**Sharon:** Gosh. I wasn't expecting that.

**Carl:** Yeah, but really, it's the point of the whole thing. In fact, we believe this kind of storytelling is important for capturing what we learn while we're out there volunteering. That's why we do the photos. A photo is a tangible reminder of the story. Before every volunteering event, we hold a brief to make sure everyone knows what we're doing and why. We cover all of the important stuff. Even some of things I was talking about in my friend's story, about how to listen and fit in rather than assume you are just going into another business activity. We make presentations at staff meetings, involve people in round-table discussions and we make sure to tell anyone who's volunteered to share their story with others and ask them what they think about it. We also encourage employees to use social media to write blogs, create video logs, or use Twitter or Facebook to tell their friends and family about some of their experiences. It's a powerful way to understand what we've learned.

**Sharon:** Amazing. Do people do it?

**Carl:** Yes. A lot actually. You see the results around you, hanging on the walls. People love to tell stories. And we all like to share our own experiences. So yes. As long as the company keeps encouraging it and listening, it's a popular cultural piece of how we engage our community and each other. You can see it all on our Facebook and Twitter and Blog pages — all the URLs are on my card. Also, you should check out the Intel blog, for example, CSR@Intel.[21] Their posts are truly engaging and full of spirit. They send their employees all around the world with Intel Service Education Corp, to educate different groups in computer skills. They blog about their experiences at each location. It's very moving, actually, to read these first-hand insights and stories, often with photos of local people, sat at Intel-powered laptops and learning what to do with them. It is clearly very empowering for the Intel people, as much as it is for the local communities they serve.

**Sharon:** Yes, someone else mentioned that recently. I'll check it out, for sure, as well as all your websites and blogs.

**Carl:** Hey, guess what, it's after four already. You have a train back home at five, correct?

**Sharon:** Yes.

**Carl:** In that case, there's just time for a few questions before you leave. Anything we haven't covered?

**Sharon:** Carl, you have covered more than I thought could possibly be covered. Frankly, I thought I was coming to hear about some nice programmes, and the way you encourage and reward volunteers. In fact, I have received what seems like a doctorate in volunteering. Just hearing

21  blogs.intel.com/csr.

you and Jenny and Brian talking today has been pretty transformational in itself, even before I have gone out and done anything for anyone else. I have many questions, but I won't offload them on you now, as I want to think through everything you have said, and how we should be going about things in my company. Carl, thanks so much for taking the time to share all this with me. It is crystal clear to me that HR has a strong contribution to make.

Sharon felt she couldn't thank Carl enough. But Carl wasn't looking for thanks; he was happy. He loved talking about his work and loved helping others. In fact, he felt that he had had a transformational day also.

# 11
# Employees and the environment

There was just one thing that Sharon felt she hadn't got to the bottom of completely, and that was what employees can do in the workplace to support the company's environmental efforts and become more environmentally conscious citizens. It was clear to her that understanding company policy and procedures was one thing, but that employees could also make a significant difference to the company's day-by-day performance by supporting environmental initiatives. She also thought that this was an area in which she could make some quick wins by reducing costs, developing team work and supporting the organisational culture. It was the kind of thing that most people could relate to. Something you didn't have to spend hours explaining. People understood quickly. In fact everyone was talking about green office, green building, green teams, green this, green that, green pretty much everything.

It was Saturday afternoon, and Sharon was at home with a cup of coffee, contemplating what she would make for dinner that evening. Robert had taken the children ice-skating at a new rink that had opened not too far away. She had a good couple of hours before she had to get into the kitchen and start rattling those pans. The environment was on her mind. She hadn't really wanted to think about work, but ideas kept popping up. It was one of the final pieces of the CSR jigsaw puzzle that she needed to think about before she could start pulling everything together and developing some sort of plan. She started with a quick Internet search. She soon came across an article about how Deloitte deals with green issues in its business.

# Deloitte: Best Practices for Going Green[1]
## By Deborah Fleischer, President of Green Impact

What do you think of when you hear Deloitte?

You might think of a professional services firm or Big Four auditor. Today, the company has also put a big green stake in the ground, both looking internally to green its operations and as an offering in its consulting practice. Two aspects of this work are worth noting: Deloitte's internal green team, working to engage employees in sustainability, and its Green Sync™ tool.[2] I had the chance to have an e-mail exchange with Thomas Dekar,[3] vice chairman of Deloitte LLP, regional managing principal of the North Central Region and corporate responsibility officer for the Deloitte U.S. Firms. He shed some light on the origins of Deloitte's programs and offerings. Read on to learn about Deloitte's best green business practices for engaging employees in sustainability.

### Internal green team

In January 2008, a Green Champion was selected, and green teams were formed, in each office. An Office Greening Toolkit, with projects covering the key aspects of sustainability, was distributed, and shortly thereafter, a 'How green is *your* footprint?™' survey was made available. The Green Leadership Council (GLC) was established in August 2008 as a voice for employees to help shape national programs.

The GLC is composed of senior representatives from each of the eight regions in the US and India as well as representatives from Talent, Community Involvement, Field Operations, Information Technology and the Enterprise Sustainability group. The council maintains a constant dialogue between national leadership and people on the ground in offices across the country.

The GLC's broad role is to assist in implementing a sustainable green culture at Deloitte, develop and share green ideas across regions, participate in the development of greening goals, track and monitor performance in implementing ideas and achieving greening goals, and identify and address challenges and opportunities related to greening Deloitte.

---

1   Deborah Fleischer, 'Best Practices for Going Green', 1 February 2010, www. triplepundit.com/2010/02/best-practices-for-going-green, accessed 6 June 2010. Reproduced with permission of the Deborah Fleischer, President of Green Impact (www.greenimpact.com), a strategic environmental consulting practice that helps companies engage employees, strengthen their relationships with stakeholders, develop profitable green initiatives and communicate their successes and challenges.

2   www.deloitte.com/view/en_US/us/article/be64066f0f001210VgnVCM100000-ba42f00aRCRD.htm, accessed 6 June 2010.

3   www.deloitte.com/view/en_US/us/About/article/710e1dd26f00e110VgnVCM100000ba42f00aRCRD.htm, accessed 6 June 2010.

## The biggest wins and best green practices

'The most important factor in our success has been the widespread engagement and participation of our people. We believe this has come about in large measure from our approach to greening at Deloitte,' explained Dekar. He outlined six key characteristics of the program:

- **Opt-in:** The green programs operate on an opt-in basis, because Deloitte recognizes that making responsible decisions can't be forced; people have to want to be 'green.'
- **Focus on raising awareness and education:** Much of the focus has been on communication that generates awareness and education regarding the impact the company makes on the environment.
- **Empower at the local level:** Green Teams empower greening at the local level. The national office provides direction, materials and support, but sustainability is ultimately local and in the hands of its people.
- **Small changes can make an impact:** 'We place emphasis on the importance of everyone's individual actions; and offer the perspective that small changes when multiplied by the 45,000 people of Deloitte can result in a huge impact. Consistent with that approach, through the green footprint surveys we focus on the positive aspect of increasing a green footprint by being more environmentally responsible,' commented Dekar. Thus far, 29,000 people have taken the office footprint survey.
- **Transparency:** He continued, 'Another strategy is to be open and transparent about the progress of our offices in completing the 50 greening projects contained in the greening toolkits. This encourages friendly competition among office and regions. An interactive GreenDot Scorecard available to all was created to publicize results covering over 100 locations.'
- **Collaboration:** Most recently, GreenShare, a mega collaboration site was established. It provides real-time discussion and a repository of best practices, providing opportunities for employees to participate and collaborate.

### Green Sync

In addition to the green team efforts, Deloitte also developed a tool to support employee and stakeholder engagement. I have not had the opportunity to see the tool in action, but Dekar commented, 'Green Sync™ is a framework providing actionable solutions to increase employee engagement and support sustainability goals and associated business objectives.'

The elements of Green Sync™ include the following:

- **Strategic visioning:** Developing strategic goals in a clear and actionable manner, thus setting the direction for all other related activities.
- **Stakeholder alignment:** Facilitating stakeholder and leadership buy-in, and synchronizing messaging.
- **Communications and branding:** Using communication tactics to inspire and motivate change, while reflecting the organization's vision and brand in all messages in such a way that the brand is enhanced.

- **Learning:** Using delivery methods to educate employees on how their individual actions can make a positive impact on the organization.
- **Culture:** Cultivating an environment that supports sustainability initiatives.
- **Rewards:** Establishing recognition and/or reward programs for employees who demonstrate commitment to sustainability initiatives.

Dekar explained, 'Because people are the most important asset of any organization, companies can benefit through increased recognition as an employer of choice — one that recruits and retains the best, most diverse talent, and has a collaborative culture that engages employees in achieving sustainability.' He outlined other business benefits from Green Sync, including:

> **"** It helps organizations fulfill their sustainability vision by 'walking the talk,' and avoiding 'greenwashing.'
> - From a bottom-line perspective, it provides innovative opportunities to reduce costs and reap long-term benefits while also increasing employee morale and commitment to the organization.
> - It helps an organization positively impact the environment while enhancing its internal and external brand.

**To learn more**

To learn more about Deloitte's green programs, see its 2009 Corporate Responsibility report.[4]

*Deborah Fleischer is president of Green Impact, a strategic environmental consulting practice that helps companies engage employees, strengthen their relationships with stakeholders, develop profitable green initiatives and communicate their successes and challenges. You can follow her occasional tweet @GreenImpact.*

Sharon was impressed by this article. She thought that Deloitte clearly seem to have taken this environmental approach seriously. She also liked the article and looked for more by Deborah Fleischer. Just as quickly as she had come across the first article, she came across a second.

4  www.deloitte.com/view/en_US/us/About/corporate-responsibility/index.htm, accessed 6 June 2010.

# 10 Best Practices for Building Green Teams[5]
**By Deborah Fleischer, President of Green Impact**

GreenBiz.com and Green Impact have partnered to release a new report, 'Green Teams: Engaging Employees in Sustainability.'[6] Based on interviews with green team leaders from Intel, Yahoo!, eBay and Genentech, as well as a review of the latest literature on employee engagement and green teams, the report provides an overview of the best practices companies are using to support and guide green teams. It is divided into four key sections: making the business case for green teams; getting started; four emerging trends; and green team best practices.

It is a great resource for companies and organizations just beginning to think about creating a green team and for those ready to take their existing program to the next level.

## What is a Green Team?

Green teams are self-organized, grassroots and cross-functional groups of employees who voluntarily come together to educate, inspire and empower employees around sustainability. They identify and implement specific solutions to help their organization operate in a more environmentally sustainable fashion. Most green teams initially focus on greening operations at the office, addressing such issues as recycling in the office, composting food waste, reducing the use of disposable takeout containers and eliminating plastic water bottles.

This focus on operations is evolving and some green teams are beginning to focus their efforts on integrating sustainability into employees' personal lives, while others are bringing consumers into the equation and aligning their efforts to support broader corporate sustainability objectives.

## The Business Case

Because most companies do not track metrics related to green teams, it can be challenging to make the business case for investing resources to support them. However, based on a review of existing green teams and interviews with experts, the business case includes:

- Cost savings by integrating energy efficiency into the workplace and products and services;
- Attracting and retaining the best and brightest talent who want to work for companies with an authentic green commitment; and

5  Deborah Fleischer, '10 Best Practices for Building Green Teams', GreenBiz.com, 7 December 2009, greenbiz.com/blog/2009/12/07/10-best-practices-building-green-teams,

6  Deborah Fleischer, 'Green Teams: Engaging Employees in Sustainability', *GreenBiz Report*, 7 December 2009. www.greenbiz.com/research/report/2009/12/03/green-teams-engaging-employees-sustainability, reproduced with her permission.

- Increased market share and revenues resulting from a stronger brand and new, innovative green products and services.

Carrie Freeman, a corporate sustainability strategist at Intel, commented, 'When it comes to looking at ways to reduce our footprint, we very much see a direct correlation between reducing our costs and engaging our employees.' Be it changing light bulbs, turning off the lights or getting your employees to innovate greener solutions in their jobs, engaging your employees to identify easy, low cost efficiency initiatives can result in significant cost savings.

The National Environmental Education Foundation's (NEEF) recent report 'The Engaged Organization: Corporate Employee Environmental Education Survey and Case Study Findings'[7] stresses, 'By engaging employees, companies can spark innovative changes in everyday business processes that save money and reduce environmental and social impacts while also inspiring employees to make sustainable choices at home and in their communities.'

According to a case study by BSR[8] on Intel's green teams, 'It may seem like a distraction in these times of financial instability to focus on employees' passion for sustainability, but efforts toward employee engagement will strengthen a company's employee base-which will be a crucial element in recovering from the recession. And maintaining employee loyalty and high productivity will help companies position themselves for success as the economy revives.'

And eBay's volunteer Green Team leader in Omaha stresses, 'Having a Green Team gives people something to believe in; something that is a tangible, visible representation that we are a company that cares.'

## Best Practices

The report concludes with a detailed summary of 10 best practices for green teams, with specific examples from leading companies. The best practices detailed include:

1. Start with the visible and tangible: focus on internal operations
2. Get senior management involved, but don't lose the grassroots energy
3. Engage employees to capture ideas
4. Communicate and share best practices
5. Engage employees with their bellies: the low carbon diet campaign
6. Engage employees in their personal lives
7. Engage customers to be part of the solution
8. Use art to raise awareness
9. Create a toolkit to support and guide green teams
10. Align green teams with corporate sustainability goals

---

7 www.neefusa.org/business/report_2009.htm, accessed 6 June 2010.
8 Blythe Chorn, 'Case in Point: How Intel Engages Employees in Sustainability', Business for Social Responsibility, 25 August 2009, images.carbonrally.com/assets/BSR_Insight_Intel_Employee.pdf, accessed 6 June 2010.

Download the report[9] to learn more about these best practices and for a comprehensive list of available resources on employee engagement and green teams (a summary table is included below).

**Resources for Learning More**

- Building an Organizational Culture of Sustainability[10]
- Corporate Green Teams: A New Social Trend at Work [11]
- Crossing the Green Divide[12]
- Corporate Green Teams: Sustainable Business from the Bottom Up[13]
- eBay Green Team[14]
- Employee Transportation Coordinator Handbook[15]
- Employee Engagement for Sustainability: A Survey of Emerging Best Practices at 30 Large Global Organizations[16]
- The Engaged Organization[17]
- Green Genes at Genentech[18]
- How Intel Engages Employees in Sustainability[19]
- How to Build a Green Team: The First Step to Sustainability[20]
- How to Start an Employee Commute-Benefits Program in 10 Easy Steps[21]
- Leading From the Middle: The Power of the Green Champion[22]

9 www.greenbiz.com/research/report/2009/12/03/green-teams-engaging-employees-sustainability, accessed 6 June 2010.

10 www.triplepundit.com/2009/09/building-an-organizational-culture-of-sustainability-employee-engagement, accessed 6 June 2010.

11 www.altaterra.net/resource/dynamic/blogs/20080721_144258_24980.pdf, accessed 6 June 2010.

12 www.deloitte.com/view/en_US/us/Services/additional-services/Corporate-Responsibility-Sustainability/article/15fae890a620e110VgnVCM100000ba42f00aRCRD.htm, accessed 6 June 2010.

13 www.greenbiz.com/news/2008/06/07/corporate-green-teams-sustainable-business-bottom?page=0%2C2, accessed 6 June 2010.

14 www.ebaygreenteam.com, accessed 6 June 2010.

15 www.climatebiz.com/research/report/2000/11/19/employee-transportation-coordinator-handbook, accessed 6 June 2010.

16 www.groomresearch.com/ee.pdf, accessed 6 June 2010.

17 www.triplepundit.com/2009/09/employee-engagement-three-tips-for-engaging-employees-in-sustainability, accessed 25 August 2010.

18 www.triplepundit.com/2009/07/green-genes-genentech-green-teams-go-biotech, accessed 6 June 2010.

19 images.carbonrally.com/assets/BSR_Insight_Intel_Employee.pdf, accessed 6 June 2010.

20 www.greenbiz.com/news/2009/05/05/how-build-green-team-first-step-sustainability, accessed 6 June 2010.

21 www.greenbiz.com/research/report/2008/09/14/how-start-employee-commute-benefits-program-10-easy-steps, accessed 6 June 2010.

22 www.greenbiz.com/news/2008/10/12/leading-middle-power-green-champion, accessed 6 June 2010.

- Making Your Impact at Work[23]
- The Role of Human Resource Management in Corporate Social Responsibility[24]
- Sustainable Silicon Valley Green Team[25]
- Ten Keys for Educating and Engaging Employees[26]
- Top Strategies for Getting Employees Behind Sustainability[27]
- Three Tips for Engaging Employees in Sustainability[28]

'What amazing insights and a wealth of information,' thought Sharon. She asked herself when she could possibly make the time to read all these articles and reports. Each one seemed to her more interesting than the previous one. She wanted to devour every single one and learn all there was possible to learn about engaging employees in environmental teams. The Andromex Green Team. Her head was already buzzing with possibilities, and she hadn't even read one of the resources quoted in the article. However, what this told her was that there is power in the environment. Organisational power. It is something that can create a sense of common mission and activity which affects everyone, both in the workplace and in the home, and which no-one can dispute. It is not a political thing, not a charity/do-good thing, not something which anyone could have any objection to. Especially as greening the organisation would save the organisation money in the long run, and even perhaps in the short run. Greening the organisation has the power to unite people and create a consensus in a non-threatening way.

Sharon remembered something else she had come across when she was reading CSR reports about how companies make changes in the way employees commute to work to reduce environmental impact. She also recalled an interesting blog-post that referred to a survey in the USA about biking to work. The survey had found that 40% of Americans would be happy with the opportunity to bike to work, if safe facilities were available. The blog-post,[29] by Julie

23 netimpact.org/displaycommon.cfm?an=1&subarticlenbr=2745, accessed 6 June 2010.

24 www.greenbiz.com/research/report/2009/09/19/role-human-resource-management-corporate-social-responsibility-0, accessed 6 June 2010.

25 www.sustainablesv.org/dms/sustainability-teams/launching-green-team, accessed 25 August 2010.

26 www.greenbiz.com/research/report/2000/11/09/ten-keys-educating-and-engaging-employees, accessed 6 June 2010.

27 greenimpact.wordpress.com/2009/10/26/bsr-2009-top-strategies-for-getting-employees-behind-sustainability, accessed 6 June 2010.

28 greenimpact.wordpress.com/2009/09/22/three-tips-for-engaging-employees-in-sustainability, accessed 6 June 2010.

29 Julie Urlaub, 'Get Paid to Bike to Work', 9 February 2010, blog.taigacompany.com/blog/taiga-company/0/0/get-paid-to-bike-to-work, accessed 6 June 2010.

Urlaub of Taiga Company,[30] a consulting firm advising businesses on green and sustainability issues, makes the point that

> commuting to work by bike can be a component of a business sustainability programme. Cycling as alternative transportation helps the environment by keeping $CO_2$ out of the air and bikes require far less materials, energy and waste in their production than even the 'greenest' car.

In the USA, biking to work is recognised as a fringe benefit for tax purposes and all costs related to bicycle maintenance are even tax-deductible. Sharon wondered if that was also applicable in the UK. In addition, however, Julie Urlaub states that becoming a 'bike-friendly office' is easy and that there are many benefits to employers in adopting a bike commuting programme. Sharon read Julie's list as it appeared on the Internet:

- Increase worker productivity: Fit employees are more alert, more productive, perform better and more efficiently.

- Improve employee health.

- Lower health care costs: healthier employees can reduce health insurance costs.

- Reduce parking cost.

- Reduced carbon emissions.

- Reduce turnover: Employers who appreciate workers' personal needs have less employee turnover.

- Supporting bike commuting is less expensive than an in-office fitness facility.

- Improve work/life balance: Bike commuting can be substituted for the gym, saving employee's personal time.

- Community engagement: Bicycles can be produced and maintained locally by local bike shops contributing to local job opportunities as part of a sustainable economy.

- Improve company image.

- Expand eco awareness within the organization and community.

- Link wellness programmes with the corporate sustainability plan.

Sharon felt this could be a very interesting experiment. She wondered if a green team could also examine employee habits in commuting to work and how many of the benefits on Julie Urlaub's list could be realised at Andromex.

---

30 www.taigacompany.com/about/3.

'Integrating sustainability into employees' lives', as Deborah Fleischer had put it. Sharon was quite taken up with this thought. She realised that there was another element of corporate social responsibility which was inviting her, as an HR manager, to explore, develop, lead, create, innovate and more. She again wondered how on earth she would be able to absorb all this knowledge in order to make sensible recommendations to her boss and the Exec team on how to leverage this overwhelming opportunity.

Then Sharon had a brainwave. She remembered that one of her new HR recruits, responsible for HR processes in the Sales Division, had said that she was involved in an EcoTeam in her neighbourhood. This was one of these teams involving community members who get together to learn about environmental practices in the home and implement them together as a community.[31] Sharon hadn't thought too much of it at the time, but now it suddenly came back to her. She had said that she had been involved in this EcoTeam for over a year now, and that they had saved money on electric bills, and on a few other things, though she couldn't recall what. Sharon remembered that she said she really enjoyed being a member of the team, and that she had come to know her neighbours more closely and made new friends: she had hardly exchanged two words with them before, and now they were all practically best friends, socialising and taking trips with the children, an involvement far beyond their initial interest in protecting the environment. 'That's it,' she thought. 'Joann is the one who is going to lead our Green Team. Joann the Green. Green Joann. The Andromex Green Team, let's make it a reality, Joann.' Sharon laughed to herself and thought that come Monday morning, Joann was going to get an assignment she hadn't expected. A green assignment.

Sharon was still taken up with all her green thoughts as she realised that time was getting on and she had better cook up something tasty for the returning Ice Champions.

～

It was Monday afternoon and she and Joann were sitting in Sharon's office, talking about Joann's work programme and the problems of recruiting good sales people. She needed two new sales managers for the UK, as one had left after two years, and another was needed for the sales restructure as the business was developing.

**Sharon:** What's the problem in recruiting sales people, Joann? This has never been an issue before.

**Joann:** Sharon, I know, but let's face it, we are not all that attractive compared to other companies operating in our sector. Our terms and conditions are average, our career progression opportunities are reasonable, but we just don't have anything that stands out as a unique and attractive employer brand. I have been meaning to talk to you about this.

31 ecoteams.org.uk.

**Sharon:** Yes, I've been thinking a lot about this too. When I was in San Diego, I learnt many new things about employer branding and corporate social responsibility. One of the aspects of this is how potential employees view us as operating responsibly. Actually, I have been thinking a little about this and putting two and two together to come up with something that might help, and which I think you might find interesting.

**Joann:** I get it. You have something you want me to do. I haven't been here all that long, but your reputation precedes you.

**Sharon:** Good. No surprises then. (They laughed.) Corporate social responsibility is an important element in building an employer brand these days. I remember the stories about your Eco-Team in your local neighbourhood. I was thinking that perhaps you would like to lead a green team network of volunteers at Andromex. We haven't got a corporate policy on this yet, and I was wondering if we could start to build things up from grassroots level. There must be a host of other employees who are interested in protecting the environment. Perhaps you could start something up on a small scale, as a pilot, in one or two departments, and see how it catches on?

**Joann:** You mean like a neighbourhood EcoTeam, where employees monitor their own personal environmental impacts?

**Sharon:** I was thinking more along the lines of how employees behave at work with regards to saving resources, recycling, reducing waste and so on, though there is no reason they cannot apply this to their personal and home lives. What I really want is to deliver several benefits: (1) Employees will make changes in their behaviour at work and improve our impact on the environment and save money for the company, (2) Employees will be engaged in a team project thereby improving dialogue and team work, (3) Employees will have the opportunity to do something meaningful beyond their daily work, which will give them added motivation. The outcome of this will be a benefit to the environment, to the employees themselves and to the company. Ultimately I want to use the data from this pilot to gain management support for a company-wide programme and the development of a clear policy on environment. An added benefit of course would be benefits to employees in their personal and home lives. Eventually, this should have an influence on our reputation and attract potential employees who feel it is important that companies play a role in improving the environment. It's not an immediate solution to the recruitment issue, but the sooner we get started, the sooner we will gain the benefits. What do you think?

**Joann:** I love it! It will be a lot of fun. It will be a kind of extension of our local EcoTeam. I can bring in our Team Coach to train up the group as we get started. It's a great idea. Thank you for asking me to do this, Sharon. Where do you think we ought to start? Which department?

**Sharon:** I suggest you float the idea with a few people. Talk to the rest of the HR team and others in different departments. Start where you can get a critical mass of motivated people. What is most important at this stage is a successful pilot that can be a basis for bigger things. You can also talk to Liam from IFC. He is the Environmental Officer at their plant in the USA and he led the development of green teams there. Here is his card. He said he would be happy to help.

**Joann:** Fine, thanks. Starting with the most motivated people sounds like a good idea.

**Sharon:** Objectives? Can we set a tentative plan? Thinking aloud here — two teams of at least five people each in six months having made a measurable difference in the way they do things? You can think about what and how to measure and we can discuss it. This is just an initial level of measurement. Later we can talk about the more complicated things. How does that sound?

**Joann:** It sounds fine, Sharon. I hope to be able to do better than that but I won't promise. Under-promise, over-deliver. I learnt that from you.

**Sharon:** You are a fast learner. I hope to learn a few things from you as well, in the next few months, about the environment. Keep me posted.

**Joann:** Sure. But what do I do about our recruitment issues in the meantime?

# Part II
# **Embedding CSHR**

# 12

# The employee life-cycle

Having spent the last few weeks since the flight to San Diego learning all about corporate social and environmental responsibility, and having systematically gathered her thoughts about each one, Sharon was ready to propose a strategy and a five-year plan to ANDEX. She knew that no ANDEX leader was taking the lead on this, and, although it shouldn't necessarily fall to HR to lead the corporate CSR programme, she was anxious to move things forward. All that she had heard had convinced her that businesses that do not operate in a sustainable way are not highly regarded and face real risks of losing a competitive edge. She felt that she had a duty to drive this, just as the company had a duty towards its stakeholders. She had to think about how she would put the strategy together. The business case was fairly straightforward. There were many studies and positive examples she could pull together to make a compelling argument for CSR at Andromex. The HR piece was about turning employees into CSR ambassadors, both in the way they approached their jobs and in their communications internally and externally.

Sharon had always worked systematically and thoroughly. She liked to think that this was one of the key ingredients in her success: understand the implications and possibilities, envision a direction or an end-point, and build an opinion or a plan from there. Her team often commented on how this helped them as she was always writing briefing papers and case studies that provided them with the rationale behind their work and the context they operated in. Even ANDEX relied on her to present briefing papers for all her HR proposals, and she knew they read them because discussions in meetings often referred to points she had raised. It always made her discussions both with colleagues and with her team more effective. More importantly, this discipline, which she had developed early on in her career, forced her to focus her mind and develop absolute clarity before she imposed her ideas on others. So it was now, as she started to concretise her thoughts about CSHR and what she might do to create a CSHR approach within her function. She knew that CSHR could not operate in a vacuum, and that, in developing her CSHR strategy, there would have to be a minimum level of acceptance from ANDEX and a level of organisational readiness that would enable plans to be integrated into an evolved working culture. She knew she couldn't ignore this. However, as a first step, she thought, she must understand the implications for her own function. Systematic and well-ordered as she was, Sharon set aside two weeks for this process. She blocked out three hours a day on about six days in this period, and allocated this time to 'CSHR functional review'. Her secretary, Amanda was perplexed.

**Amanda:** Sharon, what's this CSHR that's taking up so much time over the next two weeks? Is it a new project you are working on?

**Sharon:** Yes, I need time to work out the basics.

**Amanda:** OK. I will try to work around it but you ought to know that George is scheduling quite a lot of meetings and has blocked out large chunks of time for the IPO discussions and planning. Can't this project wait till that's all over and done with?

**Sharon:** No, Amanda: CSHR is urgent. It will also help us approach the IPO and future growth.

**Amanda:** OK, what is it then, Change Systems in HR? Culture Shock for Human Resources? Creative Strategy for HR?

**Sharon** (laughing): Funny, you are on form today. No, it's not any of those but it includes all of them.

**Amanda:** Well, what is it then?

**Sharon:** It's Corporate Social Human Resources.

**Amanda:** What on earth is that?

**Sharon:** I'll tell you what. As soon as I have prepared the groundwork, in these sessions I have blocked out, you will be the first to see the output and then you will know exactly what CSHR is. OK?

**Amanda:** OK. But I hope it's worth it. This CSHR is going to cause me a whole load of scheduling headaches over these two weeks.

**Sharon:** Come on, Amanda. You're a champion. You'll do it.

Sharon laughed to herself and Amanda waltzed out of her office, and waltzed back in again five minutes later with coffee and some biscuits. Sharon decided to start with a briefing paper covering the areas in which the business impacts on the employee and his or her life-cycle with the company.

# Employee life-cycle and CSHR

The company impacts employees in two cycles that progress simultaneously: the employee's professional cycle and the employee's personal cycle. These cycles run in parallel, though each employee's phasing of each stage in each cycle will be different.

## The professional cycle

### Pre-hire phase

In this phase the company reaches out to potential employees, impacting their potential employability and opportunity to gain first-time employment or improve their professional development by changing jobs.

The company may start this process early on through involvement in the community and community empowerment programmes, or contribute in a more focused way to education or vocational study in order to create the conditions in which individuals may develop in a way which gets them ready for the job market, or provides them with additional skills to advance in the job market.

An important element in this programme is the company's reach-out to universities and other employment establishments to identify candidates for graduate intake and graduate development programmes. The choice of educational establishments, the responsiveness to student's demands, the ease with which potential employees may find out about the company, the framing of the company's job requirements and the attractiveness of the employer brand all impact the kind of candidates who will be eligible and motivated to apply for a job with the company. By encouraging, for example, minority groups, the pre-hire phase impacts on the chances of individuals from these groups to enter the job market.

In the pre-hire phase of the employee life-cycle, the company's CSR programme impacts the ability of all individuals to **enter or improve their position in the job market**. Elements of the CSHR programme which drive these impacts are:

- Community involvement and investment in education or vocational skills
- Employer brand which includes the company's social and environmental mission
- Recruitment proactive reach-out to a diverse pool of potential candidates
- Company responsiveness to queries from potential employees

### Hire phase

In this phase, the company selects those candidates which it assesses will best assist in meeting the company business objectives from a wide range of candidates which may come from outside or inside the business. The way the company makes this selection has a significant impact on individuals.

In the hire phase, the company must ensure equal opportunity for all individuals, and fair and equitable selection and recruitment processes. The recruitment process considers both internal and external candidates and therefore must consider the needs of both. In the case of mature candidates, who are changing jobs rather than entering the job market for the first time, the company has an impact on the potential of individuals to enhance their professional portfolio of skills and experience. In the case of candidates who have been made redundant, the company impacts their ability to maintain the continuity of their professional development.

In the hire phase of the employee life-cycle, the company's CSR programme impacts the ability of all individuals to **enter or improve their position in the company**. Elements of the CSHR programme which drive these impacts are:

- Equal opportunity recruitment processes
- Attractive remuneration and benefits packages
- Company promises with regard to potential opportunities

**On-boarding phase**
In this phase, the company creates the framework in which new employees may start to develop their contribution to the company. This has a long-term impact on the employee and in some cases, may even determine the quality of the individual's contribution and the length of his tenure with the company.

The on-boarding phase should ensure the individual gains:

- The initial professional skills and knowledge in order to do the job for which she or he was hired
- Clear grounding in the company mission, values, principles and code of ethics
- Training in health and safety policies and practices
- Understanding about remuneration and benefits and all entitlements
- Introduction to relevant colleagues and contacts, or social groups within the business, who can support the individual during the on-boarding phase and possibly longer term
- Guidance about the physical working environment and familiarity with the physical workplace

This phase impacts both on the initial capability of the individual to do his or her job, and the working environment which the individual needs to navigate. It is important in this phase not only to add skills and knowledge, but also encourage a supportive, open, friendly, caring spirit, which will cause the individual to feel respected and empowered.

In the on-boarding phase of the employee life-cycle, the company's CSR programme impacts the ability of all individuals to **start or maintain their professional development**. Elements of the CSHR programme which drive these impacts are:

- Training in initial company requirements
- Corporate culture
- Processes which empower the new hire
- Establishment of a supportive network for the new employee

**Development phase**
This is the period from start of employment to end of employment and represents the longest and most complex phase of the employee life-cycle. It covers the way the company adds professional value to the employee so that he or she can learn and grow, develop professional skills, move into roles of increasing scope and/or responsibility, achieve and contribute. Typical elements of this phase are encompassed in the core elements of the company's human resources approach and will include:

- **Training.** Professional skills training and personal competency training. This may extend to formal external educational or vocational programmes
- **Performance reviews.** Feedback about the individual's performance and programmes to assist improvement
- **Performance development.** Investment in programmes which contribute to the individual's performance and contribution

- **Professional development.** This may include coaching and mentoring programmes
- **Career counselling.** Advice to the employee about potential career development routes and opportunities
- **Personal support.** For employees experiencing change in their personal life-cycle in accordance with their needs
- **Community involvement.** Opportunities for the employee to be involved in social or environmental contribution to the community

In the development phase of the employee life-cycle, the company's CSR programme impacts the ability of all individuals to **significantly improve their professional value and future employability**. Elements of the CSHR programme which drive these impacts are typically included in an advanced human resources strategy, but will be supplemented with:

- Diversity and inclusion programmes to ensure all individuals have a fair opportunity
- Corporate culture development to ensure individuals are motivated, empowered, respected and engaged
- Programmes which support employee well-being

**Leaving phase**

In this phase, the company creates the framework in which employees may leave the company after a short tenure (voluntarily or through dismissal) or after a lifetime of employment and enter into retirement. The ways in which employees leave the company are critical to the individual's ongoing employability (if mid-career) or to the employees' ongoing ability to maintain a decent lifestyle in retirement.

The company impacts the employee who leaves the company in mid-career through the way it provides recommendations for future potential employees, assists employees in finding alternative employment, and maintains contact with 'alumni' who may be potential re-recruits in the future. The company impacts retiring employees in the way it prepares them for retirement and maintains support for them after retirement.

In the leaving phase of the employee life-cycle, the company's CSHR programme impacts the ability of all individuals to **change or end their professional development**. Elements of the CSR programme which drive these impacts are:

- Outplacement programmes for retirees
- Guidance for leavers
- Ongoing support for retirees through maintaining contact and welfare benefits
- Support for an alumni programme

## The personal cycle

This is the cycle that runs parallel to the professional cycle and can have significant impact on the way an employee performs and develops through time. This cycle operates at the interface between the employee as a resource and the employee as an individual person, and the complex matching of the needs of both. Each individual has different needs at different times throughout his or her life-cycle and different phases of the professional cycle intersect with different factors of the personal cycle at different times and in different ways. Most companies tend not to pay too much attention to the personal cycle, believing this to be within the employee's own sphere of responsibility. The critical difference in a CSHR approach is that it accepts the employee holistically as a total individual, with both personal and professional needs, has understanding for the individual's personal needs and offers supportive and flexible frameworks to address these.

The factors in the personal cycle do not progress in a linear way. Sometimes employees may access education later in life, some may start a family and only then look for employment, some may maintain a career and think of family at a much later stage, some may divorce and remarry, etc. Most factors in the personal cycle continue in parallel but not necessarily with synchronicity throughout the employee's life and cannot be planned or predicted.

### The education factor

Typically, the education factor is about an individual gaining education to enable him or her to become employable. In underprivileged communities, access to education may be problematic for all, and for some population groups, such as women in certain societies, access to education may be denied. A company demonstrates its corporate responsibility though influencing access to education and supporting enhanced access for all individuals. In addition, a company impacts employees' ability to continue their education while in employment through support for academic education and flexibility to allow for study time. Examples of CSHR programmes that the company could adopt to enhance academic education for employees are:

- Community investment in education and enhancement of access to education
- Academic study grants
- Partnerships with academic institutions which provide frameworks for employees continued education
- Vocational academic programmes aligned with company functional opportunities

### The personal growth factor

Employees, as individuals, continue their personal growth throughout their lifetime. The essence and directions for personal growth will often be influenced by the employment context of an individual. Each employee is exposed to a range of influences in the workplace, which are described in the professional cycle. These influences continue throughout the employees' professional cycle and may be highly formative, providing opportunities for unique experiences, challenges and insights. This may include travel, living in different countries on expatriate assignments, meeting many different types of people, cultures and communities, formation of friendships and connections and much more. All these elements can significantly affect an individual's personal values, spiritual growth and overall ability to maintain a fulfilling life and contribute to society. Examples of CSHR programmes that the company could adopt to enhance personal growth for employees are:

- Opportunities for spiritual development
- Cultural learning programmes
- Values and personal insight exploration and development programmes
- Enrichment lectures, workshops, experiences
- Community volunteering opportunities

## The family factor

This factor may see the employee marry and start a family. Some employees may choose same-sex partners. Some employees may have problems starting a family and elect to adopt or foster children. Some employees may not enter into personal relationships, but, as they get older, may assume responsibilities for elderly parents or siblings depending on personal family circumstances. Employees will build their homes, perhaps buying housing or moving home from time to time. Grandparents, parents or siblings may die, causing great emotional trauma. Children may move away from home to study or marry. Each of these and a million more instances of personal circumstances will impact the employee's ability to be motivated and engaged at work at different times throughout her or his professional cycle. All personal life elements relating to family needs and experiences will require different levels of the employee's personal energy, emotion, commitment and time and will influence the amount of energy, emotion, commitment and time the employee will have for professional development and work contribution. A company demonstrates its corporate responsibility though attentiveness and responsiveness to this multitude of changes in an employee's personal life-cycle and through the adoption of flexible and supportive policies and practices which take into account the employee's differing level of contribution at different times, while maintaining opportunities for the employee to continue professional development over time. A CSHR approach will impact the employee's ability to successfully navigate professional and personal demands and gain maximum growth in both life-cycles. Examples of CSHR programmes that the company could adopt to enhance this ability are:

- Work–life balance programmes
- Employee affinity groups or networks.
- Sabbatical, unpaid leave, maternity/paternity leave programmes
- Child adoption support, childcare support, parental care support
- Social and psychological counselling programmes

## The financial stability factor

Most employees, at different stages of their life, will desire to enhance their financial standing so as to become financially stable and have the ability to maintain their life quality throughout their lifetime including after retirement from employment. Some employees may have difficulty managing their finances and fall into debt or experience significant stress. Other employees may just not take an interest in personal finances and reach a stage in their lives where they suddenly realise they do not have the financial resources to fulfil their dreams or maintain their lifestyle as anticipated. These issues may cause some of the most significant disruptions to an employees' ability to contribute in the workplace.

Examples of CSHR programmes that the company could adopt to enhance the ability of an employee to become financially stable are:

- Education programmes on personal finances and household management
- Insurance, pension and savings plans
- Secured loans for employees for big purchases such as homes or cars
- Crisis funds which assist employees in times of particular hardship
- Personal financial counselling
- Payment of a living wage, and fair benefits

## The health factor

An employee's health is arguably the single most significant factor that will impact an employee's contribution at work. Employees may invest in their own health and well-being, but many may not. Similarly, factors in the workplace may affect employees' health, ranging from practical issues relating to occupational health and safety, to less direct issues such as the availability of healthy food in the workplace, to less quantifiable issues related to stress, relationships and personal work habits. Additionally, employees, through no fault of their own, may succumb to sickness that may prevent them continuing the same work as previously, or even require them to cease working altogether. Companies that invest in providing platforms for assisting employee awareness of healthcare issues and support the development of a working environment in which health impacts are understood and addressed are likely to create a healthier workforce which contributes in a healthier way to delivering business objectives. Examples of CSHR programmes that the company could adopt to enhance the health of employees are:

- Health insurance programmes
- Comprehensive work health and safety policies, plans and implementation
- Health crisis funds for serious instances of long-term sickness
- Health education for the employee and family members
- Fitness programmes, sports clubs, weight reduction, substance abuse elimination programmes, stress management workshops, time management training

## The legacy factor

This is something that is becoming increasingly important in today's fast-paced society. Many studies show that employees want to do meaningful work that goes beyond advancing the interests of business profits and growth, and also contributes to the society and the sustainability of the planet. This is more prevalent now among young people, but also with mid-career managers who reach a certain realisation that work should be about more than making money and should provide some additional spiritual and community value. Many mid-careers leave companies to seek paid work in not-for-profit organisations with clear social or environmental missions. The not-for-profit sector has become a very significant employer and is participating in the war for talent, offering the opportunity to earn a living while doing good. More people are realising their need to 'leave a legacy for future generations' that will outlive them as their contribution to a better world. The way a company offers opportunity for employees to satisfy these higher level aspirations has an impact on the way they engage in the workplace and the nature of their contribution.

Examples of CSHR programmes that the company could adopt to enhance the legacy that employees can leave are:

- Community partnership or volunteering programmes
- Short-term sabbaticals in not-for-profit organisations
- Involvement in company green teams
- Appointment as ethics or diversity officers
- Company community donation schemes

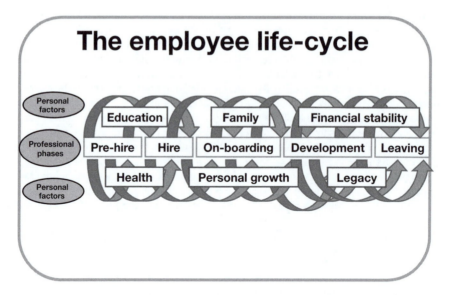

Sharon felt pleased with this. There were things she had forgotten or left out, she felt sure, but it could serve as a basic overview of the interrelationship of impacts in ways which traditionally the HR function has not addressed. She plotted this out on a roadmap type of template:

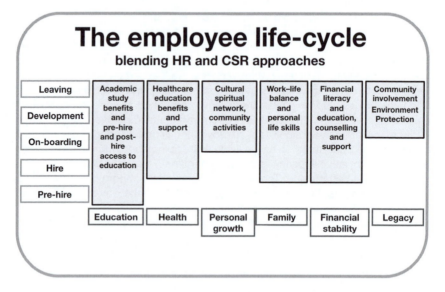

Sharon felt this was a good exercise. This was surely a model that could present a good start for the purposes of considering and planning how the HR function could develop policies, plans and programmes that could support both the business strategy and the need to develop greater corporate responsibility. The next step was to consider the different ways employee impacts in the workplace are enhanced and enriched by a CSHR approach.

This exercise had taken Sharon some hours and she felt she had better get back to the day to day before she was accused of slacking. Thinking about impacts, she decided to have an impact on her stomach, and called up Patricia from her team to see if she was ready for lunch.

# 13

# Employee impacts

Sharon settled into her next task, which was to think about the ways in which employees make an impact. Considering how to go about that was a challenge. 'When it boils down to it,' Sharon thought, 'everything that an employee does, even if it is outside working hours, impacts on the business, or on the employee's role in the business.' Then, thinking back to models of corporate responsibility, and something that Arena had told her right at the very beginning of her CSHR education, she decided to develop an employee stakeholder model. If she thought about who the stakeholders of employees were, she would understand where employees were impacting. She made a first attempt at defining the stakeholders of employees.

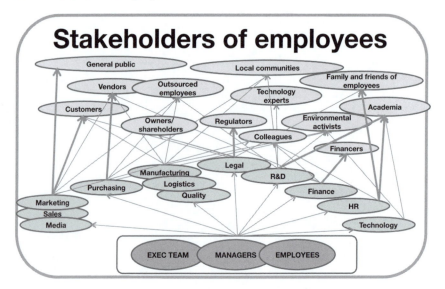

Sharon realised this wasn't going to get her anywhere. Every employee was connected to every stakeholder in some way. She had tried to show a primary stakeholder relationship with thicker lines on the chart, but it wasn't clear. No one would have a hope of understanding this. She tried another approach.

This was much clearer, she felt. With the employees and the organisation hierarchy at the base of the big bubble, Sharon felt this represented how every single employee, whether directly or indirectly, could have an impact on both internal and external stakeholders of the organisation. Clearly, employees in different functions would have different relationships, many of which were not shown in detail on this chart. In general, the principle is that every action and every decision of every employee has the potential to reinforce the organisation approach to corporate responsibility, or to erode it. Typically, she had heard, that people recount their positive and negative experiences to several friends and acquaintances. She thought to herself that Andromex had 2,500 employees. If each one talked to 15 people from their personal circle of family and friends at least once a month about something that was going on at Andromex — for example, some good thing that Andromex had done for the community — that was 450,000 contact points per year. Add to that an average of 100 external conversations or emails per working day across the organisation with all external stakeholders, that's over 60 million contact points per year, each of which results in a reinforcement of reputation or an erosion of reputation. Nothing is neutral. Either employees are adding or they are detracting from company reputation with their actions and interactions. Sharon thought that this was the key to corporate reputation management.

She recalled the significant recent corporate scandals such as Enron, World.com and players in the banking sector in the financial crisis of 2008–09.

These were the results of corporate culture perhaps, but also the actions and decisions of individuals. She felt that the way to corporate responsibility was to ensure that each and every employee understood his or her personal stakeholder network and the opportunity to deliver added value at each contact point. This, of course, providing that the employees themselves were positive about the company, identified with the values and felt they themselves were benefiting, as a result of internal corporate responsibility as she had defined in her previous work-session.

She decided to develop this using a few case study examples she had come across in recent months.

## H&M case study

### The issue

In January 2010, the Swedish global fashion retailer H&M[1] learnt a lesson in New York, when an insightful and bold young woman, Cynthia Magnus, found 20 discarded bags of unwanted clothes outside the back of H&M's store on 34th Street, New York. Clothes in the bags — gloves, socks, jackets, shirts, etc. — had been intentionally damaged to prevent re-use; clothes that needy families could derive great benefit from. After receiving no response to the attempts to contact the company, Cynthia went to the press. The story was reported in the *New York Times* on 5 January 2010[2] and did not omit to make reference to H&M's statements of commitment to corporate social responsibility. Within hours, cyberspace was alive with comments from all corners of the globe expressing anger, indignation, scorn, incredulity, cries for boycott, accusations of irresponsibility, analyses, commentaries, tweets and Facebook posts. By 6 January, it was the number 2 trending topic on Twitter. And H&M published their response on Twitter to the effect that H&M was investigating and that this was not representative of their policy. A search for 'H&M destroying clothes' on Google brought up over 70,000 references. Actually, bags of discarded Wal-Mart clothes were found too but H&M bore the brunt of the outrage. All major news publishers took up this story. And it seems as if everyone had something to say.

H&M is actually considered a positive company in terms of CSR. They have produced an annual CSR report since 2002. All H&M's reports are downloadable from their website,[3] as is their Code of Conduct in 25 languages and a range of other responsibility-related materials,[4] The company has made significant progress in developing sustainability strategy and was one of the first to speak out against Uzbekistan's forced labour and child

1 www.hm.com.

2 Jim Dwyer, 'A Clothing Clearance Where More Than Just the Prices Have Been Slashed', *New York Times* (5 January 2010).

3 www.hm.com/us/corporateresponsibility/sustainabilityreporting__csr_report2009. nhtml, accessed 7 June 2010.

4 www.hm.com/us/corporateresponsibility/downloads__downloads.nhtml, accessed 7 June 2010.

labour in the cotton-picking fields. The CSR Manager of H&M, Ingrid Schull-ström, maintained a blog on the H&M CSR home page.[5]

As chance would have it, she wrote on 29 December, just a few days before H&M hit the headlines that she would not be posting during January and February 2010 due to extended leave and 'should something exceptional happen in the field of CSR during my absence, one of my colleagues might post an update in this column'. The headline 'H&M donates clothes to charity' appears in bold on the same page.

Later, H&M made a further statement and promised to review policies, but not without quite some harm having been done to this apparel retailer's reputation.

## The stakeholder issue

- There were a small number of employees directly involved in the incident itself:
- Store employees who decided to destroy and discard the clothes
- Warehouse employees who had selected to simply discard the clothes on the street for everyone to see
- Sales/Store Manager who had not clarified policy and/or ensured adherence
- Who were the stakeholders affected and which employees in the business could have influenced the positive handling of this issue?

## H&M case study: stakeholder impacts

| Stakeholder | Reaction | Employee touch point after incident |
|---|---|---|
| General public: (potential consumers, or friends of potential consumers) | Outrage at destruction of good clothes depriving poor people of the chance to receive them at zero or low price | • **CEO and/or other senior manager**: statements of apology and redress.<br>• **Sales/store managers**: revision of discarding clothes policy to prevent recurrence<br>• **Store employees**: review and understanding of policies<br>• **Designers**: review of types of clothes discarded and why so as to prevent recurrence |
| Media | Love a good scandal | • **PR manager**: clear statement of apology and explanation |

5  www.hm.com/us/corporateresponsibility__responsability.nhtml. Author's note: Since writing this article, Ingrid Schullström, who was head of CSR at H&M at the time, has now left her position. There is no indication that there is a connection between this incident and her departure from this role.

| Stakeholder | Reaction | Employee touch point after incident |
|---|---|---|
| Consumers (current customers) | Indignation at the fact that they had paid money for clothing that the company throws away | • **Sales/store managers:** communication with consumers in the stores<br>• **Managers/employees**: to assist with managing social media backlash in a considered way |
| Social activists or community groups | Anger that underprivileged people are deprived of an opportunity | • **PR manager and CSR managers:** explain to local community partners |
| Environmental activists | Outrage at waste and method of disposal. A statement about fast fashion and its negative effects | • **PR manager**: issue apology and explain |
| Investor | Concern at bad press potential influence on stock price | • **Investor relations**: possible issue of quicker, clearer statement to investors<br>• **CFO** to calculate the financial implications of the discarding of clothes |
| Families/friends of employees: | Disappointment that family member works in a company that acts irresponsibly — desire to know more details | • **HR managers**: issue an internal statement to employees to brief them on H&M's position<br>• **All employees**: correct discussion about the issue outside of the workplace |
| Potential employees (students, new recruits) | Don't want to work for a company which doesn't have regard for the community | • **HR managers**: issue statement to academic institutions on H&M's overall position |

Sharon thought that this was clear enough. Perhaps only a small group of employees were involved in creating what was a significant PR CSR issue for H&M, but, in fact, many employees could be involved in handling the repercussions of this issue, each employee with their own specific touch point. She felt this relevant to many different issues. The degree to which a CSR mindset is embedded in the entire organisation both assists in the avoidance of potentially harmful incidents such as these, and also in their rectification. She thought back to what she had learnt about green teams and employee engagement in caring for the environment. Every single employee doing his or her bit would be sure to notice all the actions of the company that could have a negative direct impact on the environment — even simple things like printing on double-sided paper or alerting maintenance to dripping taps. The small actions of many employees add up to big impacts. 'This is what embedding CSR is all about,' Sharon thought. 'Ensuring that each and every employee understands enough to be able to notice opportunities to make a difference; ensuring that each and every employee is engaged enough to be able to take the right actions at the right time and to represent the company in the appropriate way to all external stakeholders.' Sharon felt this could be very powerful indeed. Not only was this about improving business results and making a difference to society and the environment, it was also about giving *all* employees a reason beyond opening their monthly payslip to feel they are changing the world. So this was the essence of CSR and HR. This was about creating incredible employee engagement not only about business issues, but also about society and environment issues. She remembered something that Rona Parkville often repeated when referring to employer workplace impacts: 'It's about converting the impacts on employees to the impacts of employees.'

Sharon ended this session just as the clock turned 7 p.m. She felt she had done enough and was looking forward to spending the evening with the family. She decided to leave her laptop in the office. That way, she wouldn't be tempted to log on later in the evening. Feeling rather self-righteous, she looked around her office, felt grateful that she had a job she enjoyed so much, a boss that gave her freedom to act even though he wasn't convinced, a new project that gripped her in a most compelling way, and a wonderful family to go home to. She flipped off the light-switch and headed towards her car.

# 14

# Ethics

Later that week, Sharon had fixed time with Douglas Green, the company's Legal Adviser. He was responsible for all the legal affairs of the company and everything related to regulatory compliance and matters that Sharon had some knowledge of, but still relied on Douglas for quite significantly. Sharon had wondered about ethics. She had seen that every public company she had come across had a code of ethics, or code of business conduct or something with a similar name. She knew that Andromex had such a code, but it had never been formally communicated.

**Douglas:** Ah yes, Sharon, our Code of Ethics. Technically, we don't need one, because we are not publicly traded and do not need to make legal filings to the Stock Exchange Authorities and other bodies, but we did set up a Code a long time ago. We haven't done much with it, though.

**Sharon:** Yes, Douglas, I know. I want to revive it. Make it more central to the things we communicate and observe as part of our corporate culture.

**Douglas:** Oh my goodness! Are you bored? Don't you have enough to do? The Board asked me to give them a Code of Ethics, they approved it and I filed it. We don't need a Code of Ethics to tell us what to do. We behave in an ethical and reputable manner with or without a Code. Just putting the Code on a poster somewhere won't make us any more ethical. What's the big deal?

**Sharon:** I think it is a big deal, actually Douglas. I'm not blaming you or anything. In fact, this is something I should have picked up on long before now. If we have a Code of Ethics, I think we should make sure that all our employees know about it. We can't take it for granted that every employee knows what's important or will know when to recognise an issue that may pose ethical problems. I have been learning quite a lot about this over the past few weeks, and it seems to me that there are several good reasons for us to dust off that copy you have, take a look to see if it truly represents the spirit and values of the company and develop a process of awareness. We should also ensure we have a proper process for managing ethical issues as they arise. I am sure they crop up every day in one form or another.

**Douglas:** Look, Sharon, you will have to talk to George about this. I think he has got other things on his mind at the moment. I really don't see the need for this. If anything crops up, we deal with it. That's much more important than talking about it. I don't have the time to spend in endless sessions revising an ethics code. Ours is pretty basic, covers the generic clauses that most codes of this nature cover. I did a bit of research before I developed it. But I think it does the job and if I am going to have to be involved in making changes, I want George to tell me it's a priority.

**Sharon:** OK, Douglas. I understand. Sorry for springing this on you. I will talk to George and raise it at the next ANDEX Meeting. Though if you ask me, as we prepare for the IPO, it's even more relevant.

Sharon was astounded. She had worked for this company for five years and no one had referred to the Code of Ethics. The only reason she knew about it was because she had found it in a file in her office, when she took up her role at Andromex. She didn't know whether to be pleased that the Code existed, or disappointed that no one knew it existed, except for a privileged few. The fact that the Legal Adviser didn't seem to think it mattered was also a cause for concern. As she understood it, most companies had an ethics officer, and this was not usually the HR manager. She needed to think about how to present this to George. If Douglas's reaction was anything to go by, she would hear the same words coming out of her boss's mouth. She had to be prepared. She felt that a Code of Ethics was the bedrock of her future plans to help the company develop a CSR programme. She remembered Arena telling her that leadership, governance and ethics were the framework of organisational readiness that was essential before a company could embark on a CSR programme. There had to be a basic acceptance of values and ethical behaviour before going further. Sharon thought she needed to move fast on ethics, as a first stage, and only then put forward a more comprehensive plan. In the meantime, she would do what she could with her HR team in other areas. Actually, she felt good that she had invested time and effort with ANDEX a couple of years back in developing a mission and values statement. This was something that did provide some level of cohesiveness and was used to establish expectations. It was simple and straightforward, which Sharon liked.

She used these values in training sessions for managers and was always happy when interest-

### Andromex mission

To be a highly efficient and responsive software solutions provider for clients worldwide

### Andromex values

- Respect for all
- Innovation
- Speed of response
- Integrity
- Teamwork

ing discussions took place about how the values were reflected in the everyday life of the business. She occasionally 'tested' employees when she visited different departments, asking them if they knew the five Andromex values. Most employees could name four out of the five which both frustrated and pleased her at the same time. However, it did give her confidence that ethics training was just a step away from a basic adherence to a set of defined values, and that in terms of organisational maturity, she was building on solid ground. She had read in one of the magazines she had picked up on business ethics that there is no point in developing an ethics code unless the organisation has first defined its core values. At least there was one thing less to do, she thought, though she did wonder whether it might have been more effective to have a process whereby more people in the company contributed to the development of the mission and values. Having the top executive team decide about values and impose them on the organisation was missing an opportunity to engage more people and ensure the values were really those that fitted the organisation and that people could identify with. However, she was not going to open all of this up again as she had enough on her plate developing the ethics programme. If she were to do this over again, she felt she would develop a statement of corporate values in a more participatory way. She remembered talking to an HR person who described a four-day off-site process involving 50 managers in which an updated set of values were agreed.[1] She thought this sounded very worthwhile.

By the time Sharon got to see George, she was ready for all his objections. George was actually less of a barrier than she had imagined, perhaps because the thought of becoming a public company was on his mind. Public companies have codes of ethics, ethics officers and other processes for managing ethics on a going basis. George agreed to table this at the next ANDEX meeting for approval by the team. Sharon was pleased and got to work on a short presentation. She didn't want to make it too complicated or threatening, so she kept the concepts to the bare minimum.

The ANDEX meeting was scheduled to start at 2 p.m. though, as usual, it was closer to 2.17 before they got going. This was something that always irked Sharon; something about the culture of arriving and starting meetings on time was one of the things that she hadn't sorted out in her organisation yet. Maybe she could turn it into an ethical issue, she thought to herself. Something about respecting the time of others. But before she could get carried away, Tony the CFO was on his feet to present the quarterly results and propose a review of

---

1  The author actually participated in such a session for Middle East and Africa region senior managers in a four-day programme held in France, and assisted in the facilitation of a similar session in Unilever Israel during her time as VP Human Resources. This was part of a global roll-out of a workshop for all senior teams around the Unilever world in 2002–04, designed to realign the business in support of new focused objectives.

off-shore operations costs, which were yielding greater benefit than had been anticipated. He was proposing moving more of the UK operations off-shore. Sharon was prepared for this, she had seen his recommendation, and she was clear about the effects this would have on the local workforce. There was a long discussion, the cost differentials weren't massively significant, and Sharon was pleased when the consensus was to review again in another three months, after the IPO direction was becoming clearer. It wouldn't be good just now to create a significant change that could affect reputation and destabilise part of the operations. Sharon was also pleased because this issue had ethical implications as well. She had said in the meeting that it was not just a decision about money, but also a decision about people and all stakeholders. Some disagreed, but others were supportive. This led her into the proposal on ethics.

Sharon opened with what she felt was something non-threatening. She said that Andromex was an ethical business. She was not criticising anyone, just making a proposal to safeguard the future of Andromex as an ethical business. She saw her colleagues nodding around the room. She felt good so far.

The other tactical decision she had taken was not to propose a review of the Code of Ethics too early. She was asking for a process of embedding ethics, not starting from scratch.

Sharon ran through the reasons briefly. They were largely self-explanatory, she felt. She told a short story about how ethics can be misunderstood and mis-interpreted through lack of knowledge rather than desire to behave unethically, and another about the need for new frameworks as the world is dynamic and new ethical debates come up every day such as ethical use of social media during work hours. The ANDEX team did not raise any objections, so Sharon proceeded with a proposal for the Ethics Programme Framework, which included the inclusion of ethics in different elements of HR processes, and what she had learnt to be necessary in terms of structures to support ongoing performance.

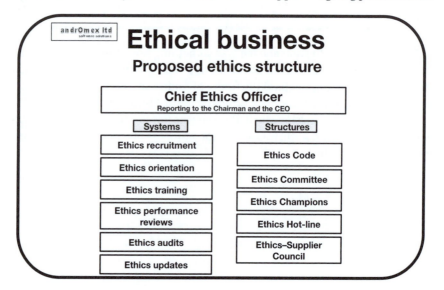

Sharon's proposed structure generated some discussion. Everyone thought it was rather too much and would take too much time. There was a debate about who should be the Ethics Officer — Sharon as HR Manager or Douglas as the Legal Adviser — and the consensus, which Sharon was very happy about, was that it should be Douglas, while she would sit on the Ethics Committee. The ANDEX team was nervous about an ethics hot-line and felt this would open up a Pandora's box of unjustified complaints. Sharon explained that, as Andromex was an ethical company, they should have nothing to fear. She was pleased with that one; they had all nodded at her first chart so now they couldn't disagree. She also said that this was not the experience of other companies, all of which have established hot-lines. ANDEX agreed to a hot-line, but an internal hot-line, not an externally managed hot-line as other companies have adopted. No point in hanging out Andromex's dirty laundry for everyone to see, they had said. Although Sharon felt this was a little cowardly, she thought it was a good start. Finally, ANDEX was concerned about spending time training everybody in the company and wondered if she had taken into account the time and cost of this exercise. Sharon explained that the broad-scale training for all employees would be handled by internally trained Ethics Champions, and conducted during team meetings as far as possible so as to cause as little disruption and extra cost as possible. She then presented the proposed timetable.

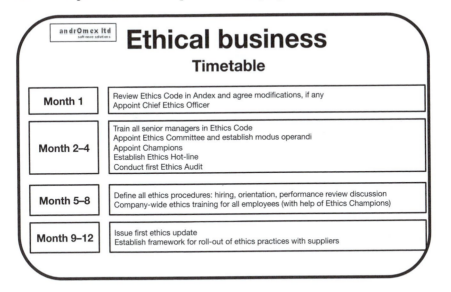

Sharon was proposing a 12-month programme, which was certainly, she told her colleagues, manageable and not overambitious. She looked around at her colleagues, rather satisfied that she had presented in a compact way, no high-flying theories, and no scaremonger tactics. George even laughed and said they had already completed half of the first month's tasks by appointing the Ethics Officer. Her Board members agreed to the programme, with the request that

Sharon take into account all other priorities when scheduling training and other activities that would involve employees in their divisions. Sharon promised she would, and felt she had taken her first step in becoming a CSHR manager and making the world a better place. She immediately texted Amanda to ensure an ANDEX day was scheduled within the next month to run the session on the current Code of Ethics. A day well spent, she thought to herself, on her way home that evening after another few hours with her ANDEX colleagues on a host of subjects. 'Sharon', she said to herself 'you are on your way!'

# 15
## Leadership

Sharon felt she had just one more barrier to overcome before she started developing her plan: leadership. Although as the HR Director, she didn't have a problem with getting things moving, she felt she needed a stronger endorsement from her CEO, George, for a more comprehensive approach to corporate responsibility. She didn't want to push too far too early, but at the same time, it didn't make sense for her to start a rollercoaster unless she knew that her boss was not only supportive, but also prepared to lead. At their next meeting, she broached the subject.

**Sharon:** Thank you George, for your support on the ethics programme. I think it's the right thing to do, and I'm glad you do too.

**George:** That's OK, Sharon. I knew it would cost me more headaches to disagree.

**Sharon:** But you believe it's the right thing to do.

**George:** Yes, I do. I think it's a good move.

**Sharon:** George, I wanted to talk to you about corporate responsibility in a broader sense.

**George:** OK, what?

**Sharon:** I think we ought to develop a full corporate responsibility strategy. That's much more than a Code of Ethics, it's about considering the environment, contributing to the community, thinking about social and environmental considerations when we design our software solutions as far as we can, about the way we hire people and develop them, the way we contract and maintain relationships with suppliers and much more. There are many reasons to do this, it's becoming more and more the way companies do business these days, and there are so many business advantages to this approach.

**George:** What did you have in mind, Sharon? Remember we have a lot on our plate in the coming months. You are talking about quite a major process. Of course, I am aware of the talk about sustainability and the responsibilities of businesses. I see that most global corporations have adopted that route to some extent or another. I've read, or at least, partially read, several CSR reports, especially those in our sector or in the high-tech field. Companies such as Cisco, Symantec, SAP and Intel. They are quite impressive, I have to say, even though I am a little unsure if all the good news they write in these reports is actually true. Even if some of it is, it's in the right direction. But frankly, we are in a different league. We are a small multi-country but far from global B2B player, fighting to stay competitive in a fierce market. I don't have the resources to put against writing glossy reports or contributing millions to alleviate poverty in the underdeveloped world. I may agree that it would be nice to do all of that, but I would be out of a job long before I had a chance to accomplish anything worthwhile. Do you understand?

**Sharon:** Yes, George, I understand. I fully understand that our first priority is to be a successful business and continue to grow. I am not suggesting we lose our heads here. I would like us to take a more strategic approach, define a five-year plan with some key areas we would address as a company, and move forward at a pace we can manage. There are things, such as environmental activities, which will actually save us money and enable us to become more efficient in the short to medium term. As with any change process, I fully understand that the scope and the pace of change needs to be carefully planned and managed, in a way which supports the business and doesn't disrupt it.

**George:** Yes, I know you understand the business.

**Sharon:** What I was thinking was that we should take this year to do a study of where we are. There are some international guidelines, such as the Global Reporting Initiative,[1] which is used for writing CSR reports, or the United Nations Global Compact,[2] which has over 5,000 business participants, many of them smaller companies than Andromex. We could map ourselves against these guidelines to see where we stand and highlight opportunities and risks. It would take a few months to do it. I know a consultant who works with IFC, the food company, who is an expert, who could do such a study and make recommendations. That's a decision point. The sole extent of your commitment at this point would be to support the study. This is a business issue, really, not an HR issue, so it's not something I should lead for the long term, but in the meantime, I admit I would be interested in doing this. During my trip to San Diego, I talked

1  www.globalreporting.org.
2  www.unglobalcompact.org.

to so many people about CSR. I am totally convinced it will be positive for the business and I can bring you as much data as you want to demonstrate that. But as a first stage, mapping where we are seems to me to be the right way to go.

**George:** More consultants. More management time. More cost. Frankly Sharon, I can't agree to this right now. It may be right for the future, but you know what, we are doing OK, and we have agreed to work on ethics – I think that's enough.

**Sharon:** George, I am not going to let this go easily. People want to be part of a business that is demonstrating its commitment to something more than profit. We have a hard time recruiting as it is, being one of the smaller players. All our larger competitors are speaking the language people want to hear. They are talking carbon footprint, recycling, diversity and inclusion, water consumption reduction, community partnerships, sustainable development. We haven't even registered what all that means for us yet. I know we might not aspire to be market leaders, but the gap is widening between corporations who are talking responsibility and sustainability and those who are not.

**George:** Sharon, look, let me think about it, OK? I don't want to overstretch our resources now. Come back to me in two months and we will see how things stand.

Sharon knew when to stop. She also recognised the beginning of a promise. She knew that when she went back to George in two months, there would be a good chance he would agree to let her do a mapping study of the total corporate responsibility status of the company. She didn't push. She resolved to do a few things:

First, to move her HR team in a CSR direction as far as was possible within her jurisdiction without alienating George or her ANDEX colleagues

Second, start pumping George with new data about the benefits of a CSR strategy for medium-sized businesses.

Third, to try to interest her ANDEX colleagues in business-related activities that have social and environmental added value, without risking profitability.

Fourth, keep learning.

She would train up her HR team in the meantime, to make sure they were all on board and ready to become CSHR champions. She knew George, and she understood his position. Don't step onto the diving board unless you are prepared to jump. If it's not broken, don't fix it. But sometimes, she thought to herself, you don't know it's broken. Sometimes, you have to get your act together before it gets you together. Somewhat deflated, but not broken, Sharon told herself that at least George had listened to her. She knew she would get what she wanted over the next few months. It made sense. All she wanted was for her business to be a better business. How could anyone disagree with that?

# Part III
# The CSHR infrastructure

# 16
# HR stakeholders

**Sharon:** Bye, Arena. Looking forward to seeing you before Christmas.

**Arena:** Bye, Sharon. I can't tell you how pleased I am with what you are doing at Andromex. I have never seen anyone take something on board as you have with such drive. When I think back to that flight to San Diego, and the look on your face when I suggested we talk instead of watching a movie, I can't help but laugh. Look at you now! You are transforming your role. You can't know how happy that makes me.

**Sharon:** You never know; maybe one day I will write a book for HR managers.

**Arena:** Hey, we will co-author it.

**Sharon:** It's a deal. Have a great rest of the week, and thanks again for everything.

Arena and Sharon had met for lunch in London, in a small place near Blackfriars. They had spent some time talking about their families and general developments in the HR function, the job market, the effects of the financial crisis, recruitment problems, a particular case of sexual harassment that had been rather unpleasant for Arena in IFC, and the quality of clothes in fast-fashion chains. Among other things. Sharon had been pleased to meet Arena in order the check her CSHR roadmap. She had her bi-annual team review meeting coming up next week and was to present the CSHR concept to them, together with an action plan that was based on moving the HR function forward in the absence of a comprehensive corporate CSR strategy. She had done quite a lot of independent research over the past few weeks and had built a framework for action that she felt was on the right track. The opportunity to bounce it off Arena was just what she needed. She had also talked to Rona from the CSR consulting firm, who had given her some insights, so she knew she wasn't too far off the mark. She had asked Arena what she felt about the skills HR people needed in order to manage CSHR.

**Arena:** There are several articles and studies about what makes a good manager of sustainability, but no one, as far as I know, has written about what it takes to make HR people good CSHR managers. I will have to think about that. Essentially, a lot of CSHR leadership is about indirectly influencing others. Creating strategy and processes and relying on others to put them into practice. Recruitment, for instance. We define the process but it's the line manager at the end of the day who makes the decisions. CSHR is more of that, just that the processes are a little different. I tend to think that part of the transition to CSHR is about gaining new knowledge of areas that are not traditionally core to HR, such as employee impacts on the environment, or knowledge of the charity sector for the development of community partnerships. However, there are things which require a different kind of skill-set, I think. Take, for instance, the opportunity to integrate community work into performance reviews, or the way we select HR vendors, or the way we write employee surveys. All of these things look different when a CSHR manager does them. It's about thinking in a different way about strategy and about processes. What does that require of us that we don't already develop as HR managers? Broader strategic capabilities? New ways of maintaining dialogue with external organisations? New understanding of the corporate volunteering environment so as to assess its value in employee development? I don't think these are skills that HR managers don't have, but in the CSR context, they do become more critical.

**Sharon:** How do you feel you have changed, Arena, since you became more CSR-oriented?

**Arena:** Well, I have become more outspoken. I have become more prepared to take a stand for what's right, just because it's right, and not because I can justify every last penny of expenditure. I find myself listening to everything through two filters — my regular HR filter, which is about contribution to the business and contribution to individuals, and through the filter of our broader community and society and environment.

Last week in IFC there was a discussion about closing one of our remote manufacturing plants in Europe and moving production to the UK. The plant is small, employing only 230 people or so, and its output can easily be handled by one of our larger plants. I found myself thinking about the effect on the total community if the plant were to close down, rather than the effect on individuals. I saw the employees going home to their families and not being able to find alternative employment in such a small place. I saw the kids suffering as their parents are out of work. I saw small store owners in that small town start to lose income and possibly going out of business as a result of our plant ceasing operations. I realise we have a business to run, and that any global business has to make economies of scale, but the enormity of our responsibility in a community has to count for something. I immediately said that we have to take this into account. At first, the CFO and some of the others looked at me as though I had converted to another religion or something. But I explained to them that 230 people are a community, and they are directly connected to a community of several thousand people who are connected to our factory — their families, local businesses, haulage companies, all sorts of small and large suppliers, etc. We had to consider more than just the act of making 230 people redundant. I said that we had to have a process of stakeholder engagement in that community and look at how we could phase out while leaving a positive footprint and not a gaping hole in a community. I said that we can't expect this not to impact our global reputation, and that the time had passed when we could make these sorts of decision in isolation. I could never have said those things a few years back. In fact, I probably wouldn't have thought those things a few years back. I would have said we have to let the people go in a decent way, and perhaps help them find alternative employment, though, between you and me, there is a fat chance of that, the economy being the way it is. I would have left it at that. These days, I don't let anyone make these decisions without considering the entire scope of consequences and all stakeholders. I have enough insight and information now to make an intelligent case. I may make people uncomfortable, but at least I am doing it intelligently! I think one of the big differences between an HR manager and a CSHR manager is that I am able to make these connections and refer to a wealth of information and data that I otherwise wouldn't have been aware of.

The European Operations Manager, who actually doesn't really want to close the plant, had worked there for a time and was on my side. There was a big discussion about what our responsibility really is or isn't. The CFO kept repeating that there was a business case for closure and that that had to be our first thought. He admitted that he also didn't like the idea of making people redundant but that we couldn't ignore the costs involved. I said we have to consider the total cost — the cost in management time of dealing with negative outcomes, the cost in reputation, the cost in demoralisation of employees in the rest of the business, and the cost when we destroy small communities and the repercussions of people having no money to be our consumers any more. They didn't like the sound of that.

The outcome was that the Exec team agreed to opening up a process of dialogue. We will create a multi-sector team around the plant and engage in dialogue about alternatives, which includes keeping the plant open, but will also include the alternative ways of closing it for the maximum benefit to all. The Exec team charged our CSR Director with setting up that team. He was on vacation. Probably he would have spoken up before me if he had been around. In any case, I will be on the team and involved in the process of dialogue, primarily regarding the aspects relating to our employees. I am glad I learnt mediation skills all those years ago. But even so, as an HR Manager, I was never faced with these sorts of issues. This is a real core business issue. Money versus values. It's only as a CSHR-minded manager that I can recognise it, influence it, and be a good business partner to manage an optimal business and social outcome. Anyway, I am going to be flying out to Romania several times over the next few months, I guess. Does that story help?

**Sharon:** That's some story. Fascinating. It makes it very clear what sort of influence CSR thinking can have on the way HR managers contribute. It is clear that the skill is one part understanding the new business context, and the second part is an involvement in wider social issues rather than the internal ups and downs of employees. I wanted to share with you a thought about cause marketing. We don't sell branded products like IFC, so we don't have a consumer end-user to win over. We do need to create some added value for ourselves in competition with larger IT companies for software contracts and new models, and at the same time, we need to boost our reputation as it is not so easy to recruit. I was thinking that it would be easier for me to sell a marketing campaign internally than to get a budget for contribution to the community at this stage. I was wondering how I could hook these two together. Our marketing is mainly direct marketing to clients, rather than mass marketing or consumer direct marketing. Our clients are small to medium-sized firms; not all of them have CSR awareness or programmes, and I am not sure how important it is to them. Our end-users tend not to know who we are. It's not like you — IFC brands are well known. I thought that if we developed a software kit to help school pupils understand basic programming language, and ran courses for underprivileged school kids, perhaps even involving some of our programmers on a volunteer basis, this would be a good thing. Our contribution to the community. We could publicise this in the communities in which we operate. We could run a mailshot to our clients, advising them of this new initiative and offering to allocate a percentage of all revenues from them to this project. That way, our clients get to contribute indirectly to a community project, we get to improve our reputation both with our clients and in the community, and we contribute to strengthening the community. At the same time, we create an opportunity for our employees to volunteer on a small scale. What do you think of that? Marketing-wise, it's not complicated. At least, I don't think it is.

**Arena:** Yes, it's certainly a creative programme. It's not quite on the same scale as big-brand cause marketing, but it sounds interesting. It would be quite a lot of work to develop a kit and get it into the education system. Quite a lot of bureaucracy to overcome. I can't say how your Marketing people would feel about it. They have probably never had to deal with a suggestion like this before. But it's worth a try. Perhaps even the suggestion might start them thinking a little differently about the way they talk to clients and potential clients. And even if the Marketing people don't agree, it sounds like a good community project anyway. You could perhaps involve students in developing the kit, and that will hook you into universities and colleges, which might be a potential source of new recruits.

**Sharon:** OK, thanks. I will have a chat to our Marketing Director. In the worst case, he throws me out of his office. But that's nothing new (laughing). You know, I find it quite amazing that we are having this conversation in the first place. Here we are, HR managers, talking about using the business to help with HR processes like recruiting. Isn't this the tail wagging the dog?

**Arena:** Yes. But sometimes you get the best results if you work at problems from different angles. If there is something that the Marketing Department can do to help their business **and** give you an added advantage as a recruiter, then everyone wins.

After that, they had talked some more and Arena had given Sharon some pointers about the CSHR roadmap, and after around two hours and a nice, light lunch, they had said their goodbyes.

Sharon's first step in developing her CSHR roadmap was defining who HR stakeholders were.

She identified these in a basic table. It took her quite some time because she hadn't thought about this before, and she wasn't certain that she had it 100% right, but it was a start. She felt that discussion in her HR team would identify any gaps. She also knew that this needed to be drilled down to the levels of individual departments and people, rather than just the generic headlines she had noted. She felt this was as good a basis for discussion as any.

## Who are the HR stakeholders?

| Stakeholders | What they need from the HR function | How they influence HR performance | What the HR function needs from them |
|---|---|---|---|
| ANDEX | Skilled workforce at compatible cost and positive corporate culture | **Direct — High** Agrees strategy, allocates resources, leads performance | Openness to HR processes and ideas, collaboration |
| Managers | Same as ANDEX in own departments, same as employees, training in people processes | **Direct — High** Allocates resources, partners in implementation | Partnership for implementation of processes, motivated performance |
| HR Team members | Same as employees and personal HR job satisfaction and opportunity | **Direct — High** Ability to achieve HR objectives | Professional, competent, motivated performance |
| HR vendors | Opportunity to supply, fair treatment, clarity of requirements | **Direct — High** Ability to achieve HR objectives and meet budget costs | Competitive, professional, ethical supply of goods and services |
| Recruitment firms | Recruitment orders, information | **Direct — Medium** Ability to hire best people | Excellent and timely service, good people |

| Stakeholders | What they need from the HR function | How they influence HR performance | What the HR function needs from them |
|---|---|---|---|
| Employee Council members | Employee rights, recognition and respect | **Direct — Medium** Influence employment costs and benefits, and some processes | Understanding of business needs, collaborative approach |
| Legal Department | Compliance with all regulations | **Direct — Medium** Advice on changes in law, resolution of claims and issues | Support, advice, information |
| Academic institutions | Opportunities for collaboration | **Indirect — Low** Recruitment attractiveness, possibility for collaboration on projects | Assistance in recruiting, collaboration in research programmes |
| Regulators | Adherence to all labour laws | **Indirect — High** Ability to determine new labour laws affecting the business | Reasonable legislation, flexibility, understanding of business need |
| Employee families | Family member who is happy at work | **Indirect — Medium** Motivation of employees | Support for employees |
| Potential employees | Attractive, ethical workplace with opportunity to develop | **Indirect — Medium** Application for open positions | Application to work for the company |
| Employees | Attractive, ethical workplace with opportunity to develop | **Indirect — Medium** Influence the work and culture of the organisation, assimilate HR processes | Engagement in the company's objectives and values |
| HR professional associations and networks | Involvement and support of HR | **Indirect — Low** Possible avenues for developing HR competencies | Opportunities to network and learn and share |
| Retired employees | Ongoing care and contact | **Indirect — Low** Effect on current employees or community | Positive feedback |

Sharon was not surprised when she worked through this exercise that employees were not at the top of the list, though she felt this would be contrary to everyone's expectation. She knew, however, that general employees were less relevant to the HR function because HR did not manage them directly (apart from those employees in the HR function). Employees were the responsibility of the line and staff managers. HR was responsible for creating the policies, plans and processes to enable employees to gain the skills and knowledge they needed and performed in line with expectations, but HR worked through managers and company teams. As Sharon often repeated at ANDEX meetings, if the workforce is not effective, most of this can be attributed to managers who are not effective at leading, clarifying expectations, giving feedback or maintaining an appropriate monitoring system. In any event, Sharon had surprised herself by coming up with such a long list of stakeholders. She felt sure this would generate a good discussion in the next team meeting.

# 17
# CSHR job description

Patricia arrived, as punctual as ever. Sharon had asked her to meet her briefly to review the CSR roadmap that she was to present to the HR team.

**Sharon:** Hi, Patricia. Look, I want to bounce this off you. At the HR Team Half-Yearly, I want to present the CSR roadmap concept. I want you to work through it with me now and give me your feedback. You are the only one who really knows enough about the subject.

**Patricia:** Shoot.

**Sharon:** First, look at this map. Around the points of the star are the traditional HR functions. We need to look at all of these from a stakeholder perspective.

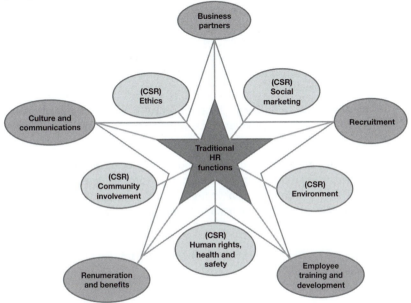

The modern role of HR covers core processes of business partnership, recruitment, employee training and development, remuneration and culture. Our role is about enhancing business capabilities and enhancing individual capabilities. Taking the concept of CSR on board, we need to do two things: first, we need to look at our traditional roles and examine where these interact with CSR themes; and second, we need to look at the way the organisation is evolving and adopt some new roles which require us to learn some new things. Does this make sense?

**Patricia:** Yes, sure it does. In recruitment, for example, we need to ensure we have ethics, diversity and gender balance in our recruiting process. Recruitment is something HR has always done, but a CSR mind-set requires us to do it differently. Another example might be the training and development programmes, which should leverage CSR and not just focus on professional or traditional leadership skills and competencies. In the new skills, I must say that human rights aren't something I have ever thought about as an HR manager. I mean, we don't have a problem there in our business, unless you call gender imbalance a violation of human rights, which I think it is, but I would never have thought of our role in those terms. I would like to understand more about that.

**Sharon:** Yes, Patricia, I think you have understood. Good. That means it is clear. When I was at the ASTD conference, I heard a fascinating lecture on human rights and how it interlinks with our HR role. I will let you have a copy of the slides.

**Patricia:** Thanks.

**Sharon:** Let's move on. A few years ago, the CSR Academy published the CSR Competency Framework. The CSR Academy was a collaborative project started by the then UK Department of Trade and Industry (DTI) and then developed under the leadership of Business in the Community, a non-profit promoting socially responsible business.[1] The Framework was developed for the DTI and based on research commissioned by the DTI with support from other groups. The purpose of the Framework was to help organisations develop and integrate CSR learning and skills. Although this was several years ago, the core competencies still seem quite relevant. There are six core areas:

1. **Understanding society.** Understanding how the business operates in the broader context and knowing the social and environmental impact that the business has on society

2. **Building capacity.** Building the capacity of others to help manage the business effectively. For example, suppliers understand the business's approach to the environment and employees can apply social and environmental concerns in their day-to-day roles

---

1  www.bitc.org.uk/cr_academy. The DTI is now the Department for Business Innovation & Skills (BIS).

3. **Questioning business as usual.** Individuals continually questioning the business in relation to a more sustainable future and being open to improving the quality of life and the environment

4. **Stakeholder relations.** Understanding who the key stakeholders are and the risks and opportunities they present. Working with them through consultation and taking their views into account

5. **Strategic view.** Ensuring that social and environmental views are included in the business strategy such that they are accepted as integral to the way the business operates

6. **Harnessing diversity.** Respecting that people are different, which is reflected in fair and transparent employment and business practices

In a report by Ian Redington,[2] published by the CIPD to support the use of this Competency Framework, Redington writes:

> strong HR involvement is a key factor in good CSR policies and procedures should not be any surprise. Having a good CSR reputation implies that a company's behaviour — and that of its people — is consistent and is of a particular standard. So CSR values must be embedded throughout the business, and good HR practices make this happen.

This report contains many case studies from a range of companies who have implemented all or part of the Framework and support the delivery of CSR through strong HR practices.

More recently, in March 2010, a paper was published by the Institute of Sustainability Professionals[3] that outlined the required competences of sustainability professionals based on a comprehensive survey they undertook of nearly 400 sustainability professionals. Their key findings in terms of skills needed were:

**Hard skill needs**

- Strategic planning
- Systems thinking
- Project management
- Financial analysis
- Auditing

---

2  Ian Redington, *Making CSR Happen: The Contribution of People Management* (London: Chartered Institute of Personnel and Development, 2005, www.cipd.co.uk/subjects/corpstrtgy/corpsocres/_mkngcsrhpn.htm, accessed 7 June 2010).

3  Marsha Willard *et al.* 'The Sustainability Professional: 2010 Competency Survey Report' (International Society of Sustainability Professionals, 2010, www.sustainabilityprofessionals.org/files/ISSP_Competency_Study_Special%20Report_3.10_final.pdf).

**Soft skill needs**

- Communication with stakeholders

- Problem solving

- Inspiring and motivating others

- Flexibility or adaptability

- Team-working or collaborating

As you can see, strategy and stakeholder communications stand out in both frameworks. However, aside from this focus on stakeholders and, in the CSR Academy Framework, a focus on understanding society and environment, these competences could also describe the skills we expect of good HR managers.

In thinking about this, I have developed a job description for the CSHR Manager, which includes the key elements of the CSHR role and the competences required. This is for a generalist HR manager in a business partnership function within a business. Later, we can look at specific job descriptions for training managers, recruitment managers and employee relations managers, etc. Take a look:

## Job description: CSHR Manager

### Job purpose

The CSHR Manager is responsible for developing and assimilating tools and processes that enhance business and individual capability, in a way that develops a positive and healthy organisational culture, upholds business principles and values, and maintains accountability for the effects of business and individual actions on all stakeholders including society at large and the environment.

### Job objectives

- Support the delivery of business strategy, objectives, goals and targets through the effective engagement and deployment of people

- Assure the resourcing of the business with appropriately skilled talent, in the right place at the right time to perform the required tasks

- Contribute to the development of a corporate culture that encourages dialogue, support for individuals, openness to new ideas and the ability of each individual in the organisation to achieve professional and personal fulfilment

- Assure the understanding of people in the business of the impacts of all their activities on stakeholders, society and environment, and support programmes in which all may contribute to improving these impacts

### Key areas of responsibility:

- **HR strategy.** Development and implementation of HR strategy that is aligned with business objectives and supports business strategy delivery through all professional HR functions in a responsible way

- **HR stakeholder engagement.** Identify all direct and indirect stakeholders of the HR function in the business and engage with them in different ways to ensure complete understanding of their needs and aspirations, and ensure responsiveness to these needs
- **Personnel planning and resourcing.** Analyse the long-range resourcing needs of the business in the context of changing market and business dynamics, and manage processes to ensure that people with the right skills are available as needed to perform tasks as required
- **Organisational culture.** Promote the development of an ethical, inclusive and diverse organisational culture based on respect and values, in which all are able to contribute in a context of open information and dialogue, acceptance of continual change and focus on professional leadership and personal accountability
- **HR functional contribution.** Develop, deliver, monitor and measure processes and tools to ensure effective attraction, recruitment and retention, training and development, remuneration and reward, performance management, and employee relations in the business, in line with the principles and practices of social and environmental responsibility
- **Internal communications.** Ensure a high, dynamic and interactive level of internal communications in which all employees are engaged and can feel part of the business community
- **Sustainability.** Ensure the HR function is aligned with the business's sustainability strategy by providing sustainability awareness training for all employees, and developing HR programmes that support sustainability strategy, which may include community involvement and volunteering programmes and environmental activities undertaken by employees, among others

## Key measures:

- Employee satisfaction and inclusion
- Employee diversity
- Stakeholder satisfaction with the HR function contribution
- Adherence to ethics and values by employees
- Attraction, recruitment and deployment effectiveness
- Employee health and safety and well-being
- Employee retention and turnover rate
- Individual skill development (training)
- Performance review implementation
- Employee engagement in internal communications
- Employee volunteers and hours volunteered in the community
- Employee contribution to reduction of the business's environmental footprint

**Key knowledge and skills required:**

- Business strategy, processes, performance drivers, risks and opportunities
- Sustainability and corporate responsibility principles and practices
- Business and sustainability issues in the wider societal context
- HR strategy development
- Stakeholder engagement and dialogue processes
- HR functional development and implementation expertise in all HR sub-functions
- Human rights, labour codes, health, safety and well-being frameworks
- Communication tools including advance application of social media internally and externally

**Key competences required:**

- Leadership, clarity of purpose, long-term thinking and visioning skills
- Ability to challenge the system using an enquiring mind and analytical skills
- Listening, mediating, integrating and influencing skills
- Commitment to help people grow and develop (in alignment with business needs), and a passion for business with social and environmental responsibility
- Outstanding prolific communicator via diverse channels
- High degree of integrity, personal ethics and commitment to social justice
- Optimism and a sense of humour

**Sharon:** What do you think? It's different from the traditional HR job descriptions we have written so far, and it makes very clear the HR role in supporting sustainability and CSR objectives. Does it go too far?

**Patricia:** It's quite a lot to take on board. The job description makes it very clear that the HR Manager focus must be not only on the business itself, but also on the impacts of people in the business and all the business activities on environment and society. It requires the HR Manager to have a triple focus at all times: the business, the people and the world.

**Sharon:** Yes, not unlike the concept of triple bottom line coined by John Elkington — people, planet, profit — which is used widely today as a framework for referring to CSR.[4]

**Patricia:** In looking at the areas of responsibility, I notice you include community volunteering and environmental activities. I understand that this is part of a CSR culture and has to be essential to the HR role. These

4  John Elkington, *Cannibals with Forks.*

things won't happen in a business if HR does not provide the organisational platforms to enable these and engage employees in these things. Another thing that strikes me is the key measures. There are some things there that are quite different from our traditional HR focus, for example, measuring diversity, which we don't do, and the issue of stakeholder satisfaction with the HR function. I have seen some companies do internal service surveys in which different departments rate others on the levels of service and contribution they provide. Is that what you mean?

**Sharon:** Yes, that could be a good tool — I've also seen it used in some companies. But stakeholders are both internal and external. Employee families, for instance, are stakeholders. Community partners are stakeholders, regulators, and our Executive Committee, which doesn't usually participate in such surveys. A true stakeholder engagement programme for HR would include both internal and external stakeholders.

**Patricia:** I understand. It's good, Sharon, I like it. It would make us much more in tune with what people want from us and what people think of us. It would give us as an HR function much greater legitimacy with management. I would really like to work on a process like that.

**Sharon:** Great! Though you can be critical, you know. I am not asking your opinion just so that you can tell me everything is wonderful.

**Patricia:** Come on, Sharon, you know me better than that.

**Sharon:** What about the skills and competences? What do you think of that and where do you see the key challenges for us?

**Patricia:** Many of them are what we do now, of course. The key differences are in this understanding and familiarity with the sustainability concept and context, and working out what that means for our business. The dialogue with stakeholders is something we haven't really had practice in. Human rights and labour codes are not things we tend to refer to, and I am not sure we always equate our role in HR with social justice. None of these things seem to me to be totally divorced from the kinds of skill that experienced HR managers need to have. For the more junior managers, or those focused on HR sub-functions, such as recruitment or training or compensation, there would need to be a much clearer set of guidelines, as you mentioned. However, nothing here seems to me to be completely foreign to our HR mind-set, though there is definitely a shift required.

**Sharon:** OK. Thanks. That is useful input. I am planning to present this at the HR Half-Yearly and propose an initial plan of action limited to the things we can do in the HR function, given that we don't have a clearly declared corporate position on CSR to date. I'm working on George on that, but with the IPO at the top of his mind, that might take some time. But I see no need to delay, do you?

**Patricia:** Of course not. Many of these things are within our own remit and will only enhance our ability to support the businesses. I see no reason for us not to proceed in some areas. After all, if we start to practise what we preach we may find that it accelerates our ability to influence management.

Sharon was pleased with this discussion, and even more pleased at the way she was methodologically working through the total scope of CSR. She felt quite the pioneer, and had found a new meaning in her work. Not that she had ever felt her job lacked meaning, but CSR was giving her the opportunity to consider more tangible ways to contribute to the quality of life and make her business one she would feel even prouder to be associated with. Her husband was also beginning to be influenced by this. He had even asked her the other day if she was going to stop buying a certain chocolate bar because of the company's use of palm oil, which endangered the habitat of orang-utans in the Indonesian forests.[5] She was blown away by that question. But she was certainly choosier in the brands she purchased when she did her weekly shop, now that she was more aware of the companies that practised CSR. She was also more in awe of the ones who did, now that she understood the scale of the transformations she was trying to effect.

In addition, Sharon wondered just how many of the clients that Andromex served were engaged in this thinking process. At this point, until Andromex developed a comprehensive strategic approach, she didn't feel that she would have much opportunity to engage customers in the CSR discussion, though clearly that was something to look at later on. However, if, as a result of her efforts in HR, Andromex program developers and engineers did produce software that had the potential to reduce environmental impacts, this would be another beneficial impact of her work. Green IT was a topic of much discussion, she realised. She recalled reading about an application that Intel had developed to convert spare computer power from any computer into computer processing energy that could be transferred to non-profit organisations or those involved in climate change.[6] This was incredible use of programming technology for improved environmental impact. 'I must find that article and send it to our Apps people,' she thought. 'Maybe someone will take the hint!'

5  A reference to the Greenpeace campaign against Nestlé, makers of KitKat, regarding their use of unsustainable palm oil: www.greenpeace.org.uk/blog/forests/kit-kat-give-orang-utan-break-20100317, accessed 8 June 2010.

6  blogs.intel.com/csr/2009/08/progress_thru_processors.php, accessed 8 June 2010.

# 18

# The HR CSR roadmap

It was time for the HR Half-Yearly. This was a practice Sharon had instigated in the same year she started her role with Andromex, six years ago. It was a two-day session, every six months, in which one day was spent reviewing the achievements of the last six months against the objectives, goals and targets the team had set themselves, and the second day was a review of changing externals, new demands, new insights, thoughts, ideas and plans. Given that her HR team was fairly stable, and most had been around for at least three years, the atmosphere in these meetings was professional and business-focused while being familiar, informal and the chance for a catch-up on personal news and even a little company gossip. Sharon always opened the two-day session, which was held off-site at a local hotel, with a round of personal news. Everyone had the chance to say what was going on in their personal lives, show the latest pictures of their kids or new family pet, share things that were on their mind, totally unrelated to the business. Everyone had a chance to be heard in these meetings, and everyone usually felt at the end of the two days that they had had an influence in some part of the process.

Sharon always presented the team with a small gift at the end of the Half-Yearly. This time, she had decided not to buy a gift, but to use the funds to make a donation of one thousand pounds in the name of the Andromex HR Team to a local charity, which she would ask the team to vote on at the end of the meeting. She felt this would give them a chance to understand what she would be talking to them about on the second day of the meeting, both in terms of CSR and in changing behaviours and perspectives.

It had taken Sharon some time to find the right formula for these meetings, but after several years Sharon was pleased with the arrangement, and she was looking forward to this meeting both with a degree of excitement and some trepidation, given the scale of change she would be asking her team to consider on the second day. Fortunately, the evening in between both days was one when they all let their hair down a little. Usually they visited a local nightclub, or a wine bar, and people relaxed and enjoyed each other's company. After that, she joked to herself, they would be receptive to almost anything she dared to propose to them. However, she knew she was regarded by her team as highly professional, a great boss, on the whole, and someone who was able to effect change in the organisation and, most importantly, someone they could trust. They knew she had their interests at heart and did her best to provide the kind of supportive environment and backing that they needed in order to produce their best work. Sharon was sure that they would hear her out and give her the benefit of the doubt, even if they didn't quite understand the magnitude of the change she would be recommending to them.

As people started to arrive, Sharon looked around with pride at her team and was anxious to get the two days under way. The first day went pretty much as expected. Each team member presented his or her own scorecard, successes, difficulties, and key priorities for the coming half-year. There were no surprises for Sharon, and it felt good to get everyone on the same page. Recruitment and retention had shown up as one of the key issues — all the team were feeling some pressure here — and possible solutions were discussed. There had been rather too much unplanned turnover in the last six months, and not enough agility in recruiting to funnel the business growth occurring in parts of the organisation. The team was seeing this as largely outside their control, believing it to be related to aggressive recruiting tactics of the larger companies, including higher compensation levels and joining incentives, but Sharon felt that elements of her CSR approach would provide a new perspective on solutions in this area. Sharon updated the team on the key learnings from the San Diego conference, handing out CDs with notes and presentations for them all to review in their own time. She mentioned some aspects of HR related to CSR, but she didn't dwell on this as a key item, thinking it best to leave this to the following day. On the evening of the first day, the team voted to go to the local bowling alley, rather than a night-club, though the amount of beer consumed significantly reduced the number of spares and strikes scored. It was a fun evening, and the team were once again bonded and re-energised and ready for some tougher discussions the following day.

Sharon opened up Day 2 with a presentation about CSR, the importance for the HR function, the CSR contribution of the HR function, the HR stakeholders and the CSHR job description. She recounted her discussion with the CEO, and expressed her desire for the HR function to show leadership in the areas where they were able, even without a corporate strategy led by the Executive Committee.

She was pleasantly surprised that her team got it, without significant discussion. They seemed to understand that this was not only the right thing to do, but that it would help them in supporting improved business results. There were long discussions about the Andromex employer brand and how this could be developed to present a more responsible and meaningful picture to future recruits. There was strong support for a more defined approach to community involvement and the possibility of getting out into the community to do some good. There was massive support for stronger internal communications and the development of a company blog — suddenly everyone had stories they could write about. There was enthusiasm at the development of a code of ethics and a company-wide assimilation process, which ANDEX had already approved. All in all, instead of, as Sharon had feared, significant resistance, her team had strongly endorsed the general concept of leading HR with a CSR flavour. In fact, they all started to joke about how they would change their business cards to read CSHR Training Manager, CSHR Recruitment Manager, etc. After two hours of presenting and discussing the theory of CSR (Sharon thought to herself: 'Two hours on something I have spent three months researching and defining'), Sharon presented the roadmap for HR as she saw it:

Thanks everyone for being so positive so far. Remember, in an ideal world, we would expect the Leadership Team to move us forward as a company on corporate social responsibility. Our mandate to act would be derived from the corporate approach, mission and sustainability intent. Currently our leadership is not in that position. I want to make it absolutely clear that my proposals are not a criticism of them. ANDEX is leading the business to greater achievements and we are becoming bigger and stronger as a business. As we grow and develop, we observe all laws and do not breach any serious codes of ethical behaviour as far as I am aware. As your HR Director, I have always felt proud to be associated with a company led by a team with integrity and a caring approach to people. As you know, ANDEX have approved the Business Ethics Programme. The fact that CSR does not figure as a corporate priority is a shame, because I believe we, as a company, are missing out on the potential benefits and opportunities. As HR Director, however, I have decided to progress what I feel we can progress in the absence of a definitive position by leadership, for five reasons: (1) Any future CSR programme, and I am sure this will happen sooner or later, requires HR as critical partners and a certain organisational readiness. I would prefer to get us in position ahead of time, so that when the leadership is ready to move, we will be on the ball. (2) Our development of CSR within HR strategy is not counterproductive — it remains in line with our role in supporting the delivery of organisational objectives and will enable us to address HR processes in a more comprehensive way and deliver greater value for the organisation. (3) Our showing leadership in this area will provide a good example for the rest of the company and will help us influence the leadership in this direction. We will be able to influence from a position of practical experience and strength, rather than just citing theories and activities of other companies. (4) In the area of people, community and environment, I believe we will be able to make a meaningful contribution. And (5) I believe this is a more fulfilling and meaningful approach to HR for each and every one of us on a personal level. It will enrich our professional lives and make us more aware of the context of our roles in the business and in society.

Finally, you all know me. You know that when I believe in something, I go for it. Fortunately, George Felton is giving us a wide berth and I believe he will be supportive on the whole. A key tenet of our progress along the CSHR roadmap will be our continuous updating of ANDEX and communication on our progress in all areas. At all stages we will make sure to get as broad endorsement as possible from ANDEX and others in the business. Wherever we are making fundamental changes or require operating budgets, we will ask ANDEX for authorisation as we usually do. We will progress ahead of the pack but we must remember that we are not going to operate in a vacuum, in secret or in a way that could cause the company embarrassment at any stage. Is that clear to everyone?

The team all nodded. No one said anything. Sharon was quite serious and had that determined look on her face. They knew they had to listen.

I have developed a roadmap in four stages. There's a chart for each one. The first stage is about understanding the conditions in which CSR can develop in our company, facing the internal and external realities, and creating a basic level of organisational readiness.

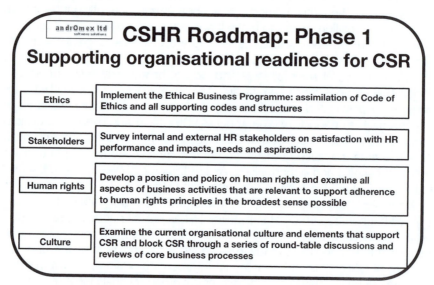

The second stage is about energising people in community and environmental activities, which will bring some fairly quick wins in terms of cost savings, team working and motivation, as well as benefit to society and the planet.

**andromex ltd** *software solutions*

# CSHR Roadmap: Phase 2
## Engage with community and environment

**Community**
- Develop a community involvement cross-company steering team to establish potential for employee volunteering
- Survey employees for potential interest and readiness for volunteering activities
- Meet potential community partners
- Develop a policy and plan for volunteering activities

**Environment**
- Establish pilot green teams comprising employee volunteers in different departments
- Train green teams in basic elements of environmental protection, consumption reduction, recycling, waste disposal, commuting to work, etc.
- Measure cost savings and impact reductions as a result of green team activity. Reward green teams for cost savings and benefits achieved.
- If successful, roll out to all company departments.

The third stage is the adaptation of key HR processes. I haven't listed everything but the areas we should start with are on the map.

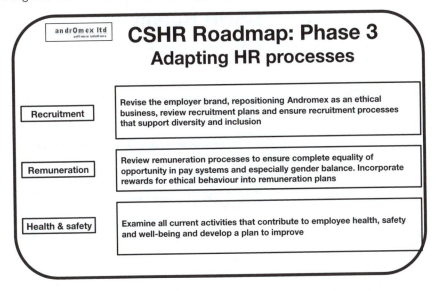

**andromex ltd** *software solutions*

# CSHR Roadmap: Phase 3
## Adapting HR processes

**Recruitment**

Revise the employer brand, repositioning Andromex as an ethical business, review recruitment plans and ensure recruitment processes that support diversity and inclusion

**Remuneration**

Review remuneration processes to ensure complete equality of opportunity in pay systems and especially gender balance. Incorporate rewards for ethical behaviour into remuneration plans

**Health & safety**

Examine all current activities that contribute to employee health, safety and well-being and develop a plan to improve

The fourth stage is about consolidating the embedding of this entire approach through training and communications.

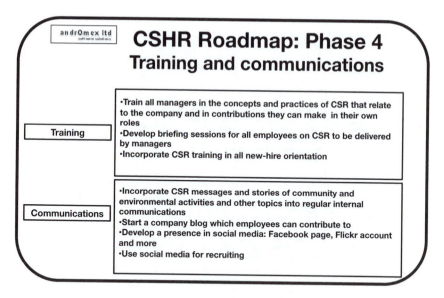

And this chart shows the phases over three years.

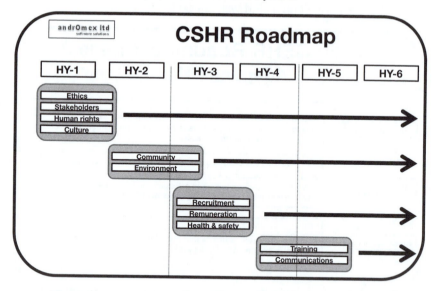

And just so that you don't think I am inventing all of this, here is a quote from the Chartered Institute of Personnel and Development[1] in a guide they produced some years ago.

---

1 The Chartered Institute of Personnel and Development (CIPD) is the professional body for those involved in the management and development in the UK.

# A word from the CIPD

The argument for HR people taking the CSR agenda seriously can be summarised as follows:

• Companies are increasingly required to take account of the impact of their activities on society

• The credibility of CSR is dependent on delivery, not on rhetoric

• HR is responsible for many of the key systems and processes (e.g. recruitment, training, communications) on which effective delivery depends

• HR people have relevant knowledge and skills in relation to e.g. organisational learning and culture change

• Managing trust and risk raises fundamental issues about how people are managed

• CSR offers the HR community opportunities to demonstrate its strategic focus

**The CIPD Guide to Corporate Social Responsibility**
**www.cipd.co.uk**

OK, folks. That's the plan — it's a broad direction we can take over the next three years focusing on organisational readiness, value-creating actions, adapting HR policies and plans, and consolidating this position through focused training and communications. I think this is the best we can do until ANDEX moves into the driving seat. We may find some things move more quickly, some more slowly than this outline; we may find that there are blockers along the way and that a change of course might be necessary. However, I would like to hear your feedback on this, and understand where you all are, because the next step will be to assign leadership to each of the different elements and set ourselves some objectives and targets.

By the way, this plan is not an excuse for not doing those things that we have already committed to doing in our HR work-plan for this year, which we are half way through. We will continue to do all those things and add a certain CSR flavour wherever possible. In recruiting, for example, we may find that our CSR approach actually helps us deliver, though I doubt we will be able to make massive advancements during the next six months as a result of this. However, there are some things we can do. We will use the services of a consultant to assist us in the early stages, as I cannot claim to be an expert. Anyway, I have talked enough. What do you think?

Sharon waited for the first response. It was Patricia, her number two and generally the one with the most to say. Patricia, it was no surprise, was fully supportive and felt that this programme would be a credit to the Andromex HR function and to the business. Others followed suit, with questions and comments. One of the biggest concerns the group had was the HR stakeholder survey. They felt this would open up a number of issues that it might be better not to confront. Some felt that HR would not have all the answers so why raise the questions. Others wanted reassurance that they would not be creating unrealistic expectations that would come back to haunt them at a later stage. In general, no one came up with any major issues and the energy in the room, even after two days of discussions, was upbeat. Sharon felt good, though she knew her task was not entirely over.

With an endorsement from her team under her belt, Sharon booked time at the next ANDEX meeting to brief her colleagues about the direction she was taking. She was certain that she wouldn't meet any resistance, as this would be seen as something within the HR function. A few employees volunteering on their own time or printing fewer documents would not be much of a concern to her business-focused, IPO-focused colleagues, she told herself. However, she could not progress without updating her colleagues as a sign of respect for them, and also to catch any objections at an early stage, if there were any. Also, she thought, briefing the executive team is part of the process of engaging and influencing them.

# 19

# CSHR: a critical business partner

It was late Friday afternoon and Sharon was still wrapped up in the positive vibes from her Half-Yearly, though at this point in the week, her thoughts were starting to turn to the upcoming weekend, which was rather packed with family events. Her daughter Michelle was due to turn nine on Monday, and the entire family was to descend on the Black household for lunch on Sunday in honour of the youngest of the Blacks. Sharon's thoughts of how to decorate Michelle's birthday cake were interrupted by an SMS from Cathy Joseph,[1] who was asking Sharon if she had time to Skype. Sharon quickly SMS'd back with a yes, picked up her headset and logged in.

Sharon and Cathy were good friends, having met when Cathy was working as a consultant on a project to develop workforce initiatives to increase staff engagement at the company Sharon had worked for before Andromex. Cathy had been in the UK on a three-month assignment for that project and two

1  Cathy Joseph is a real person, who has been of assistance in writing this chapter, specifically in reminding the author of the great contribution of the Prahalad article quoted, and also in reading the draft manuscript and offering many insights. Cathy is a consultative professional who uses a strengths-based approach to driving enterprise-wide, workforce strategies and programmes that have positively impacted both performance and the bottom line. At Cengage Learning, Time Warner, Gartner and GE Capital, she successfully integrated this approach, while demonstrating her strong abilities to assess organisational development challenges, mobilise commitment and drive positive change. In addition to serving as a collaborative business partner, Cathy has been recognised for her intuitive abilities to engender trust and foster engagement across global employee populations of up to 5,000. She can be contacted via Twitter at www.twitter.com/cathyj131.

other assignments, running simultaneously. Sharon had been the key partner from the HR function and they had forged a friendship. Cathy lived and worked in the USA, in Stamford, so they rarely saw each other. She had hoped that Cathy would make it to the ASTD conference, but a client assignment had prevented that. However, they kept in touch via email and a call on Skype every couple of months. Sharon was glad to take some time out to chat to Cathy. After a catch-up on what both had been doing and, of course, Sharon's telling Cathy all about Arena and her new CSHR focus, Cathy had some thoughts of her own to share. Cathy was an organisational change strategy professional, with many years of experience in supporting change in very large organisations, and she said that she was exploring opportunities to leverage her organisational development skills as a catalyst for change in the field of CSR best practices in employee, stakeholder and community engagement.

**Sharon:** Ah, so you are becoming a CSHR manager too?

**Cathy:** A CSHR consultant, I suppose, in a way.

**Sharon:** Wow. I could have just asked you to come over here and teach me what I have been spending the last few months researching and learning the hard way.

**Cathy:** Yes, Sharon. Why didn't you think of that? What are friends for?

**Sharon:** I will bring you in at Phase Two.

**Cathy:** I am writing that down.

**Sharon:** Seriously, do you think what I am planning makes sense? I haven't really got George's support beyond the ethics programme and a promise to think more about it. What happens when the Exec team start telling me there is no budget for CSR? What about the cost of it all? Will we really be able to lead change if the Exec team is not on board? I am moving forward, and my HR team is very supportive, even more so than I'd imagined, but when I stop to think, I have to wonder if I am overstretching. What do you think, Cathy?

**Cathy:** I think what you are doing is brave and absolutely correct. If every manager sat around waiting for the CEO to tell them what needed to be done, businesses wouldn't move very fast. You are a model of the sort of proactive initiative-taking leader that I so often teach about in sessions with employees. And frankly, between you and me, and I will deny this if you quote me, there are so few HR managers who demonstrate this level of bold action and act as true leaders, and that is what is such a shame about the HR profession. HR managers are so often busy with dealing with what's directly under their noses that they don't have time to truly envision a different type of organisation.

My experience of CSR on organisation culture has been very positive. One of the key differences some of my clients have perceived is the way innovation gets managed and developed. There was an article in the

Harvard Business Review in 2009 by Prahalad and some others.[2] You've heard of Prahalad, right? He died in April.[3] He was the one who wrote the Fortune at the Bottom of the Pyramid,[4] which changed the entire perspective of how businesses view business opportunities in low-income underdeveloped countries. That book was revolutionary and changed the thinking on many aspects of CSR highlighting the infinite business opportunities for making a profit whilst contributing to the advancement of social issues such as poverty and the quality of life. He seemed to prove that the fact that people were poor did not discount them as a massive potential consumer opportunity if approached in the right way. Anyway, in this article, he maintained that only companies that make sustainability a goal will achieve competitive advantage, and pointed to two key things: innovation, saying that 'sustainability should be a touchstone for all innovation'; and cost, saying that 'becoming environmentally friendly can lower your costs and increase your revenues'. This was a very important and influential article because it added two very key insights to the debate. The first was that it addressed many people's view that the cost of establishing and maintaining a sustainability programme is high and too much of a burden on companies. Prahalad made it clear that sustainability is not a 'burden on the bottom line' and is actually a good investment with a rapid return. After studying the sustainability activities of 30 different companies, he concluded that sustainability enables a company to reduce cost in many areas.

Actually, this is now borne out by practitioners. The CEO of Marks & Spencer, Sir Stuart Rose,[5] said that their Plan A programme for sustainability became 'cost-positive' after only two years out of their five-year plan. Ray Anderson, the Chairman of Interface Flooring,[6] said that sustainability at his company is self-funding — the elimination of waste serves to fund all the other initiatives. This is a very good argument for your CEO and your management team. But Prahalad and his co-authors in that HBR article said that there is more. They said that the sustainability approach actually drives a different way of thinking about the business and the way it manufactures products, and technologies, processes and business models. As a result, businesses can exploit a range of new opportunities they weren't capable of doing before. This applies to all kinds of businesses, not just manufacturing. They quoted Cisco as an

2   Ram Nidumolu, C.K. Prahalad and M.R. Rangaswami, 'Why Sustainability is Now the Key Driver of Innovation', *Harvard Business Review* (September 2009), www.hbr.org.

3   Prahalad was Paul and Ruth McCracken Distinguished University Professor of Strategy at the University of Michigan's Ross School of Business and a member of the board of directors of the World Resources Institute. He died in April 2010.

4   C.K. Prahalad, *The Fortune at the Bottom of the Pyramid* (Upper Saddle River, NJ: Wharton School Publishing, 2006).

5   www.sustainablelifemedia.com/content/story/brands/m_and_s_say_its_eco_plan_is_cost_positive, accessed 8 June 2010.

6   theenergycollective.com/TheEnergyCollective/49002, accessed 8 June 2010.

example of a company who, after re-examining their policy of scrapping old equipment, moved to higher levels of re-use, reduced recycling costs by 40% and turned recycling into a profit centre that contributed to the bottom line. In the area of HR, for example, they talked about working from home as a new opportunity that reduces cost and enables a different kind of collaborative working.

So think about it Sharon, which two priorities are always at the top of any CEO's list? Innovation and cost. These are two of the most powerful arguments for sustainability as they make it very clear that you don't have to sacrifice profit for sustainability. On the contrary, sustainability makes you more profitable. Sooner or later, your Exec team will understand this and when they do, they won't have any time to waste. The fact that you are proactive in putting in place a culture that will support this is tremendously important.

**Sharon:** What a great perspective, Cathy. I knew we were friends for a reason. You have certainly reinforced my thinking. What are you doing in this area?

**Cathy:** Well, as you know, my strengths and experience are in organisational development and workforce engagement and empowerment initiatives. I have good experience in engagement both internally and externally. These days, I am using this to help organisations create the cultural infrastructure in their business that will support dialogue and involvement, which are the key elements of an innovation and sustainability culture. I love it.

**Sharon:** Any plans to be in the UK this year?

**Cathy:** Not until you invite me to do a project at Andromex.

**Sharon:** I will include you in my budget, but you will have to lower your rates; we can't afford a big invoice from an American super-consultant.

**Cathy:** Funny. Just think of me as an investment in innovation. The profits Andromex will make will be more than enough to fund a few weeks of consulting time. Also, I will come and stay at your house so the accommodation costs will be lower.

**Sharon** (laughing): OK, it's a deal.

**Cathy:** Great, keep me posted on how you are doing. I am so glad we touched base today. Oh, and Michelle has a birthday coming up soon, right?

**Sharon:** Hey, that's amazing of you to remember that. Yes, she's nine next week and we are having the 'Gathering of the Clans' at our house on Sunday. I just hope that no bright spark thinks to bring her an iPhone or something like that, though that's probably what she would like most. At age nine. Can you believe it? It takes me all my time to keep her away from Facebook.

**Cathy:** Well, I hope you have a great family celebration, kisses and hugs to Robert and all the kids, talk to you again soon.

**Sharon:** Sure, thanks. And thanks for some great thoughts about cost and innovation.

No sooner had Sharon logged off from Skype than her phone rang. She was about to ignore it, as it was after six and she wanted to finish some emails and get home, but the name showing up on the screen compelled her to pick up. It was Arena.

**Arena:** So, how did it go?

**Sharon:** It went wonderfully, actually. My HR team is really on board, and my briefing of the Executive Committee was a doddle. I am not sure if they were totally hooked, but no one objected. So, now I have a three-year programme to make happen.

**Arena:** That's fabulous, Sharon. You have done so well. I am sure you will enjoy the journey. I was thinking that we should have a joint meeting of our HR teams. You could bring your people and I will bring my top team and we can share best practices in HR and CSR and CSHR. If we can help you with policies that we have so that you don't have to reinvent the wheel, where relevant, I would be happy to do that. After all, we all need to help each other out, right?

**Sharon:** Yes, Arena, we do. Thank you so much. I think you have given me more help than I could ever have imagined, though I don't see me being able to route much help in your direction.

**Arena:** Don't worry about that. Your time will come. And teaching you what I know has helped me to reinforce my own thinking about CSR and where we are at as a company. It's a never-ending cycle, you know that.

**Sharon:** Yes, I do. When I met you on the San Diego flight, I felt that HR was a critical partner in the business. Now I know that CSHR is an even more critical partner. Our role is not only focusing on internal business events and practices, it's about our indirect impact as a function and how we manage ourselves in the business to deliver broader impacts beyond the business. The more I realise this, the more I realise just how critical a partner we should be.

**Arena:** Great. Let's set a date for that meeting and, you know what, we ought to fly away together again sometime soon.

They both laughed and simultaneously clicked the 'End' button on their phones. Sharon felt she was already flying.

# Appendix
## Companies referenced

| Company | Reference | Chapter |
|---|---|---|
| 3BL Media | CSR communications | 3 |
| Adidas | CSR in the supply chain | 1 |
| ANZ | Employee engagement | 2 |
| Aviva | Employee well-being | 2 |
| Bank Leumi | Spirituality in business | 2 |
| Ben & Jerry's | Values | 1 |
| | Human rights | 4 |
| Chesapeake Energy Corp | Remuneration and benefits | 5 |
| Chevron | Employee well-being | 2 |
| Cisco | Community activity | 8 |
| Coca Cola | Recruitment | 7 |
| comme il faut | Values | 1 |
| | Employee dialogue | 3 |
| Danisco | Recruitment | 7 |
| Danske Bank | Employee development | 8 |
| Deloitte | Green activities | 11 |
| Deutsche Bank | Community activity | 8 |
| eBay | Remuneration and benefits | 5 |
| | Employee volunteering | 10 |

| Company | Reference | Chapter |
|---|---|---|
| Eileen Fisher | Values | 1 |
| | Employee engagement | 3 |
| Eli Lilly | Employee volunteering | 10 |
| EOG Resources | Remuneration and benefits | 5 |
| FedEx | Communications | 9 |
| France Telecom | Employee well-being | 6 |
| Gap Inc | Values, supply chain recruitment | 1 |
| | Employee dialogue | 3 |
| | Human rights | 4 |
| General Electric | CSR strategy | 1 |
| General Motors | Employee well-being | 2 |
| Genentech | Remuneration and benefits | 5 |
| GlaxoSmithKline | Recruitment | 7 |
| Google | Remuneration and benefits | 5 |
| H&M | Employee impacts | 13 |
| Intel | HR Manager article | 9 |
| | Remuneration and benefits | 5 |
| | Communications | 9 |
| Interface | CSR benefits | 1 |
| | Cost of CSR | 19 |
| JC Penney | Human rights | 4 |
| Johnson & Johnson | Employee well-being | 2 |
| KPMG | Remuneration and benefits | 5 |
| | Community activity | 8 |
| Lafayette Mining company | Stakeholder engagement | 3 |
| Levi Strauss | Human rights | 4 |
| Microsoft | Remuneration and benefits | 5 |
| MITRE | Remuneration and benefits | 5 |
| Nike | CSR in the supply chain | 1 |
| | Human rights | 4 |
| | Recruitment | 7 |
| Nordstrom | Human rights | 4 |
| Novartis | Living wage | 2 |
| Optus | Employee volunteering | 10 |

| Company | Reference | Chapter |
|---|---|---|
| Patagonia | Values | 1 |
| Procter & Gamble | Employee well-being | 2 |
| | Remuneration and benefits | 5 |
| Puma | CSR in the supply chain<br>Human rights | 1<br>4 |
| Royal Dutch Shell | Human rights | 4 |
| Serco Sodexo Defence Services | Remuneration and benefits | 5 |
| Starbucks | Stakeholder engagement | 3 |
| | Recruitment | 7 |
| Tata Steel | Remuneration and benefits | 5 |
| Tate & Lyle | Human rights | 4 |
| The Body Shop | Values | 1 |
| The Walt Disney Company | Recruitment | 7 |
| Timberland | CSR leadership | 3 |
| | Human rights | 4 |
| Twinings | Recruitment | 7 |
| Unilever | Responsible marketing | 2 |
| | Remuneration and benefits | 5 |
| | Employee volunteering | 10 |
| Vattenfall | Gender | 7 |
| Vodafone | Employee dialogue | 3 |
| Wal-Mart | CSR purpose | 2 |
| | Remuneration and benefits | 5 |
| | Recruitment | 7 |
| Westpac Bank | HR strategy | 7 |
| Zipcar | Communications | 9 |

# Index

Page numbers in *italic figures* refer to illustrations